The Trouble with Terror

What is terrorism and can it ever be defended? Beginning with its definition, proceeding to its possible justifications, and culminating in proposals for contending with and combating it, this book offers a full theoretical analysis of the issue of terrorism. Tamar Meisels argues that, regardless of its professed cause, terrorism is diametrically opposed to the requirements of liberal morality and can only be defended at the expense of relinquishing the most basic of liberal commitments. Meisels opposes those who express sympathy and justification for Islamist (particularly Palestinian) terrorism and terrorism allegedly carried out on behalf of developing nations, but, at the same time, also opposes those who would tolerate any reduction in civil liberties in exchange for greater security. Calling wholeheartedly for a unanimous liberal front against terrorism, this is a strong and provocative attempt to address the tension between liberty and security in a time of terror.

TAMAR MEISELS is Lecturer in the Political Science Department at Tel-Aviv University. She is the author of *Territorial Rights* (2005).

The Trouble with Terror

Liberty, Security, and the Response
to Terrorism

TAMAR MEISELS

CAMBRIDGE
UNIVERSITY PRESS

CAMBRIDGE UNIVERSITY PRESS
Cambridge, New York, Melbourne, Madrid, Cape Town, Singapore, São Paulo, Delhi

Cambridge University Press
The Edinburgh Building, Cambridge CB2 8RU, UK

Published in the United States of America by Cambridge University Press, New York

www.cambridge.org
Information on this title: www.cambridge.org/9780521728324

First published 2008

Printed in the United Kingdom at the University Press, Cambridge

A catalogue record for this publication is available from the British Library

Library of Congress Cataloguing-in-Publication data
Meisels, Tamar.
The trouble with terror : liberty, security and the response to terrorism / Tamar Meisels.
    p. cm.
ISBN 978-0-521-89948-2
1. Terrorism. 2. Terrorism–United States. 3. Terrorism–Government policy.
I. Title.
HV6431.M435   2008
323.325–dc22
                                        2008025646

ISBN 978-0-521-89948-2 hardback
ISBN 978-0-521-72832-4 paperback

For Abigail and Martha

Contents

Acknowledgments

This book consists of seven chapters written at various times throughout the six years following September 11, 2001. Most of these chapters are versions of articles that have already been published. I begin by thanking the editors of the following journals for allowing me to use these materials here:

"Targeting Terror," *Social Theory and Practice* 30 (3), July 2004, pp. 297–326.

"How Terrorism Upsets Liberty," *Political Studies* 53, March 2005, pp. 162–81.

"The Trouble with Terror," *The Journal of Terrorism and Political Violence* 18, 2006, pp. 465–83.

"Combatants – Lawful and Unlawful," *Law and Philosophy* 26, January 2007, pp. 31–65.

"Torture and the Problem of Dirty Hands," *The Canadian Journal of Law and Jurisprudence*, January 2008, pp. 149–73.

I am grateful to Richard Bronaugh, editor of the *CJLJ*, for his detailed comments on this last article.

Next, I must thank my daughters, Abigail and Martha, for allowing me the time and quiet necessary to write all this. I thank them for agreeing to share my attention with this long and time-consuming project; for their support, understanding, and cooperation. Above all, I thank them for their friendship.

In the course of writing these articles, and later adapting them into this book, I have been fortunate to receive extremely helpful comments from a number of colleagues, who are also very dear friends: I am most grateful to David Enoch, Cecile Fabre, and Guy Sela, for their patience in reading previous drafts and versions of these chapters, and for their important suggestions and help throughout.

Special thanks are due to George Fletcher for comments on previous versions of Chapters 4 and 5, as well as for the very useful and enjoyable conversations we have had on war and terrorism during his visits to Israel. I am particularly grateful for his participation in a conference on terrorism that I organized at Tel-Aviv University in March 2004. I learned a great deal from the paper he presented there on "The Problem of Defining Terrorism," which first called my attention to the questions I address in Chapter 1. His book *Romantics at War* had a great influence on me when setting out on this project. All this is greatly appreciated.

I am also indebted to Alan Dershowitz for his helpful points of clarification on an early version of Chapter 7. His comments have helped make this chapter much better, and more accurate, than it was in its original form.

Meir Dan-Cohen's "acoustic separation" sparked some of the ideas in Chapter 7. A very memorable conversation we had with some others in the lobby of the Tel-Aviv Hilton, as army helicopters circled above at the beginning of operation "Defense Wall," first raised the question, "What's wrong with killing the bad guys?" which gave rise to Chapter 5 of this book. Aside from which, he deserves special thanks for being a real friend at a time of personal need, helping to resolve disputes and restore calm, without which I doubt this book could have been completed.

Last, and most important: my deepest thanks go to Jeremy Waldron for his invaluably helpful comments on the various chapters in this book. Though we do not always agree, the influence of his work on terrorism and torture is apparent throughout this book. I am especially grateful for the discussions we have had on these issues, and for the opportunity to benefit from his scholarly criticism, learned comments, and illuminating suggestions. Like Waldron himself, his contribution to this work is in a league of its own.

Introduction

In the days following September 11, 2001, many foreign nationals paid homage to New York's victims by laying wreaths and writing inscriptions in memorial books. Among those paying their respects and offering condolences were a large number of Israeli visitors and ex-patriots who, whether individually or collectively, had already experienced several decades of terrorist atrocities. While the collapse of the twin towers was indeed a uniquely momentous event – a horrific spectacular carried out on the world's largest stage – the Israeli New Yorkers had already witnessed the essence of this horror before. They had smelled the smoke and witnessed the carnage. They had seen such devastation and destruction – the bodies, the families, the loss, the death, and the bereaved. They had already buried many victims of terrorism and embraced many survivors. No one could have been more sympathetic to New Yorkers on that fateful day.

One Hebrew inscription attached to a wreath sticks in the mind. Summoning up the words of the prophet Jeremiah, one anonymous Israeli in the crowd wrote of her pre-September 11 American friends: "they had eyes, but could not see."[1] A week later, former Israeli Prime Minister Benjamin Netanyahu expressed similar sentiments when addressing the US Congress. He said America had received a wake-up call from hell.[2] His words were received with loud, unanimous applause by members of the House. America may once have been blind, but now could see.

---

[1] The reference is to Jeremiah 5:21, KJV: "Hear now this, O foolish people, and without understanding; which have eyes, and see not; that have ears, and hear not."

[2] Netanyahu's speech in the US Congress, September 20, 2001, reprinted in Benjamin Netanyahu, *Fighting Terrorism* (New York: Farrar, Straus, and Giroux, 2001), p. xix.

Let there be no misunderstanding from the outset. This is a book about terrorism, but it is also, and most definitely, an argument against terrorism. It draws on the existing theoretical, primarily philosophical, literature on terrorism, and argues with much of it. The first part of the book argues against a growing academic reluctance to define terrorism as a specific and fiendish deed. Later, it offers a systematic normative evaluation of the phenomenon of terrorism and of various forms of contending with it from the perspective of liberal morality. Beginning with the definition of terrorism, proceeding to its possible justifications, and culminating in proposals for combating it, this book suggests that regardless of its professed cause, terrorism is diametrically opposed to the requirements of liberal morality and can only be defended at the expense of relinquishing the most basic of liberal commitments. It argues against a considerable body of literature that expresses sympathy, and at times outright justification, for Islamist (particularly Palestinian) terrorism and terrorism allegedly carried out on behalf of developing nations. It takes on the apologists for terrorism and refutes their arguments.

On the other hand, and not one whit less important, this wholehearted call for a unanimous liberal front against terrorism does not bear the practical implications that some self-interested state leaders wish to accord it, nor should it always supply them with the legal and political license they seek to acquire when confronting terrorist threats. Part II looks to liberal democracies and asks how the freedom and security of their citizenry, as well as the rights of suspected terrorists, should be handled by liberal democratic legal systems in an age of terror. Domestically, it questions whether civil libertarians ought to resist any readjustment of civil liberties, even at times of grave security threat, but at the same time argues against those who would tolerate any diminution of civil liberties in exchange for greater security. I sketch my argument on this internal issue in terms of classic social contract theory, which I believe contributes to an illumination of the frequent debate on the supposed tension between liberty and security, particularly in times of crisis.

Part II also offers an analysis of the debate over the legal status of terrorists and their rights. It defends the contemporary American labeling of irregulars as "unlawful combatants" and offers an argument for denying them prisoner of war status as well as the rights of internal due process accorded common criminals. On the other hand, I also argue adamantly for upholding the basic human rights of irregular combatants and against the more draconian measures implemented by the US Bush administration against terrorists and terrorist suspects.

Internationally, Part III defends particular methods of combating terrorism which are often objected to by liberals. In particular, it defends targeted assassination, and entertains the possibility of employing harsher interrogation techniques for questioning terrorists in life-threatening situations. Crucially, however, the last two chapters deal at length with the specific issue of torturous investigations and with arguments from extreme emergency, and ultimately uphold and defend the age-old liberal commitment against outright torture.

Finally, the outcome is a complex set of views, but hopefully not an incoherent one. Our views on these various issues should be complex and perplexing, not necessarily sitting well with any one political party, state agenda, or world leadership. We live in truly complicated times, and should think accordingly.

Defining and Defending Terrorism

1 | Defining terrorism – a typology

As the leaders of Western democracies and their security forces increasingly struggle with terrorism, their lawyers and philosophers continue to struggle with its definition. Several recent studies point to the inconsistencies and inadequacies of existing legal definitions, as well as to the contradictions among them.[1] C.A.J. Coady suggests that there are more than a hundred modern definitions of "terrorism."[2] George Fletcher mentions only dozens, concluding that no one of them is definitive.[3] Consequently, there is no globally agreed, unambiguous definition or description of terrorism – popular, academic, or legislative. Igor Primoratz complains that "Current ordinary usage of the word displays wide variety and considerable confusion; as a result, discussing terrorism and the array of moral, political and legal questions it raises is difficult and often frustrating."[4] Wilkins does not altogether exaggerate when he writes that the number of definitions of terrorism equals the number of works dedicated to the subject.[5] By 1984, Alex Schmid had collected 109 different definitions of terrorism.[6] Later, he states that he "cannot offer a true or correct definition of terrorism" and that "[t]errorism is an abstract phenomenon of which there can be

---

[1] Jeremy Waldron, "Terrorism and the Uses of Terror," *The Journal of Ethics* 8 (2004), pp. 5–35; George Fletcher, "The Problem of Defining Terrorism," paper presented at a conference on "Terrorism – Philosophical Perspectives," at Tel-Aviv University (organized by the Department of Political Science and the Minerva Center for Human Rights, Tel-Aviv University Law Faculty), March 2004; and in George Fletcher, "The Indefinable Concept of Terrorism," *Journal of International Criminal Justice* (2006), pp. 1–18.

[2] C.A.J. Coady, "Defining Terrorism," in I. Primoratz (ed.), *Terrorism – The Philosophical Issues* (New York: Palgrave Macmillan, 2004), p. 3–14.

[3] Fletcher, "The Problem of Defining," p. 2.   [4] Primoratz, *Terrorism*, p. xi.

[5] Burleigh T. Wilkins, *Terrorism and Collective Responsibility* (London: Routledge, 1992), p. 2.

[6] Alex P. Schmid, *Political Terrorism: A Research Guide to Concepts, Theories, Data Bases and Literature* (Amsterdam: North-Holland Publishing, 1984), pp. 119–58.

no essence which can be discovered or described," commenting that "authors have spilt almost as much ink as the actors of terrorism have spilled blood."[7] Indeed, to date, academic standpoints remain diverse. When it comes to defining terrorism some, like Walter Laqueur, seem to forego analysis in favor of platitudes, in the belief that "[a]ll specific definitions of terrorism have their shortcomings simply because reality is always richer (or more complicated) than any generalization."[8]

At least one reason for the disparity of definitions stems from the variety of objectives we have in defining terrorism. Lawyers desperately require definitions in order to prosecute and sanction "terrorists." They must distinguish terrorism in precise legal terms from other forms of crime. Social scientists aim to describe this phenomenon in a way which will better our sociological and psychological understanding of it and enable us to face this modern challenge more successfully.[9] Heads of state and politicians often adopt definitions that serve their national, political, or ideological agendas. Naturally, they usually define terrorism as a form of violence that is carried out exclusively by non-state groups. As Primoratz puts this: "Nobody applies the word to oneself or one's actions, nor to those one has sympathy with or whose activities one supports."[10]

Recently, both George Fletcher and Jeremy Waldron have questioned whether we should spend time worrying about definitional issues at all. Fletcher suggests that, "when it comes to terrorism, we know it when we see it – as Justice Stewart famously said about pornography."[11] According to Fletcher, while people have strong intuitions about what is and what is not terrorism, no definition of terrorism can be filtered from a specification of necessary and sufficient conditions.[12] Specific forms of conduct, he claims, cannot be identified as terrorism by simply running a relevant test on them. Instead, he probes the relevance of eight variables on the contours of terrorism: violence, intention, the victims, the wrongdoers, just cause, organization, theater, and what he calls the "no guilt, no regrets" of the

---

[7] Alex P. Schmid and Albert J. Jongman, *Political Terrorism: A Research Guide to Concepts, Theories, Data Bases and Literature*, 2nd edn. (Amsterdam: North-Holland Publishing, 1988), p. xiii.

[8] Walter Z. Laqueur, *The Age of Terrorism* (Boston: Little, Brown, 1987), p. 145.

[9] Waldron, "Terrorism," p. 6.   [10] Primoratz, *Terrorism*, p. xi.

[11] Fletcher, "The Problem of Defining," p. 2; Waldron, "Terrorism," p. 6.

[12] Fletcher, "The Problem of Defining," p. 3; Fletcher, "The Indefinable Concept of Terrorism," pp. 16, 18.

perpetrators.[13] Drawing on Wittgenstein's "relationships of family resemblance," Fletcher argues that terrorist acts do not presuppose necessary and sufficient conditions. Instead, a given terrorist act may resemble a second terrorist act in some respect, and a third terrorist act in another. The features of the second and third terrorist acts that resemble one another may be different as well. There is, however, no common denominator for all acts of terrorism, apart, perhaps, from their theatrical nature.[14]

In "Terrorism and the Uses of Terror," Waldron pursues some interesting distinctions among, for example, "terror," "terrorism," and "terrorization," and reveals some psychological insights into the fearful elements of terror, but he concludes that no canonical definition emerges from these observations.[15] In one such invaluable insight, Waldron ascribes the term "terrorization" to the type of action that induces desperate panic and overwhelms a person's rational decision-making capability, and distinguishes it from coercion, which concerns actions that leave room for rational deliberation on the part of the victim.[16] Nonetheless, he argues ultimately that defining "terrorism" is difficult and not an enterprise worth undertaking, except for specific legal purposes.[17] While Fletcher and Waldron both expend the necessary effort in investigating this definitional question, they essentially concur that, in the end, "The quest for a canonical definition of terrorism is probably a waste of time."[18] This book argues, to the contrary, that a canonical and consistent definition of "terrorism" can and should be pursued, particularly by philosophers.

In his recent and provocative book, *What's Wrong with Terrorism?* Robert Goodin humorously accuses political theorists, myself included (in a slightly different connection) of having "a limited range of tools in their intellectual toolkits. Presented with real world events, they rummage around to see what among their standard equipment best fits this occasion, rather than necessarily doing any first order philosophy on the situation at hand."[19] Goodin is probably right, and it is not

---

[13] Fletcher, "The Indefinable Concept of Terrorism," pp. 8–16; Fletcher, "The Problem of Defining" considers only the latter six of the eight variables mentioned above.

[14] Fletcher, "The Problem of Defining," throughout; Fletcher, "The Indefinable Concept of Terrorism," esp. p. 18.

[15] Waldron, "Terrorism," esp. pp. 8–9, 11–12, 33.   [16] Ibid., pp. 11–12.

[17] Ibid., p. 33.   [18] Ibid., p. 5.

[19] Robert Goodin, *What's Wrong with Terrorism?* (Cambridge, UK and Malden, MA: Polity Press, 2006), p. 170.

surprising then that we have in recent years witnessed a veritable slew of academic writing on the definition of terrorism. Political philosophers are rather fond of framing classifications and typologies, and categorizing and defining. Contra Waldron and Fletcher, however, I do not consider this a waste of time. If we are to fruitfully pursue the further moral issues regarding the changing character of modern war, we must first agree on a canonical definition of terrorism. As Coady observes, "There are two central philosophical questions about terrorism: What is it? And what, if anything, is wrong with it?" We must deal with the first question because of the importance of the second.[20]

I have another piece of old equipment in my toolbox that I believe meets the occasion. Aristotle observed long ago that our definitional powers are essentially linked to our ability to distinguish good from evil. The gift of speech, Aristotle tells us, goes beyond the physical capacity to utter sounds and even the ability to recognize and name objects in the physical world. The essential attribute of human speech is captured by the ability to differentiate, categorize, and define a variety of incidents as belonging to a common genus, while excluding others. It is the capacity to distinguish and define which enables us to make ethical judgments.[21] To bring this observation into the present, the twenty-first-century philosopher's objective must be to define terrorism in order to identify its morally crucial features.

Aside from pure moral inquiry, there are also other, more practical, objectives to be served by a clear definition of terrorism. As I have said, lawyers require definitions in order to prosecute terrorists. Chapter 4 of this book looks at the legal status of irregular combatants. Chapters 5 to 7 contemplate the appropriate attitude on the part of the international community towards certain modes of combating terrorism and terrorists, specifically towards the practices of targeted assassination and investigative torture. In view of recent events, there is a great need to adapt international law to the reality of modern warfare. Legislation on terrorism, and the legitimate modes of combating it, is sorely lacking. Legally defining terrorism would be a very good place to start. An orderly definition would specify the category of persons we call terrorists for the purpose of both prosecuting and fighting them, and distinguish them from those who would categorically be immune from such repercussions. A definitive description of terrorism would enable us

---

[20] Coady, "Defining Terrorism," p. 3.
[21] Aristotle, *The Nicomachean Ethics* (London: Penguin, 1976), pp. 75–6.

to consider policies designed to combat it, such as targeted killing, without lending our hand to related practices, such as the murder of political enemies, which we ardently condemn. An internationally agreed-upon definition of terrorism is a necessary first step in the right direction.

Why are Western theorists having such a hard time agreeing on a definition of terrorism? Israeli legal theorist Alon Harel suggests that the various conflicting definitions fall roughly into two categories, each with a distinct political agenda. One large group of contemporary definitions seeks to highlight a specific aspect of terrorism that is said to single it out as a particularly fiendish and condemnable practice. In contrast, a second group of definitions aims to blur the distinction between terrorism and other violent acts, suggesting that terrorism is no worse than many forms of state-employed violence.[22] While Harel never names particular scholars in each of his categories, most authors on terrorism do indeed fall distinctly into one of the two groups.

Throughout this chapter, I pursue this distinction between two broad categories of definitions based loosely on their respective goals. I refer to them as the "inclusive" and the "restrictive" definitions respectively. In the next section, after pursuing several paradigmatic definitions of the inclusive category, I criticize this type of definition, suggesting that it is entirely politically motivated, misguided, and normatively unhelpful in understanding the modern phenomenon that is terrorism. While authors of these wide, inclusive definitions accuse their opponents of begging important moral questions – allegedly defining terrorism as unjustified – they themselves advance their political agenda by shaping definitions that suit them. Chapter 2 offers a more detailed refutation of such political agenda. This chapter, as well as the next, suggests that a satisfactory definition of terrorism must specify its uniqueness and distinguish it from other types of human activity, specifically from other types of violent action. If terminology is to contribute to ethical judgment, the definition itself ought to highlight the characteristic normative aspect of the category in question. The term "terrorism" is derogatory, at least in ordinary usage. That is why no one applies it to themselves and practically everyone nowadays attempts to apply it to his or

---

[22] Alon Harel, "Is Terrorism a Moral Category?" paper delivered at a conference on "Terrorism – Philosophical Perspectives," at Tel-Aviv University (organized by the department of Political Science and the Minerva Center for Human Rights), March 2004.

her enemies. Therefore, I argue here, the characterizing features we are looking for are bound to be at least objectionable if they are to bear any connection with ordinary speech. Finally, I conclude the present chapter by siding with what has been dubbed a "tactical definition" of terrorism; tactical in that it focuses on the specific problematic tactic of terrorism as an action category.[23] I do so without reference to the nature of the perpetrators of such a tactic or the justness of their goal and without rendering it morally and politically unjustifiable by definition. The following chapter looks more closely at political motivation and the question of justification.

Inclusive definitions

The *Oxford Student's Dictionary for Hebrew Speakers* describes terrorism as merely the "use of violence and intimidation, especially for political purposes."[24] Interestingly, this was also Leon Trotsky's understanding of terrorism: as violence intended to intimidate and thereby achieve political objectives.[25] Quite obviously, many acts of conventional warfare can equally be described as violent and intimidating for political purposes. Several modern-day theorists adopt a variety of inclusive definitions of terrorism that blur, or deconstruct, the distinction between terrorism and other forms of political violence. This type of definition aims to obliterate the distinction between terrorism and other violent acts, with the clear implication that terrorism is, in and of itself, no worse than many other practiced forms of violence which are internationally sanctioned.

Many theorists believe that the very concept of terrorism, or at least its current usage, has been molded in a sinister way in order to serve the political interests of the stronger powers within the international community, specifically those of the United States. Hence, it is argued, the United States' labeling of particular individuals, groups, states, and organizations as "terrorists" is biased and unjust.[26] There is nothing

---

[23] Coady, "Defining Terrorism," pp. 3, 7. For Coady's tactical definition, see also C. A. J. Coady, "Terrorism, Morality and Supreme Emergency," in Primoratz, *Terrorism*, p. 80.

[24] A. S. Hornby, *Oxford Student's Dictionary for Hebrew Speakers* (Tel-Aviv: Kernerman, 1991).

[25] Leon Trotsky, "A Defense of the Red Terror," in Primoratz, *Terrorism*, pp. 31–43.

[26] Virginia Held, for example, "Terrorism, Rights, and Political Goals," in Primoratz, *Terrorism*, p. 65–79.

distinct about this type of violence that has not already been employed far more extensively by the United States itself and some of its closest allies. Noam Chomsky, for example, clearly holds this view.[27] If so, perhaps the moral appraisal of any specific use of force relies ultimately on the justness of its cause rather than on the means employed in its pursuit.[28]

In "Political Terrorism as a Weapon of the Politically Powerless," Robert Young attempts to justify what he describes as terrorism in terms of "just cause." While he recognizes that states as well as groups use terror tactics, he concentrates on the latter, arguing that "the most promising way, morally, to defend terrorism not carried out by states is as a weapon which those who lack conventional political power can use to fight the just causes they are otherwise prevented from promoting."[29] He admits in advance that killing or injuring the innocent, as well as random or indiscriminate attacks – which are the features most commonly associated with terrorism – are rarely, if ever, justifiable.[30] Young's self-professed political agenda – that of justifying terrorism by the politically powerless – is then squared with his difficulty in justifying the killing of innocents and random indiscriminate violence, by attempting to evade, and subsequently obscuring, the definitional question, which he claims to avoid.[31] Instead, he lists those features which he believes provide a clear description of terrorism.[32] These include causing fear, usually by non-state actors, and a broad range of political goals.[33] Finally, he rejects those definitions that associate terrorism with random indiscriminate violence, as well as with the targeting of non-combatants, as "moralized." Recognizing that "many believe terrorism involves threatening to harm, or harming, non-combatants (which is code for 'innocents'),"[34] thus violating the classic just-war theory

---

[27] Noam Chomsky, *9–11* (New York: Seven Stories Press, 2001), esp. pp. 23, 40–54, 57, 73–4, 90–1, as well as in his numerous other similar publications.

[28] This is pointed out by Alon Harel, "Is Terrorism a Moral Category," and is exhibited in the work of Ted Honderich, *After the Terror* (Edinburgh University Press, 2003) esp. pp. 91–7, and at least implied by Jacques Derrida in G. Borradori, *Philosophy in a Time of Terror* (University of Chicago Press, 2003), pp. 85–136.

[29] Robert Young, "Political Terrorism as a Weapon of the Politically Powerless," in Primoratz, *Terrorism*, pp. 55–64 (pp. 55–6).

[30] Ibid., p. 57.   [31] Ibid., p. 55.   [32] Ibid., pp. 56–7.

[33] Ibid., p. 56.   [34] Ibid., p. 57.

principle of discrimination, Young points out, unoriginally, that civilian victims need not be "innocent" in the moral sense. They may be state officials, supporters of the government, or even heads of state, whose targeting is regarded by others as political assassination rather than terror.

Young's argument here is somewhat circular, as well as fraught with error. For one thing, the term "non-combatant" as it functions within the just-war theory principle of discrimination is not code for "innocent" in any ordinary moral sense. On the contrary, talk of targeting the innocent is shorthand, or code, for "non-combatant" – non-threatening, unarmed personnel. The terminology of just-war theory does not refer to the normal moral or judicial sense of innocence as opposed to blameworthiness, but rather to "innocents" in terms of defenseless, or not immediately threatening, individuals as opposed to armed combatants. There is, therefore, nothing novel in Young's suggestion that non-combatants may be implicated in the terrorist's grievance. This is a well-known fact, and when they are highly implicated (as in the case of politicians) many regard their murder as an act of assassination rather than random terror. Thus, Young's argument is also somewhat circular, as he defines assassination as a form of terror and then continues to argue that "terror" – though perhaps only against the guilty – can be justified.

Young continues to argue that not only does a definition which takes targeting the innocent as a defining characteristic of terrorism "beg the question of its moral justifiability, it is also unwarrantedly prescriptive about which acts of political violence may be considered acts of terrorism."[35] This objection is curious. Definitions are intended precisely to determine what does, and what does not, fall into a particular category, and they would be of little use if they did not do so. Specifically as regards terrorism, Igor Primoratz points out "a conception of terrorism that lumps together the assassination of Reinhardt Heydrich, the Reichsprotektor of Bohemia, and the killing or wounding of a group of civilians traveling on an inter city bus can be of no use in moral thinking."[36] Prescribing which acts of violence fall under the term "terrorism" and which do not is precisely what is warranted by any adequate definition. Instead, Young himself inclusively lumps together, under the joint heading of terrorism, sabotage, political assassination,

---

[35] Ibid., p. 57.   [36] Primoratz, "What is Terrorism?", in *Terrorism*, pp. 15–27 (p. 15).

and insurgent attacks on combatants, alongside random targeting of the innocent.

Nothing else Young has to say substantiates the claim that defining terrorism in terms of the just-war theory injunction against targeting non-combatants is unwarranted. His assertion that the common understanding of terrorism in terms of failing to uphold the distinction between combatants and non-combatants is "moralized" and question-begging is simply fallacious. As Coady points out, tying the widespread moral revulsion against terrorism to the fundamental moral prohibition in just-war theory against violating the rights of non-combatants actually avoids the pitfall of making terrorism immoral by definition, since its immorality needs to be established by argument for the acceptability of the principle of discrimination itself.[37] Young might do better, then, to confront the principle of discrimination directly rather than tamper with the definition of terrorism in a confusing and linguistically manipulative and inclusive manner. The inclusive definition enables Young to argue that "terrorism," as he describes it, is often justified when employed by the politically powerless in a just cause, while at one and the same time admitting that killing innocents, which is usually associated with terrorism, is seldom justifiable.

Why is it so important to Young to define terrorism in a way that obscures its most commonly objectionable features and more easily enables talk of justified terrorism? Perhaps the end of his essay is more telling than his thesis. Its last paragraph clearly takes on the Chomsky anti-American and anti-Israeli political line, which nearly always follows inclusionist definitions. Young remains hard-pressed to defend direct attacks against civilians. However, his wide definition of terrorism, which obscures this objectionable feature and includes political assassination as well as guerrilla attacks on soldiers, enables him to imply that terrorism is justified in terms of its cause; for example, when it is directed against certain US economic policies, as well as US support for "brutal" regimes in the Middle East, most notably (though not exclusively) Israel.[38]

In his aforementioned thought-provoking *What's Wrong with Terrorism?*, Robert Goodin offers a particularly inclusive definition thereof. Goodin, unlike Young, carefully criticizes classic just-war

[37] Coady, "Defining Terrorism," p. 8.
[38] Young, "Political Terrorism," esp. pp. 61–2.

theory and argues against the common inclination to equate terrorism with unjust war and the killing of innocent civilians.[39] Essentially, he takes the somewhat technical line of argument whereby just-war theory applies only to states as the sole agents entitled to wage wars, and therefore cannot serve to define the objectionable character of terrorism, which is usually (though not exclusively) ascribed to non-state actors.[40] Goodin argues instead that terrorism's defining objectionable feature is "acting with the intention of instilling fear of violence for socio-political objectives."[41] This enables him to suggest throughout that George W. Bush and Tony Blair are guilty of terrorism (though admittedly to a lesser degree than bin Laden), for intentionally frightening their publics by exaggerating the dangers of group terrorism in order to gain political advantages for themselves.[42] Once again it appears that while defining terrorism in terms of targeting the "innocent" has been accused of being question-begging,[43] those offering wider, inclusive definitions have their own clear political agenda in mind.

Virginia Held, to take one further example, persistently accuses strict definitions of terrorism of begging the question of its justification. Subsequently, she deliberately steers away from defining the factors that turn political violence into terrorism, commenting only that "perhaps when either the intention to spread fear or the intention to harm non-combatants is primary, this is sufficient."[44] She argues that popular as well as academic speech has "frequently built a judgment of immorality, or non-justifiability into the definition of terrorism, making it impossible even to question whether given acts of terrorism might be justified."[45] And she holds up former Israeli Prime Minister Benjamin Netanyahu, alongside philosopher Burton Leiser and Michael Walzer, as paradigmatic culprits.[46] While she cites comments condemning terrorism and terrorists from each of the three authors to substantiate her claim, none of them in fact builds unjustifiability into an actual definition, as she accuses them of doing. Walzer is cited by Held as proclaiming that "every act of terrorism is a wrongful act,"[47] but his classic definition is neutral enough to enable him to consider whether various aerial bombings of civilians during the Second World War were

---

[39] Goodin, *What's Wrong with Terrorism?*, pp. 6–30.   [40] Ibid.
[41] Ibid., pp. 63, 99, 105.   [42] Ibid., esp. pp. 179–80.
[43] Goodin clearly states this accusation in ibid., p. 6.
[44] Held, "Terrorism, Rights, and Political Goals," p. 65.   [45] Ibid.
[46] Ibid., pp. 65–6.   [47] Ibid., p. 66.

justified, though they fall clearly within his definition of terrorism.[48] As for Netanyahu, who certainly denounces terrorism, his theoretical understanding of it as a definable phenomenon essentially follows Walzer, whose *Just and Unjust Wars* he cites on various occasions.[49] Leiser, for his part, admittedly describes terrorism in exceptionally unflattering terms, equating it (as Netanyahu does) with piracy, referring to terrorists in several publications as "Enemies of Mankind,"[50] but he does not actually define the phenomenon in such terms at all.[51] His actual definition, distinguishing terrorism from other acts of violence, in fact addresses the very two elements mentioned by Held herself – spreading fear and causing harm to civilians.[52]

Following these inaccurate accusations, Held proceeds to argue that terrorism, undefined by her, can be justified, once again in terms of just cause. Terrorism can be justified when it is employed as the only resort to safeguarding the human rights of those whose rights are being disregarded.[53] While recognizing that terrorism itself violates rights, she suggests that it is justified, perhaps even called for, when it is aimed at members of a group that is violating the rights of others. If there are to be rights violations, she argues, justice requires that they be more equitably distributed among groups.[54] The Israeli–Palestinian example

---

[48] Michael Walzer, *Just and Unjust Wars* (New York: Basic Books, 1977), pp. 197–203. For his discussion of the Second World War terror bombings, see pp. 106–9 and pp. 255–68. Coady accuses Walzer of building a pro-state bias into his analysis of "supreme emergency" which would exclude the possibility of its use by sub-state terrorists, thus rendering group terrorism unjustifiable and inexcusable in all cases. Coady, "Defining Terrorism," pp. 88–91. This may indeed be Walzer's view, as expressed in some of his comments. Both Held and Coady refer to Michael Walzer, "Terrorism: A Critique of Excuses," in Steven Luper-Foy (ed.), *Problems of International Justice* (London: Westview Press, 1988). My point is that the unjustifiability of terrorism is not built into Walzer's definition of terrorism.

[49] See his reference to Walzer, e.g. in Benjamin Netanyahu (ed.), *Terrorism: How the West Can Win* (New York: Farrar, Straus, and Giroux, 1986), p. 132. Netanyahu defines terrorism as the "deliberate and systematic assault on civilians to inspire fear for political ends." Netanyahu, *Fighting Terrorism*, p. xxi and p. 8; Also in Netanyahu, *Terrorism*, p. 9.

[50] Both in Burton M. Leiser, "The Catastrophe of September 11 and its Aftermath," in Primoratz, *Terrorism*, pp. 192–208, which Held cites, and in Burton M. Leiser, "Enemies of Mankind," in Netanyahu, *Terrorism*, pp. 155–7.

[51] Leiser, "The Catastrophe of September 11," pp. 192–208.

[52] Leiser, "Enemies of Mankind," p. 155.

[53] Held, "Terrorism, Rights, and Political Goals," p. 75. [54] Ibid., pp. 74–5.

is not far behind, suggesting that Palestinian terrorism against Israel is in fact justified in so far as it moves towards a more equitable distribution of rights violations between Israelis and Palestinians.[55]

There are many other examples of politically motivated inclusive definitions of terrorism. Ted Honderich and Jacques Derrida put forward wide definitions that go further towards justifying specific acts of terrorism.[56] Both are discussed at length in the following chapter that addresses the justificatory issue. As we shall see, Honderich suggests, reasonably enough, that terrorism is a subset of politically motivated violence, which falls short of conventional war and is internationally illegal and (to say the least) morally questionable.[57] We cannot, however, leave things at that, as Honderich himself would have it, and "give up on the strict and careful idea of terrorism, and go on ... in our inquiry, with a more general idea of it."[58] Here, more than anywhere, the devil is in the detail.

The remainder of this chapter looks at some strict, or restrictive, definitions of terrorism. Following Coady, I refer to them as "tactical" in that they define terrorism in terms of the specific tactic employed, rather than with reference to the nature of their perpetrator or the justness of their cause. I suggest that, whatever the personal politics of their authors, such definitions are in fact far less question-begging and agenda-based than their inclusionist counterparts. Perhaps more importantly, only a definition that aspires to isolate terrorism from other forms of violence and identify its objectionable features can be normatively illuminating. As in all other spheres of life, the object of definitions is to distinguish the particular from seemingly similar phenomena. We do not define trees (to borrow from Aristotle's examples) by equating them with bushes or shrubbery, and those philosophers who followed Aristotle in seeking the defining characteristic of humanity did so with reference to those features (such as speech or the supposedly related capacity for moral judgment) which characterize humans as opposed to (other) animals. This is no more than stating the obvious.

Approaching the topic in hand, we cannot reach an adequate definition of murder by obscuring the difference between it and manslaughter or negligence, nor do we beg any important questions of justification by

---

[55] Ibid., p. 76.
[56] Honderich, *After the Terror*; Jacques Derrida in Borradori, *Philosophy*.
[57] Honderich, *After the Terror*, pp. 98–9.   [58] Ibid., p. 98.

defining it in terms of what is wrong about it – intentionally killing another human being – though I assume we all take that feature of murder to be negative. On the contrary, any adequate definition must specify precisely the wrong involved in it. Whether we then regard murder as justifiable under certain circumstances is entirely beside the point. The same goes for other morally dubious practices, such as torture. Any morally useful definition must isolate the phenomenon of torture, properly so called, from related painful practices – such as unpleasant medical procedures – and associate the former with at least prima facie evil-doing. Any definition that refrains from doing so is unhelpful and in fact makes a mockery of common language. This, however, need not, or should not, beg any questions of justification. One may still regard torture, or murder, as justifiable under certain circumstances (say, in self-defense, or on the utilitarian grounds of avoiding greater pain for the many).

The same obviously goes for terrorism. Terrorism is undoubtedly a derogatory term and we need not set out with a neutral, or objective, attitude towards it in order to avoid bias. An adequate definition of murder, theft, or torture ought to highlight these particular wrong-doings, and need not assume an attitude of moral neutrality towards their practice. Wrongdoings, however, can at times be justified, or excused, and such possibilities ought not to be excluded terminologically, thus entirely precluding further moral reflection. An adequate definition of terrorism, if it is to have any connection with common usage, must describe at least a prima facie wrong and seek to further our understanding of this term by bringing out what it is that makes terrorism morally repugnant to most of us.[59] It ought not, however, as the inclusionists argue, beg the further moral question of its possible justification.

Furthermore, the inclusionists have at least one more point in their favor, as most theorists would concede. Definitions ought not specify the nature of the terrorist perpetrator.[60] Non-state terrorism is probably no worse than certain forms of state-employed violence, which may themselves be regarded as terrorism, or something perhaps worse than

---

[59] This is also Igor Primoratz's goal in "What is Terrorism?," in *Terrorism*, pp. 15–27.
[60] For example, to name just those who have been cited thus far, Walzer, Coady, Primoratz, Held.

terrorism (e.g. genocide, mass murder, deportations, ethnic cleansing). I write these lines as Israel bombs civilian residential areas in Lebanon as part of its war against Hizbullah and Hamas. I do not regard this as terrorism, for reasons that will become apparent once the definitional issue is clarified. However, considering the possibility that states, such as Israel, commit acts of terror against civilians ought not to be precluded by definition. Quite aside from avoiding political bias in favor of states, the definition of terrorism, if it is to be helpful in assessing a contemporary moral (at least prima facie) wrong, and hopefully contribute to avoiding it, ought to describe an action category rather than narrowing the linguistic possibility of applying it to certain actors, such as states.

Restrictive definitions

What is terrorism, strictly defined as an action category, or a specific violent tactic? Michael Walzer's understanding of terrorism in *Just and Unjust Wars* forms the classic example of the stringent definition and has become the term of reference for practically every discussion of terrorism. According to Walzer, "terrorism" (as distinct from guerrilla warfare and political assassination) is a particular form of political violence: it is the intentional random murder of defenseless non-combatants (some of whom, Walzer's account implies, must be considered innocent even by the assailants' own standards, e.g. infants, children, the elderly and infirm, and foreign nationals), with the intent of spreading fear of mortal danger amidst a civilian population as a strategy designed to advance political ends.[61]

Walzer's understanding of terrorism as distinguished from other forms of violence, described derogatively as the ideologically motivated random targeting of non-combatants, is echoed in many modern works. Paul Berman's *Terror and Liberalism* describes contemporary terrorism as opposed to other forms of political violence in terms strikingly similar to those of Walzer.[62] The clear distinction of terrorism from all other military and paramilitary activity, along with the negative normative implications that attach to this singular category, have recently been

---

[61] Walzer, *Just and Unjust Wars*, pp. 197, 203.
[62] Paul Berman, *Terror and Liberalism* (New York and London: Norton, 2003), pp. 35–6.

restated by Jürgen Habermas in his post-September 11 reflections on terror.[63] Not surprisingly, this is the common Israeli approach to terrorism amongst politicians and academics (left and right) alike. It was no coincidence on Held's part to mention Michael Walzer and Benjamin Netanyahu in the same breath in this connection. Like Walzer, Netanyahu defines terrorism as "the deliberate and systematic assault on civilians to inspire fear for political ends."[64] And he regards the essence of terrorism as "the purposeful attack on the innocent, those who are *hors de combat*, outside the field of legitimate conflict."[65]

Primoratz also regards "violence against non-combatants, civilians, the innocent, as the central defining trait of terrorism,"[66] and Saul Smilansky (following Tony Coady) describes the ethically significant feature of terrorism as the intentional targeting of non-combatants.[67] I have already suggested that terrorism must be distinguished from other forms of political violence if this term is to be of use in any moral context. It remains to be seen whether this particular line of definitions is sufficiently descriptive. As we saw in the previous section, the strict definition of terrorism as the random targeting of "innocents" is widely resisted. Walzer's definition in particular is often criticized on several grounds relating to the randomness of victims and their alleged innocence. I will argue briefly that such accusations are unfounded.

First, Walzer has been criticized for arguing that terrorists choose their victims at random, or indiscriminately. He places great importance on this feature, stating with regard to terrorism that,

its method is the random murder of innocent people. Randomness is the crucial feature of terrorist activity. If one wishes fear to spread and intensify over time, it is not desirable to kill specific people identified in some particular way with a regime, a party, or a policy. Death must come by chance to individual Frenchman, Germans, to Irish Protestants or Jews, simply because they are Frenchmen or Germans, Protestants or Jews, until

---

[63] Borradori, *Philosophy*, pp. 33, 56.
[64] Netanyahu, *Fighting Terrorism*, p. xxi and p. 8. See also, Netanyahu, *Terrorism*, p. 9.
[65] Netanyahu, *Fighting Terrorism*, p. 8.
[66] Primoratz, *Terrorism*, p. xii and pp. 15–30.
[67] Saul Smilansky, "Terrorism, Justification, and Illusion", *Ethics* 114 (4) (July 2004), p. 790. C.A.J. Coady, "Terrorism," in Lawrence C. Becker and Charlotte B. Becker, eds., *Encyclopedia of Ethics*, 2nd edn. (New York: Routledge, 2001), p. 1697. See also Coady, "Defining Terrorism," pp. 3–14.

they feel themselves fatally exposed and demand that their governments negotiate for their safety.[68]

It has been pointed out more than once, both by opponents of this definition and by its defenders, that terrorists do not choose their victims at random, striking altogether blindly and pointlessly, but rather choose their target carefully in view of their objectives.[69] George Fletcher argues, against Walzer, that describing terrorism as random contradicts its definition as politically purposeful. The key to understanding terrorism, he argues, cannot be that it is both random and intentional at one and the same time.[70]

Terrorists are not indiscriminate in their choice of victim in the sense of acting irrationally or in a random manner.[71] Clearly, they put much thought into the choice of their target. September 11 is a case in point. The twin towers were not chosen at random, out of a hat, as it were; this was no "shot in the dark." The target was chosen intentionally as a symbol of American financial might. Objections to Walzer's definition, which emphasizes the random, or indiscriminate, choice of victims on the grounds that terrorists choose their targets rationally, build a straw man only to be knocked down by this artificial objection. Clearly, as both Primoratz and Coady explain almost unnecessarily, "random" or "indiscriminate" in this type of definition does not stand for "irrational" or "arbitrary." Instead, these terms refer to a particular lack of discrimination, that between combatants and civilians, which is assumed to be morally valuable and is enshrined in just-war theory,[72] alongside a disregard for the particular identity of the victim. Bin Laden clearly chose his target with care, but he did so with disregard for the rules of war, alongside his indifference to the personal identities of those who showed up for work in the twin towers on that fateful morning. The first point is captured in Netanyahu's reference to the purposeful attack on those who are "*hors de combat*, outside the field of legitimate conflict."[73] The second is depicted perfectly in Paul Berman's retelling of a previous terrorist incident in New York. In 1920, a member of the Luigi Galleani

[68] Walzer, *Just and Unjust Wars*, p. 197.   [69] Primoratz, "What is Terrorism?", p. 17.
[70] Fletcher, "The Problem of Defining Terrorism," p. 2. See also Fletcher, "The Indefinable Concept of Terrorism," p. 8.
[71] Coady, "Defining Terrorism," p. 7.
[72] Ibid., p. 7; Primoratz, "What is Terrorism?", p. 18.
[73] Netanyahu, *Fighting Terrorism*, p. 8.

anarchist group planted a bomb on Wall Street. In general, the group opposed the injustice of capitalism and exploitation. More particularly, the bomb was intended to avenge the arrest of Sacco and Vanzetti: "The bomb killed a random crowd of thirty-three people ... Why detonate an explosive on Wall Street? For symbolic reasons, of course. And why kill those thirty-three people in particular? For no reason. Because they happened to be walking by."[74]

Randomness in this double sense, as Walzer clearly intended it, is indeed descriptive of terrorism. It disregards the principle of discrimination (which can admittedly be questioned) and it is blind to the particular identities of its victims. For Walzer, this is a crucial point about terrorism: it is not aimed at particular people. Furthermore, as Primoratz points out, terrorism is indiscriminate in the further sense that it is difficult to avoid. This is a defining factor of this tactic, as it is what makes it so fearful and effective: "One can never count on keeping clear of the terrorist by not doing the things the terrorist objects to, by not joining the army or the police, or by avoiding political office. One can never know whether, at any time and in any place, one will become a target of a terrorist attack."[75] This is precisely because the terrorist strikes at random, in the sense specified. In fact, as Netanyahu, points out, "the more removed the target of the attack from any connection to the grievance enunciated by the terrorists, the greater the terror."[76]

Do terrorists target the innocent in particular? This close relative of the non-random objection is a further source of criticism aimed at the Walzer-type definition. Victims of terrorism are not, it has been argued, necessarily innocent. Perhaps terrorists do not aim to target the innocent at all, as Walzer and others accuse them of doing by definition. Honderich, for example, more than implies that adult Israelis at large, as well as Americans, most notably those associated with Manhattan's center of finance, are not innocent of complicity in the grievances confronted by Islamic terrorists.[77] Alternatively, it has been suggested

[74] Berman, *Terror and Liberalism*, pp. 35–6.
[75] Primoratz, "What is Terrorism?", p. 19.
[76] Netanyahu, *Fighting Terrorism*, p. 8.
[77] Throughout *After the Terror*, Honderich places a great deal of blame on ordinary citizens of Western democracies, particularly the US and UK, for the ills of developing nations. Aside from which he specifically holds Israeli civilians responsible for their government's actions vis-à-vis the Palestinians, e.g. Honderich, *After the Terror*, p. 151.

that if terrorism targets the innocent specifically, it is not so indiscriminate and random after all.[78]

First, it must be restated that 'innocent' in this context stands for civilians or non-combatants. Terrorism, is, by this account, the indiscriminate targeting of those who in classic just-war theory ought to be immune from attack. This still leaves ample room to argue about the normative distinction drawn by such theory between civilians and soldiers, as well as its applicability to modern conflicts and revolutionary warfare, in which the line drawn between civilians and combatants is far less obvious than it was on the medieval battlefield.[79] Classifying terrorism in this way – as essentially harming non-combatants – thus remains neutral in that it leaves open the question of justification, which in turn hinges largely on the moral validity of the debatable principle of discrimination.[80] There is also room to argue over who are and who are not properly defined as 'non-combatants' within specific contemporary conflicts. The boundaries in this case, however, are less fuzzy than is sometimes assumed. It is quite clear, for example, that 3,000 inhabitants of commercial office buildings are 'non-combatants', whatever the extent of moral blameworthiness attributed to them by the terrorists for compliance with American capitalism. On the other hand, talk of terrorism as *random* violence against non-combatants clearly excludes the deliberate targeting of particular agents of state as well as of particular terrorists themselves.[81]

Second, and obviously, while terrorism is defined here as the deliberate targeting of non-combatants, terrorists have no qualms about harming combatants and non-combatants within a single operation. As Primoratz observes, when terrorists bomb a civilian commuter bus, "if a couple of soldiers get on ... they will not see that as a fly in the ointment" but rather as an added bonus.[82] Terrorism is indiscriminate in this sense

[78] Primoratz, *Terrorism*, pp. 19–20, cites Walter Laqueur claiming that "if it is claimed that terrorist violence is random, then it cannot also be claimed that it is directed solely against the innocent." This is obviously not what is claimed by such definitions, as Primoratz makes clear. Rather it is claimed that terrorists fail to distinguish between the innocent and the guilty, exhibiting a disregard for innocent life.

[79] Coady in Primoratz, *Terrorism*, p. 9.

[80] Arguing for the rights of insurrectionists, Palestinian historian Karma Nabulsi, for instance, rejects the stark distinctions drawn by modern laws of war between civilians and combatants. Karma Nabulsi, *Traditions of War* (Oxford University Press, 1999).

[81] Thus Walzer distinguishes terrorism from political assassination, pp. 197–203.

[82] Primoratz, *Terrorism*, p. 20.

as well. However, it is essential to regarding an act as terrorism that its primary target be civilian rather than military. As Primoratz argues, "The defining feature of terrorism, and the reason many of us find it extremely morally repugnant, is its failure to discriminate between the innocent and the guilty, and its consequent failure to respect the immunity of the former and to concentrate exclusively on the latter."[83]

In *After the Terror*, Ted Honderich attempts an appeal to the doctrine of double effect, arguing in essence that terrorists do not aim at the innocent but rather incur innocent casualties in the course of pursuing legitimate objectives, just as regular armies do in the course of just wars. He suggests that the common Western excuse as regards civilian casualties incurred in war applies equally to such terrorists as the killers of September 11. In both cases, he claims, "their deaths were not the first intention of their killers, but necessary in the carrying out of another intention, a justified one."[84] This point of similarity, however, even if conceded, has limited implications. Perhaps bin Laden's first intention was not to kill Americans, and perhaps the first intention of Palestinian suicide bombers and their organizations is not to kill Israelis (though this is by no means a foregone conclusion).[85] Their very first intention may indeed be, as Honderich suggests, achieving their political ends. If this is true, it is admittedly a feature of their action that they share with the unintentional killers of innocent non-combatants in war. It is not, however, the only, or primarily relevant, feature of their action. It remains the case that some forms of political violence are characterized by the intentional and deliberate slaying of non-combatants, rather than the accidental, or even negligent, killing of innocents that occurs in all wars. I have already pointed out that targeted civilians may include those who are innocent even on the terrorists' own account (children, for example), though they need not be in order for the act to count as terrorist. The essential point about terrorism, described well by Primoratz, is that "Terrorists do not take on the army or the police, nor do they attempt to kill a political official, but choose, say, to plant a bomb in a city bus, either because that is so much easier or, perhaps, that will better serve their cause."[86] Others argue that in some cases such

---

[83] Primoratz, "What is Terrorism?", p. 20.   [84] Honderich, *After the Terror*, p. 103.
[85] Paul Berman argues persuasively that in both these cases death is in fact the primary goal. Berman, *Terror and Liberalism*, esp. pp. 132–3.
[86] Primoratz, "What is Terrorism?", p. 20.

tactics may be a last resort, the sole remaining option for the representatives of an oppressed group, or an emergency measure. I deliberately
leave all questions of justification open here. Be that as it may, targeting
civilians is the essential trait of terrorism,[87] whether ultimately justifiable or not. This point appears to me so obvious that it hardly needs
restating at all, let alone arguing for, were it not for the voluminous
academic literature, a sampling of which we saw in the previous section,
aimed at discrediting the significance of this defining feature.

What else, if anything, is definitive of terrorism? It seems obvious to
suggest, as Walzer does, that fear is a key element as it is tied at the most
basic philological level to the term itself, as well as describing a seemingly basic feature of the phenomenon – its frightening intention and
result. Consequently, most authors include this feature – literal terrorization – within their definition or description. This element appears to
cut across political lines and is included in the widest variety of discussions on terrorism.[88] A minority, however, argue that fear is not an
essential element of terrorism. Naturally, those who refrain from defining terrorism at all, or at least from distinguishing it strictly from other
forms of violence, point out that fear is not unique to any particular type
of violent political act.[89] More interesting is the fact that Coady, who
supplies a strict definition of terrorism, makes a similar argument for
excluding the element of fear. His tactical approach, defended here
throughout, defines terrorism as "The tactic of intentionally directing
violent attacks at non-combatants with lethal or severe violence for
political purposes."[90] As for omitting the element of fear, he argues
that, while it describes a frequent sociological effect of terrorism, it is
not definitive of it since all uses of political violence generate some

---

[87] Primoratz, "What is Terrorism?", p. 20.
[88] For descriptions that include fear or intimidation, see, all along the political
spectrum: Walzer, Waldron, Fletcher, Primoratz, Goodin, Netanyahu, Held,
Trotsky, and many others, such as C. Wellman, "On Terrorism Itself," *Journal of
Value Inquiry* 13 (1979), pp. 250–2.
[89] Waldron, "Terrorism," esp. pp. 8–9, 11–12, 33, discusses fear but refrains from
defining terrorism, as does Fletcher in "The Problem of Defining Terrorism."
Honderich, *After the Terror*, pp. 98–9, and Derrida in Borradori, *Philosophy*,
pp. 102–3, define terrorism only inclusively together with other forms of violence,
including those employed by the state.
[90] Coady, "Defining Terrorism," p. 7.

degree of fear.[91] Primoratz, following Walzer, argues to the contrary that coercion through intimidation plays a central role in terrorism and that this deliberate intimidation is an additional ground, alongside targeting the innocent, for the moral condemnation of terrorism.[92] It would seem, leaving linguistics aside, that fear plays a rather essential role in what we normally take terrorism to mean. Fear is, if not the ultimate end of terrorism, at least an interim objective of this tactic, a means deliberately used in order to achieve some ultimate political goal. Fear would appear to be part of the very tactic that is terrorism.

As for political goals, there is little dispute, if any, that terrorism, whatever else it is, is violence carried out for political purposes, with "political" taken here in the widest possible sense of the term to include religious, social, and economic ends, as well as political goals in the narrow sense. In the margins of the definitional dispute we find questions such as whether targeting civilian property ought or ought not to be regarded as terrorism properly so called,[93] and whether a threat of terrorist violence, without a resulting action, should in itself count as an instance of terrorism.[94]

To summarize, I set out by arguing that terrorism ought to be defined rather than obscured. The previous section argued that wide and indeterminate definitions are insufficient and, moreover, that they are politically biased and agenda-based. This section looked at, and defended, the central attempts to define terrorism restrictively, as distinct from other forms of political violence. I refuted some basic critiques and pointed out minor differences amongst the variety of such strict definitions. Essentially, they all define terrorism as the deliberate violent

---

[91] Coady, "Defining Terrorism," p. 6. Elsewhere, his definition appears as the "organized use of violence to attack non-combatants ('innocents' in a special sense) or their property for political purposes." Coady, "Terrorism, Morality and Supreme Emergency," in Primoratz, *Terrorism*, p. 80.

[92] Primoratz, "What is Terrorism?", p. 22.

[93] Coady, "Defining Terrorism," p. 7, holds that harming essential civilian property ought to count as terrorism. Primoratz agrees only so long as the property in question is vital to the actual survival, or livelihood, of non-combatants, p. 21. Otherwise, he argues, it is unlikely to cause the type of fear, or even fury, that characterizes terrorism. Coady himself admits that harm to property of innocents is less severe and also different in kind than bodily harming of the innocent, and that the former is at times justifiable. See Coady, "Terrorism, Morality and Supreme Emergency," p. 81.

[94] Coady is inclined to think that it should not, arguing plausibly that in general a threat to do X does not amount to the crime of doing X, "Defining Terrorism," p. 5.

targeting of non-combatants and civilian objectives, ignoring civilian immunity and the just-war theory principle of discrimination, with the intent of achieving some form of "political" objective. Most agree that this tactic necessarily involves instilling widespread fear amongst a civilian population in order to achieve the desired end. Such definitions are tactical, in that they isolate a particular action category – the violent strategy we call terrorism – with no reference to its agent or cause. Stringent definitions single out the objectionable traits which characterize terrorism. It is their strength, rather than weakness, that they do so, as terrorism (like murder or theft) is a derogatory term. They do not, however, settle by definition the question of justifiability. Tactical definitions are thus far less question-begging than the allegedly neutral and objective inclusive definitions.

The strict definition of terrorism, in its various versions, relies on the just-war theory principle of discrimination and its applicability to modern warfare. Thus, the negative normative weight imparted to terrorism by these definitions hinges ultimately on the validity of this principle, which is not itself immune from attack. Furthermore, even if the principle is upheld as valid and applicable, there still remains a variety of justificatory arguments available to those who would, and do, defend terrorism. Even if terrorism is judged prima facie to be wrong, it could conceivably still be justified under certain circumstances.[95] Terrorism, strictly defined, may still be defended as the only means to gain political power for those who lack it, as Young would have us believe, or to more justly redistribute rights violations, as Held would have it.[96] Terrorism can be argued for in terms of last resort or extreme emergency, or as a morally problematic means towards achieving a worthy end. And it may be argued for as a reaction to state terrorism.[97] Terrorism may be justified on purely utilitarian grounds – achieving a greater good for a greater number. Honderich argues that it is justified as a means to attain better lives for more people. In the next chapter I reject such arguments for a variety of reasons. But the point is that they are not settled by defining terrorism stringently and even derogatively. An analytical

---

[95] Primoratz lists this possibility as an advantage of the tactical definition, "What is Terrorism?", p. 24.
[96] Young, "Political Terrorism as a Weapon of the Politically Powerless"; Held, "Terrorism, Rights, and Political Goals".
[97] Honderich, *After the Terror*.

distinguishing definition is required in order even to approach the justificatory question appropriately.

Concluding remarks

Terrorism ought to be strictly defined. It is too central a concept to the moral understanding of our contemporary world to remain obscure. Attempts to avoid its definition in terms of targeting non-combatants are terminologically evasive and unhelpful in understanding the phenomenon, and they quickly lose touch with common usage and intuitions. Terrorism is, roughly, the intentional random murder of defenseless non-combatants, with the intent of instilling fear of mortal danger amidst a civilian population as a strategy designed to advance political ends. This basic understanding (which admittedly allows for some variation and has some fuzzy edges), ought not to be obscured. Those who adopt wide and inclusive definitions claim neutrality for themselves, and accuse those who define terrorism strictly of political bias. The inclusionists, however, have their own obvious political agenda, but they also have some valid points. Terrorism ought not to be defined in terms of its agent, or presuppose the unjustifiability of its practice under all circumstances. The question of possible justification ought to be left out of the definitional question and remain unsettled by it. The following chapter considers the possibility of justifying terrorism and refutes the basic arguments offered in its defense.

2 | *The apologetics of terrorism: a refutation*

Assuming we know what terrorism is, can it ever be justified? What is the appropriate liberal, or humanist, attitude towards current events? The previous chapter concluded that defining terrorism as a distinct phenomenon leaves open the question of its possible justification. This chapter argues with those who proceed to justify terrorism under certain circumstances, and attempts to refute the central academic arguments frequently raised in defense of some acts of terrorism, particularly those directed against Israel and the US. While terrorism is far from a new phenomenon, either in the US or elsewhere, the events of September 11, 2001 have certainly pushed old questions concerning legitimate violence to the top of our agenda on good and evil. Resorting to analytical tools is perhaps no more than a philosopher's expression of despair, yet it is vital to understanding current events and appropriately influencing future ones. Philosophy, admittedly, cannot always supply one morally right answer to the exclusion of all others. At times, even strict ethical objectivism leaves room for some degree of value pluralism that enables the balancing of different morally acceptable principles against each other in a variety of legitimate ways, resulting in many cases in a plurality of morally valid political opinions.[1] Terrorism, I will argue, is no such case, at least not from any perspective that regards itself as even remotely related to liberalism. Taken from the viewpoint of liberal morality, I suggest, terrorism is one of those rare instances in which only one response is morally valid.

Recently, Western intellectuals, particularly left-leaning ones, seem increasingly confused, as traditional loyalties appear to pull in opposing directions. Liberals and leftists are accustomed to siding with the

---

[1] For the idea that morally valid views are plural, and that one reason for this may be attributed to different weight to various conflicting moral values, see Isaiah Berlin, *The Crooked Timber of Humanity: Chapters in the History of Ideas* (London: Fontana, 1990), pp. 12, 14, 17.

underdog; to supporting the self-determination of nations (most recently, fervently committed to Palestinian independence); they customarily oppose violence and war and associate with peace movements. Most versions of modern liberalism include a complicated committal to cultural pluralism and, relatedly, to the tolerance of cultures and societies, beliefs and life choices, including those which appear dramatically alien to ours. Egalitarians often support a global application of equality standards, and are therefore particularly sensitive to the plight of impoverished, developing world populations. This commits them to oppose certain Western economic policies which are associated with globalization. In the extreme it has led some to an overall anti-globalization stance, or even to the outright support of some forms of terrorism.[2] Consequently, as the leaders of liberal states increasingly view terrorism as an existential threat, some of their intellectuals argue in effect that one man's terrorism is another's freedom fight; one man's crime against humanity is another's resistance against oppression. Why, we might ask, are the desperate actions of militant groups dubbed illegitimate terrorism, while the military operations of established nations are considered legitimate warfare?

The Anglo-American liberal states – specifically the US and UK – have taken a strong public stand against any display of terrorism, and have launched a campaign – at times a violent one – against it, culminating in US President Bush's "War on Terror." The rhetoric employed by state leaders is often deliberately imprecise and inaccurate, blurring morally relevant distinctions at least inadvertently, and often scenically, with none of the analytic precision demanded in the previous chapter. Western states and their leaders employ the term "terrorism" inconsistently when confronting violence against their citizenry, and are probably often insincere in evaluating their own actions. Public political speech tends to conflate the evaluation of conflicting causes – their justness or injustice – with the legitimacy of the means adopted by either side for attaining their respective ends. None of these truisms, however, yields the conclusion that the condemnation of terrorism, and talk of waging war thereon, are forms of Western hypocrisy. If liberals have a quarrel with their governments, it ought to be over upholding the relevant distinctions, rather than dismissing them in the name of consistency. The previous chapter suggested that if philosophers have a task

---

[2] Most notably Honderich, *After the Terror*.

in this battle, it is to analyze and clarify definitions and evaluate their
normative force rather than to further obscure them.[3] This chapter
looks at some questions of moral judgment that have been thrust
upon political philosophy by current events.

Defending the undefined – justifying terrorism

In his controversial *After the Terror*, Ted Honderich takes up the
linguistic challenge discussed in the previous chapter alongside the moral
issues that flow from it. Honderich inquires at length into the definition
of terrorism, setting out more basic terms such as "violence" in general,
and "political violence" in particular.[4] "Violence" is plainly understood
to be the use of force for the worse. Honderich's definition of "political
violence" can be summed up as the internally or internationally illegal,
as well as morally questionable, infliction of harmful physical force
with political or social intentions, on a smaller scale than fully-fledged
war.[5] This includes state, as well as group, violence, either directly
engaged in or supported by financial or other means. It excludes legal,
but possibly immoral, violence (e.g. Hitler's police, or erroneous internationally endorsed wars). It also excludes "structural" injustices – such
as racism, discrimination, and immoral global arrangements. So while
the definition attaches a prima facie assumption of wrongfulness to
violence, it does not necessarily equate political violence with moral
wrongdoing.[6]

Ultimately, Honderich deliberately refrains from defining terrorism
independently of political violence in general. While acknowledging the
distinction between violence intended to create fear or outright "terror"
amongst a civilian population, as opposed to forms of "violence directed specifically at a head of state, or politicians, soldiers or policemen,"
Honderich disregards this in defining terrorism.[7] The idea that certain
forms of political violence are directed specifically at innocent people
and that this ought to be viewed as part of their particular condemnation as "terrorism," is also raised in passing and similarly dismissed out

---

[3] Honderich, in general, sneers at strict definitions and precise philosophical
  analysis, e.g. *After the Terror*, p. 94, as does Jacques Derrida, who attempts to
  "deconstruct" the concept of terrorism in Borradori, *Philosophy*, pp. 85–172, esp.
  pp. 109, 152–3, 161.
[4] Honderich, *After the Terror*, pp. 91–7.   [5] Ibid., p. 97.
[6] Ibid.   [7] Ibid.

of hand.[8] This common intuition that there is a particular wrong involved in the *intentional* killing of non-combatants and that such strikes in particular ought to be singled out as "acts of terror," is no more than momentarily considered and subsequently denied in the name of consistency.[9] After all, Western states kill innocents too, and do not condemn the death of some innocents as loudly as we denounce the death of (our) other innocents. The distinction drawn by conventional just-war theory between the intentional and direct targeting of non-combatants, versus the accidental, or additional, killing of innocents as a by-product of targeting a military objective, which admittedly occurs in all wars, receives little attention from Honderich. While all fatalities remain equally dead, there are significant differences between these modes of killing, which warrant more than a few lines of attention followed by an elegant evasion.[10]

Choosing, then, to make no definitional distinction between various forms of political violence, Honderich speaks of either *terrorism* or *political violence* as:

Violence with a political and social intention, whether or not intended to put people in general in fear, and raising a question of its moral justification – either illegal violence within a society or smaller-scale violence than war between states or societies and not according to international law.[11]

In defense of this inclusive definition, Honderich argues that making people in general fearful is not a significantly distinctive factor between forms of violence: "The main thing is getting political and social change," and this characterizes all forms of political violence as defined.[12] So Honderich's self-professed excuse for not singling out and condemning the specific sort of violence which we would usually call "terrorism" is that it is actually more like all other forms of political violence than it is distinct from them. Whatever their particular mode of operation, all aspire to bring about (or preserve) a social and political end by means of inflicting harmful force. There is then, in his view,

---

[8] Ibid., p. 95.
[9] Ibid., p. 103. Noam Chomsky repeatedly makes similar points concerning the inconsistent and self-serving use of the term "terrorism" on the part of the US, which he regards as a terrorist state. See, for example, Chomsky, *9–11*, esp. pp. 23, 40–54, 57, 73–4, 90–1.
[10] Honderich, *After the Terror*, p. 103.
[11] Ibid., pp. 98–9.   [12] Ibid., p. 99.

nothing unique or particularly condemnable about any one specific type of political violence, aside from the prima facie assumption of possible wrongfulness, which attaches to the infliction of all injury and harm.[13]

This inclusive definition of terrorism bears clear normative implications. It "does not by itself morally condemn in a final way anything that falls under it. It leaves open the possibility that there was justification of, say, the particular terrorism that led to the existence of the state of Israel. So with the attempt on Hitler's life and attempts to kill Osama Bin Laden in the years before September 11."[14] Since Honderich's definition of terrorism makes no distinction between various forms of political violence, it justifies the subsequent comparison between these three examples and the case which appears to form the hidden (though not well enough) agenda of Honderich's entire volume. It paves the way towards arguing that Palestinian terror against Israeli civilians is, in fact, justified. As Honderich puts this: "I myself have no doubt, to take the outstanding case, that the Palestinians have exercised a moral right in their terrorism against the Israelis ... and those who have killed themselves in the cause of their people have indeed sanctified themselves."[15]

The events of September 11, on the other hand, are dubbed "wrong," though not automatically so by definition. As Honderich puts it: "Our definition of terrorism does not rule out the possibility that some terrorism could be justified as response to what others called structural violence."[16] Honderich's overall political argument, developed throughout several publications, is that political violence, including terrorism, is justifiable in response to the wrongs done to individuals in developing countries and the Arab world, by the immoral omissions or direct commissions particularly of the US, associated with globalization, oil and other capitalist interests, and support of Israel.[17] While the US and Israel are singled out as the primary culprits, the UK and other Western states are also implicated in the injuries inflicted upon developing countries and Arab nations: "The conclusion is that there is no simple

---

[13] Ibid., pp. 97–9. Note, in contrast, the overall thesis of Paul Berman, *Terror and Liberalism*, which involves the suggestion that real world political or social change are not always the object of political violence.

[14] Honderich, *After the Terror*, p. 99.

[15] Ibid., p. 151.   [16] Ibid., p. 100.

[17] Most notably in *After the Terror*. See also Ted Honderich, *Terrorism for Humanity: Inquiries in Political Philosophy* (London: Pluto Press, 2003).

objection of a certain kind to terrorism against us, even the terrorism of September 11. We do not have a certain imagined moral high ground to stand on in condemning terrorism against us, in explaining our revulsion for the killers at the twin towers."[18] Certainly, if terrorism is defined so widely as to include all forms of political violence with no moral distinction among them, why then "we are all terrorists," with the US, UK, and Israel at the head of a rotten bunch. Thus, Noam Chomsky, who shares many of Honderich's assumptions, states clearly and repeatedly that the US is a leading terrorist state.[19] Add to this the forms of "structural violence" – that is, the US's alleged responsibility for the bad lives of people in developing countries and Arab populations – how then can we, without hypocrisy, oppose attacks against America by those harmed by its policies? On these questionable, and question-begging, assumptions, we cannot.

Apparently, according to Honderich, anyone who makes traditional, principled, distinctions – say among killing a political tyrant, planting a bomb on a school bus, or flying an aircraft into an office building – must be some sort of Western hypocrite (probably an American capitalist, or a Jew, or a Zionist, or all three). After all, having defined terrorism with a deliberate disregard for the element of fear – the literal terrorization of a civilian population – along with the element of targeting innocent non-combatants, the convenient outcome is inevitably going to be a striking formal similarity between killing soldiers, policemen or officials, assassinating Hitler or targeting bin Laden, and blowing up a cafe, a commuter bus, or an office building, in Tel-Aviv or New York. It would seem that, according to Honderich, these are "all in a good cause."

And yet, Honderich accepts that the events of September 11 were wrong (as opposed to Palestinian terrorism aimed at Israelis), but only because they involved the use of violence *without any reasonable hope of achieving its justifiable goals*, understood as fighting off the effects of the bad policies of the US.[20] It is instructive to note the obvious here, as G.A. Cohen has recently, "that anyone who rejects terrorism on the ground that it is counter productive ... has conceded a large point of principle to the terrorists. The criticism that terror is counter productive doesn't criticize it *as* terror."[21] Indeed, Honderich more than implies

---

[18] Honderich, *After the Terror*, p. 115.   [19] Chomsky, *9–11*, pp. 23, 40, 76, 84.
[20] Honderich, *After the Terror*, p. 118.
[21] Gerald Cohen (2003), "Casting the First Stone: Who Can, and Who Can't, Condemn the Terrorists," in A. O'Hear (ed.), *Royal Institute of Philosophy Lectures, 2004–5*. www.royalinstitutephilosophy.org/index.php.

that if the attacks of September 11 could reasonably have been con-
ceived as effective means towards saving more "bad" lives (say, in
Africa) than the number of lives they destroyed in New York, then
such attacks would in fact have been justified.[22] Furthermore, future
attacks on American civilians that would explicitly place anti-globalization and US exploitation as their goals, with reasonable hope of achieving this end, would be justified, perhaps even commended by
Honderich's "humanitarian" principles, which recommend the killing
of Israeli civilians by Palestinian suicide bombers.[23]

In an engaging dialogue with Giovanna Borradori, the late Jacques
Derrida presented a far more subtle, yet not entirely dissimilar, evaluation of the events of September 11. He too discredited the commonly
attempted distinctions between terrorism and other types of violence,
such as war, pointing to the indisputable fact that states have also
employed terror tactics against civilians in wartime, as well as against
their own civilians internally.[24] Partly in view of this "state terror,"
Derrida's discussion implies that the civilian–military distinction
between wartime killing and terrorism is misplaced, although, like
Honderich, he paid this distinction little attention, remarking only in
passing, and in a somewhat offhand tone, that "the victims of terrorism
are *assumed* to be civilians."[25]

Aside from the terrorist excesses of states during wartime and otherwise, Derrida suggested that causing fear, anxiety, panic, and even outright terror among the citizenries of a state, far from being unique to any
specific type of political violence, actually characterize the very authority
of law and exercising of state sovereignty.[26] He also reminds us of the
undeniable fact that the predominant powers often use, and abuse,
terminology and definitions opportunistically in order to suit their own
partisan political advantage, and he attempts to move from this to the
disputable claim that terrorism, therefore, cannot be strictly defined.[27]
Derrida also reiterated the platitude "that terrorists might be praised as
freedom fighters in one context ... and denounced as terrorists in
another," without seriously scrutinizing this common aphorism.[28]

---

[22] Honderich, *After the Terror*, pp. 115–20.   [23] Ibid., pp. 150–1.
[24] Jacques Derrida, who attempts to "deconstruct" the concept of terrorism in
Borradori, *Philosophy*, pp. 102–7, 152.
[25] Ibid., p. 103, emphasis added.   [26] Ibid., pp. 102–3.
[27] Ibid., pp. 105, 110, 153.   [28] Ibid., p. 102.

In a vein similar to Honderich's, Derrida points out that both terrorists and states invoke self-defense as their excuse for exercising the type of violence which their adversaries regard as terrorism. Militant groups, as well as states, commonly argue that their tactics are a last resort in the face of prior and more severe "terrorism" aimed against them.[29] Derrida, however, refrains from equating US economic policies (or Israel's military strategies) with terrorism, nor does he explicitly place them on a par with the group terrorism by which they claim to be victimized. He does, however, elude to the possibility, à la Honderich, that certain forms of Western-instigated "structural violence" associated with capitalism and globalization could in themselves be regarded by some as prior incidents of state terrorism.[30] With this, Derrida joins Honderich in placing the distinctions between deliberate and unintentional actions, as well as between acts and omissions, in the philosophical waste-paper basket, alongside the earlier dismissal of the civilian–combatant distinction.[31] Thus, he also questioned whether terrorism need necessarily involve deliberately putting people to death:

Isn't it also "letting die"? Can't "letting die," "not wanting to know that one is letting others die" – hundreds of millions of human beings, from hunger, AIDS, lack of medical treatment, and so on – also be part of a "more or less" conscious and deliberate terrorist strategy? We are perhaps wrong to assume so quickly that all terrorism is voluntary, conscious, organized, deliberate, intentionally calculated ... All situations of social or national structural oppression produce a terror.[32]

Having "deconstructed" the notion of terrorism, Derrida's terminology is also deliberately inclusive. He refers only to "violence" in a general fashion, "so as to avoid the equivocal and confused words 'war' and 'terrorism'."[33] While Derrida's political conclusions are less pronounced than those of Honderich, the two are more than reminiscent of each other. Ultimately, the normative evaluation of terrorism hinges on its prospects of success. Derrida firmly believed that September 11 was wrong, but part of his reason for this condemnation is alarmingly similar to that of Honderich:

What appears to me unacceptable in the "strategy" ... of the "bin Laden effect" is not only the cruelty, the disregard for human life, the disrespect for

---

[29] Ibid., pp. 107, 152.   [30] Ibid., pp. 107–8.
[31] Honderich, *After the Terror*, pp. 73–88, 97–9, 103.
[32] Derrida in Borradori, *Philosophy*, p. 108.   [33] Ibid., pp. 127, 161.

law, for women, the use of what is worst in technocapitalist modernity for the purposes of religious fanaticism. No, it is above all, the fact that such actions and such discourse open onto no future and, in my view, have no future.[34]

While according to Derrida, its predictable lack of success in achieving its goals was not the only thing wrong with the terrorism of September 11, his account does suggest that its inefficiency is its central negative aspect. On the other hand, Derrida observed that where terrorism has successful prospects, today's terrorists may well be tomorrow's freedom fighters and heroes of national independence, or even state leaders.[35] At the very least, it is implied that where terrorists have a realistic chance of achieving their goal, say of national liberation, they may be retrospectively justified in employing terrorist tactics.

Interestingly enough, in the midst of his deconstruction project, Derrida insisted on the interjection of one analytical distinction. He suggests that:

A Philosopher would be one who seeks a new criteriology to distinguish between "comprehending" and "justifying." For one can describe, comprehend and explain a certain chain of events or series of associations that lead to "war" or to "terrorism" without justifying them in the least, while in fact condemning them and attempting to invent other associations. One can condemn unconditionally certain acts of terrorism (whether of the state or not) without having to ignore the situation that might have brought them about or even legitimated them ... One can thus condemn unconditionally, as I do here, the attack of September 11 without having to ignore the real or alleged conditions that made it possible.[36]

Derrida's unconditional condemnation of the attacks of September 11 is a welcome point of departure from the views voiced by Honderich and Chomsky. Still, it remains puzzling as to what it means to "condemn unconditionally certain acts of terrorism ... without having to ignore the situation that might have brought them about or even legitimated them."[37] The use of the word "legitimated" is particularly perplexing. I am not the first to note with reference to terrorism that "the distance from 'understandable' to 'legitimate' is a very short one."[38] Despite Honderich's refreshingly candid "moral inquiry," alongside

---

[34] Ibid., p. 113.   [35] Ibid., pp. 104, 152.   [36] Ibid., pp. 106–7.
[37] Ibid., p. 107, emphasis added.
[38] See Netanyahu, *Terrorism*, p. 203.

Derrida's elegant philosophical deconstruction, we may not yet be ready to discard the condemnation of terrorism as such.

A deadly trilogy – guerrilla warfare, political assassination, and terrorism

Michael Walzer's seminal *Just and Unjust Wars* offers a uniquely instructive (and contemporarily relevant) distinction among three categories of irregular warfare, each warranting a different appropriate moral attitude. Clearly, not all revolutionary, non-conventional, or unlawful, political violence is terrorism. First, there is guerrilla warfare, which is distinguishable from conventional war in that it involves not only the natural camouflage used so often in traditional battle, but also a form of moral disguise in which combatants customarily conceal themselves in the midst (and rely on the support) of a civilian population, traditionally protected by the laws of war.[39] Their civilian camouflage, "the use of civilian clothing as a ruse and a disguise," serves, albeit indirectly, to blur the differentiation between soldiers and non-combatants.[40] So long as they remain unidentified by uniforms or other revealing dress (identifying badges or caps), concealing their weapons and militant identity, guerrilla fighters, or partisans, are unprotected by international laws of war.[41] Guerrillas are irregulars who fight an unconventional battle, more often embedded in a civilian population, and by so doing they threaten the combatant–civilian distinction and the traditional conventions of war of which it is a part.

Guerrillas, however, do not subvert the war convention by themselves attacking civilians; at least, this is not a necessary feature of their struggle.[42] At most, "they invite their enemies to do it. By refusing to accept a single identity, they seek to make it impossible for their enemies to accord to combatants and noncombatants their distinct 'privileges ... and disabilities'."[43] Nonetheless, at least for the most part, guerrillas themselves uphold the distinction between combatants and civilians, primarily targeting the former either by direct ambush or by means of espionage and sabotage. As a rule, Walzer tells us, guerrillas do not target innocent

---

[39] Walzer, *Just and Unjust Wars*, p. 176.   [40] Ibid., p. 183.
[41] Ibid., p. 182.   [42] Ibid., p. 179.   [43] Ibid., pp. 179–80.

civilians.[44] This is a distinguishing feature of guerrilla warfare which indicates, at least intuitively, that though non-conventional, it warrants some legitimacy, though it does not render its participants eligible for the protection of international conventions and the war rights of soldiers specified in them.[45] Guerrillas make distinctions and although they do at times kill civilians (as do anti-guerrilla forces) these are not their primary targets. While guerrillas have been known to launch terrorist campaigns (for that matter, so have states), as a rule they fight against soldiers who wear uniforms: "For these reasons, guerrilla leaders and their publicists are able to stress the moral quality not only of the goals they seek but also of the means they employ."[46] Guerrillas may warrant our moral respect, at least when we identify with their cause. The French resistance to German occupation in the Second World War is a case in point.

Many guerrilla attacks are far less noble than those of the anti-Fascist partisans. At times, they are carried out by groups and individuals who may also be implicated in strikes against civilians. Some guerrilla assaults are particularly bloody and their mode of operation may push the notion of military "fair play" to its very limits. This was certainly true of the Hizbullah truck-bombing of Marines in Lebanon in 1983, and of the many attacks carried out by the same Hizbullah organization against Israeli military targets. But whatever the tragedy, so long as non-conventional assaults are restricted to combatants, we must resist the temptation of referring to them as anything but guerrilla attacks.[47]

This vital distinction between modern terrorism and guerrilla warfare, along with its normative implications, has been restated recently by Jürgen Habermas in slightly different terms. Habermas clearly distinguishes between "indiscriminant guerrilla warfare" and "paramilitary guerrilla warfare." He states that "The first is epitomized by Palestinian terrorism, in which murder is usually carried out by a suicide militant."[48] In contrast, only "The model of paramilitary guerrilla warfare is proper to the national liberation movements and is retrospectively legitimized by

---

[44] Ibid., p. 180. For a similar characterization of guerrilla warfare as opposed to terrorism, see Paul Gilbert, *New Terror, New Wars* (Edinburgh University Press, 2003), pp. 96–7.

[45] Walzer, *Just and Unjust Wars*, pp. 182–3.   [46] Ibid., p. 181.

[47] Berman, *Terror and Liberalism*, pp. 109, 201 does not distinguish clearly between Hizbullah attacks and terrorism against civilians: nor does Benjamin Netanyahu, *Fighting Terrorism*, pp. 67–8.

[48] Borradori, *Philosophy*, p. 56.

the formation of the state."[49] Contra Derrida, then, indiscriminant guerrilla warfare cannot be retrospectively legitimized by political success. In Habermas's own words: "Palestinian terrorism ... revolves around murder, around the indiscriminate annihilation of enemies, women and children – life against life. This is what distinguishes it from the terrorism that appears in the paramilitary form of guerrilla warfare."[50]

Beyond guerrilla warfare, Walzer identifies political assassination as a second distinct variant of revolutionary resistance. Despite what Honderich would have us believe, assassination is clearly distinguishable from terrorist strikes of the September 11 type, as it necessarily involves "the drawing of a line that we will have little difficulty recognizing as the political parallel of the line that marks off combatants from non-combatants."[51] When acting in the capacity of assassins, revolutionaries draw a moral distinction "between people who can and people who cannot be killed."[52] The former consists exclusively "of officials, the political agents of regimes, thought to be oppressive."[53]

Both modern history and contemporary politics supply ample examples of this type of revolutionary violence. In 1879 someone tried to kill the Russian Tsar, and in 1881 a small group of revolutionaries did kill him. Towards the turn of the twentieth century attempts were made on the lives of the Emperor of Germany and the King of Spain. The Empress of Austria was assassinated in 1898. The King of Italy was killed by an anarchist from New Jersey. In 1901, President McKinley was murdered in Buffalo, New York. In the late nineteenth and early twentieth century, tsarist officials were frequently targeted by Russian revolutionaries. Then, of course, there was the famous assassination of the Grand Duke of Serbia in Sarajevo in 1914, sparking the First World War.[54] Towards the end of the Second World War, several attempts were made on Hitler's life by a group of German generals. In November 1944, British Minister of State in the Middle East, Lord Moyne, was assassinated in Cairo by the Jewish Stern Gang, which also carried out other such attacks.[55] In 1951, Jordanian King Abdullah was murdered in Jerusalem by a Palestinian extremist. Egyptian President Sadat was

---

[49] Ibid., p. 56.   [50] Habermas, in Borradori, *Philosophy*, p. 33.
[51] Walzer, *Just and Unjust Wars*, p. 198.   [52] Ibid., p. 199.   [53] Ibid.
[54] For these examples in particular, see Berman, *Terror and Liberalism*, p. 32.
[55] For these two examples, as well as others, see Walzer, *Just and Unjust Wars*, pp. 198–203. In contrast, see Honderich, *After the Terror*, p. 99. Note the different manner in which they are invoked by the two authors.

assassinated in 1981 by an Islamist cell within the Egyptian army. Most recently, several years ago, Israeli Minister of Tourism Rechavam Zeevi was shot to death by a Palestinian gunman in a Jerusalem hotel. All these, among many others, are cases in point.

The crucial common denominator in all the illustrative examples, sadly down-played by Honderich, is that assassins do not kill indiscriminately.[56] Ordinary private citizens remain immune from attack. This distinguishing feature is often sadly missed on the other side of the political spectrum as well, by those whose extreme zeal for fighting terrorism appears to blind them from this plain observation.[57] Like conventional soldiers and principled guerrillas, assassins "aim at particular people because of things they have done or are doing" rather than "at whole groups of people, indiscriminately, because of who they are."[58]

Paradoxically, Walzer points out that "One might even feel easier about killing officials than about killing soldiers, since the state rarely conscripts its political, as it does its military agents; they have chosen officialdom as a career."[59] Ultimately, Walzer tells us, "we judge the assassin by his victim, and when the victim is Hitler-like in character, we are likely to praise the assassin's work, though we still do not call him a soldier."[60] On the other hand, where the judgments of particular political assassins differ from our own, the "political assassins are simply murderers, exactly like the killers of ordinary citizens. The case is not the same with soldiers, who are not judges politically at all and who are called murderers only when they kill noncombatants."[61] Unlike soldiers then (but perhaps not altogether unlike guerrillas), our moral assessment of assassins necessarily hinges on a political evaluation of the justness of their cause. Perhaps this is why they remain unprotected by international convention.[62] So while assassins cannot

---

[56] As Paul Gilbert puts it: "Assassination is, however, far from the worst offence against the prohibition on attacking civilians that we witness in new wars," *New Terror, New Wars*, p. 94.

[57] The distinction between political assassination and indiscriminate terrorism is overlooked by many of the contributors to Netanyahu, *Terrorism*, pp. 10, 17, 44, 48, 56, 103, 199.

[58] Walzer, *Just and Unjust Wars*, pp. 198, 199, 200 describes how at least some assassins took special measures in order to avoid civilian casualties. See also Berman, *Terror and Liberalism*, p. 32, who makes the same moral point about the Russian anarchists.

[59] Walzer, *Just and Unjust Wars*, p. 200.

[60] Ibid., pp. 199–200.   [61] Ibid., pp. 200–1.

[62] This is Walzer's guess, ibid.

claim any of the soldier's rights specified by international war conventions and treaties, they may gain some degree of respect simply because they do set limits to their actions.

In his recent *Terror and Liberalism*, Paul Berman makes a similar observation regarding the ethics of assassination. Following Albert Camus, he retells (as Walzer does) the plot to assassinate tsarist official Grand Duke Sergei by the Russian revolutionary Kaliayev in the early twentieth century: "The first time that Kaliayev set out to kill Grand Duke Sergei, he held back, because when the Grand Duke's carriage came into view, children were at the Grand Duke's side, and the children were innocent of any crime."[63] Borrowing again from Camus, Berman cites the leader of Kaliayev's revolutionary organization, Boris Savinkov, who argued against targeting a tsarist admiral on the railroad, on the grounds that "With the slightest carelessness, the explosion could take place in the car and kill strangers."[64] Like Camus and Walzer before him, Berman observes that these "terrorists ... were morally fastidious," even "delicate."[65]

Terrorism more strictly defined, however, is distinctive. It allows for no fusion of terms, or confusion of various forms of political violence of the kind attempted by Honderich and Derrida.[66] In sharp contrast with guerrillas who (as a rule) confront armies, and assassins, who target particular officials, modern terrorism upholds no distinctions. Terrorists do not kill civilians by accident, as an unfortunate consequence of their military activity.[67] All armed forces admit and profusely

[63] Berman, *Terror and Liberalism*, p. 32. Walzer, *Just and Unjust Wars*, pp. 198–9.
[64] Berman, *Terror and Liberalism*, p. 32.   [65] Ibid., pp. 33–4.
[66] Honderich, *After the Terror*, p. 99, his final definition of "terrorism or political violence." Derrida, in Borradori, *Philosophy*, pp. 127, 161.
[67] Can one terrorize without killing? This may be logically possible, but it remains highly theoretical and largely irrelevant. Killing itself appears to be an essential inherent component of modern "terrorism" as we know it. Arguing against the Doctrine of Double Effect (which is not the issue here) Francis Kamm suggests that "the big moral obstacle to terror-killing is justifying the killing rather than justifying the production of terror per se. To support this claim, imagine that we find out that noncombatants on the unjust side, whom we could not permissibly harm in any other way, will experience terror leading to the country's surrender, if we bomb some trees. (They are irrational.) If we bomb the trees, moral objections to terror bombing should not then exist, I believe, even though we intend to terrorize these people as a means to end the war. Alternatively, suppose the people are rational. We manage to convey that we are using a new terrifying weapon to destroy the trees. We do this because we know the people will see this as a threat to use the weapon on them and, hence, be terrorized. We either

regret (whether cynically or sincerely) the killing of (at times many) innocent civilians in the course of military strikes or operations. Sometimes a civilian target is mistaken for a military one, as when American air forces accidentally bombed a wedding party in Afghanistan. In other instances, targets are at times overstepped, as was the case in September 2001 when Israel fired a missile that killed two Hamas arch-terrorists, and two Palestinian children who were playing nearby were tragically struck down.[68] In July 2002, another Israeli attack achieved its goal of targeting Hamas leader Salah Shhada, but once again exceeded it, killing not only the arch-terrorist but also over a dozen civilians, including the man's wife and teenage daughter. These are, admittedly, not isolated incidents within Israel's policy of targeting arch-terrorists, nor is harm to civilians a rare occurrence in old-fashioned wars, or in the US counter-attacks in response to September 11. While there may be ample room for questioning certain military practices that result in such tragedies, they do not amount to terrorism. For terrorists, the killing of non-combatants is not a regrettable by-product or side effect, innocent victims are not an "occupational hazard." Instead, they are the be-all and end-all of this form of belligerence.

The trouble with terror

What, then, is so wrong about terrorism in particular? Terrorism, Walzer tells us, "breaks across moral limits beyond which no further limitation seems possible, for within the category of civilian and citizen, there isn't any smaller group for which immunity might be claimed ... Terrorists anyway make no such claim; they kill anybody."[69] For Walzer, this is a crucial point about terrorism: it is not aimed at particular people:

For ordinary citizens are killed and no defense is offered – none could be offered – in terms of their individual actions. The names and occupations of the dead are not known in advance; they are killed simply to deliver a message

actually have no such weapon or no intention of using it on people. Could such a threat for purposes of terrorizing be permissible in order to stop a war? I believe it could be." See Kamm's article, "Failure of Just War Theory: Terror, Harm and Justice," *Ethics* 114 (4) (July 2004), p. 663.

[68] Netanyahu, *Fighting Terrorism*, p. xxi.

[69] Walzer, *Just and Unjust Wars*, p. 203.

of fear to others like themselves … [T]errorism, because it is directed against entire peoples or classes, tends to communicate the most extreme and brutal intentions – above all, the tyrannical repression, removal, or mass murder of the population under attack. Hence contemporary terrorist campaigns are most often focused on people whose national existence has been radically devalued: the Protestants of Northern Ireland, the Jews of Israel, and so on. The campaign announces the devaluation. That is why the people under attack are so unlikely to believe that compromise is possible with their enemy. In war, terrorism is associated with the demand for unconditional surrender and, in similar fashion seems to rule out any sort of compromise settlement.[70]

Paul Berman's evaluation of modern terrorism is similar, though he is less semantically pedantic than Walzer – referring to a variety of radicals as "terrorists." Nonetheless, he marks an important transition within revolutionary movements in the twentieth century, which he eloquently describes as the point at which "the fastidious yielded to the not fastidious."[71] That is, as Berman puts it, the loss of what the Russian revolutionary Savinkov called a "terrorist conscience."[72] Berman refers to the aforementioned bombing of New York's Wall Street in the 1920s, commenting that:

Galleani and his followers had arrived at the very reasoning that would govern the attacks on Manhattan's center of finance more than seventy years later … Galleani's idea was to commit an aesthetic act of terror – "aesthetic" was his own word – in which the beauty or artistic quality consisted in murdering anonymously. Here the nihilism was unlimited, and the transgression, total.[73]

Terrorism is also a form of immoral free riding. All groups have at least some interest in upholding the distinction between civilian and

---

[70] Ibid., p. 203.
[71] Berman, *Terror and Liberalism*, p. 34. Later, Berman describes a similar transition stage for Palestinian terrorism against Israel in which fastidiousness receded into the past and was replaced by blind killing. Berman attributes this transition to the rise of the Islamist Hamas organization, which fits conveniently with his admittedly brilliant analysis of Islamic terrorism. Nonetheless, on this point there is room for doubting whether Palestinian terrorism ever exhibited any noteworthy degree of fastidiousness, for example of the type that characterized early Russian revolutionaries. Even Berman's own account of this terrorism places a serious shadow on the characterization of its early exhibits as fastidious in any way, shape, or form. See Berman, *Terror and Liberalism*, p. 111.
[72] Ibid., p. 32. [73] Ibid., pp. 35–6.

military targets. It was precisely the growing realization of the dangers of war to civilian populations, probably more than any abstract moral principle, that pushed European statesmen in the nineteenth and twentieth centuries to negotiate and regulate the manner in which wars ought, and ought not to be, fought. As war became a more popular business, states were led, largely by concern for the well-being of their own citizenry, to initiate international conventions and side with treaties that commited them to upholding distinctions between military and non-military personnel, as well as between lawful and unlawful combatants, with the proviso that others do the same.[74] Such distinctions and codes of war, which are desirable for conventional armies and the states they represent, are in fact absolutely essential for terrorists and the success of their strategy. Terrorist tactics rely entirely on conventional armies maintaining these distinctions, while they themselves openly thwart them. Terrorism wholly depends upon its opponents upholding a moral code which the terrorists themselves reject. Terrorists hitch a morally dubious free ride on their adversaries' moral code. If their adversaries were to match their nihilism by denying the status of non-combatants and the distinction between belligerents and civilians, choosing to terrorize the latter with their superior force, they would once again have the upper hand, rendering ineffective the smaller-scale terrorism of the "underdog."

In explaining why suicide terrorists almost exclusively target democracies, Robert Pape argues that "suicide terrorists ... must also be confident that their opponent will be at least somewhat restrained ... democracies have generally been more restrained in their use of force against civilians, at least since World War II."[75] The Kurds, Pape points out, are a case in point:

Although Iraq has been far more brutal towards its Kurdish population than has Turkey, violent Kurdish groups have used suicide attacks exclusively against democratic Turkey and not against the authoritarian regime in Iraq. There are plenty of national groups living under authoritarian regimes with grievances that could possibly inspire suicide terrorism, but none have.[76]

---

[74] Nabulsi, *Traditions of War*, pp. 4–18.
[75] Robert A. Pape, "The Strategic Logic of Suicide Terrorism," *American Political Science Review* 97 (3) (August 2003), pp. 343–61, p. 350; see also pp. 347–9.
[76] Ibid., p. 350.

To put this more concretely, the instigators and perpetrators of September 11 relied on the fact that the US – whatever its moral transgressions – would not, for instance, retaliate with atomic weapons against civilian Arab populations in the Middle East. Palestinian terrorists rely on the fact that Israel, while at times killing civilians, is nonetheless bound by international and internal pressures, alongside moral restraints, that prevent it from striking back at Palestinians with all its might, with no regard for civilian life. Terrorists also rely on a set of civil liberties, which they often hold in contempt, but which enables them to operate more freely than they could in their absence. Terrorism's very livelihood depends on a reversal of the Kantian imperative to "act only on that maxim through which you can at the same time will that it should become a universal law."[77] Terrorists must will, and be assured of, the precise reverse. They rely wholeheartedly on their maxim not being universalized. Where terrorists are pursued in kind, for example, by a military force that shares their disregard for human rights and moral codes, they have no hope of success.

This is less true of guerrillas and assassins, who need not be free riders. As noted earlier, guerrillas customarily take advantage of the local terrain, or civilian surroundings. Admittedly, they depend on their enemies respecting the lives of civilians and consequently refrain from pursuing them in their midst. However, for the most part, guerrillas themselves uphold the very same distinctions and standards they expect their enemies to maintain. Unlike terrorists, guerrillas draw the same fine line that their opponents do between combatants and civilians. Their strategic advantage derives from a difference in circumstances (familiarity with local topography, or the sympathy of the local population), not from the evasion of any moral code. As for assassins, the success of their operations does not, as with terrorism, depend on their opponents refraining from similar tactics – two can play at this game. To take a familiar case, Israel's policy of targeting wanted arch-terrorists does not invalidate the effectiveness of Palestinian attacks on Israeli officials, such as the aforementioned assassination of Rechavaam Zeevi. In this case, when viewed from conflicting points of view, or from a neutral standpoint, the Palestinian gunman displayed the same moral code as the one upheld by Israel's assassination policy – kill an

---

[77] Immanuel Kant, *Groundwork of the Metaphysic of Morals*, trans. H.J. Paton (New York: Harper and Row, 1964), p. 88.

(allegedly) guilty oppressor while refraining (as far as possible) from harming the innocent. Israel's frequent reference to this assassination of Minister Zeevi as "terrorism" is an unfortunate example of inaccurate political speech (though the culpable organizations are legitimately dubbed terrorists by virtue of some of their other actions).

A terrorist, as opposed to an assassin, or guerrilla, is essentially a free rider on the moral codes and political liberties of others. They are, to say the least, free riders on the prohibitions to which civilized nations adhere. Someone may respond, however, by observing that there are worse things in the world than free riding – oppression, persecution, occupation, economic exploitation, to name just a few. Perhaps something further can be said along these lines in defense of terrorism, at least when it is employed in the pursuit of a just cause. Honderich, who at least superficially renounces September 11 (primarily for its predictable inefficiency), nonetheless defends "*liberation-terrorism*," understood as "terrorism to get freedom and power for a people when it is clear that nothing else will get it for them."[78]

This argument, whereby terrorism is justified as the only means to attaining such particular political ends as overthrowing repressive regimes, liberating oppressed peoples, and founding new nations, is not a new one. Terror apologists often point out that terrorism is a weapon of the weak. Terrorists are often portrayed by their sympathizers as the underdog, at times conjuring up images of the young biblical David. This comparative weakness, it is implied, can only be overcome by the use of unconventional tactics. Such arguments sometimes imply counterfactually that the only choice faced by disadvantaged groups engaged in conflict with a stronger power is between conventional warfare, at which they are inferior to their enemies, and terrorism. We saw above that this is far from accurate. In *Just and Unjust Wars*, Walzer argued that the availability of alternative forms of irregular warfare – guerrilla tactics and assassinations – attest to the falsity of this assertion.[79] Similarly, Habermas's distinction suggests that revolutionaries may resort to "paramilitary guerrilla warfare" which, unlike indiscriminant terrorism is a proper course of action for national liberation movements and is retrospectively legitimized with the formation of their state.[80] Paul Gilbert points out that while "the militarily weaker side has little chance of

---

[78] Honderich, *After the Terror*, p. 151.   [79] Walzer, *Just and Unjust Wars*, p. 204.
[80] Borradori, *Philosophy*, p. 56.

obtaining victory by conventional military conflict, however justified its cause may be" still, "There are several possible avenues open to it."[81] One such alternative is the use of guerrilla tactics, understood by Gilbert, as well, as distinct from terrorism by virtue of its respect for the immunity of non-combatants.[82] Freedom fighters have fastidious alternatives and are therefore unjustified in turning to terrorism under the pretense of arguments of "last resort."

Honderich's paradigmatic case, that of Palestinian terrorism against Israel, is particularly curious in this respect. Palestinians clearly have a variety of effective options. Aside from the occasional assassination, Palestinians regularly attack Israeli soldiers in operations which, despite Israeli rhetoric, are not, strictly speaking, terrorism, but rather guerrilla warfare to be judged on the merits of its political goals. There is no cause to believe that guerrilla tactics are less effective than terrorist strikes against civilians. In fact, guerrilla action bears the distinct advantage that it rarely warrants large-scale international condemnation, which often makes Palestinian terrorism appear counter-productive. Additionally, quite apart from Walzer's, Gilbert's, and Habermas's alternative modes of non-conventional warfare, there is also the option of internationally supervised peaceful negotiations for Palestinians to fall back on. In fact, in the wake of Camp David, construing Palestinian terrorism against Israel as "liberation terrorism" is rather peculiar, to say the least. Paul Berman makes this point better than I could when he questions the logic of rejecting the Clinton plan in favor of suicide attacks:

Clinton and Barak had already offered a Palestinian state. Perhaps the purpose of the suicide attacks was to widen the borders of the proposed new state – though, in that case, Arafat might have haggled at Camp David for an extra slice or two, and the question of slightly wider borders would at least have been broached. Or maybe the purpose was to widen the proposed new borders by more than a slice, to obtain a Palestinian state on a different scale altogether. But the whole point of negotiating during the eight years of Israeli–Palestinian talks, beginning at Oslo, was to work out a compromise. Or maybe the purpose of the attacks was, as Hamas and Islamic Jihad forthrightly proclaimed, to abolish Israel altogether and establish the reign of Shariah in every corner of the land. But this was not within the realm of reality. Actually, none of the imaginable purposes had any chance of being

---

[81] Gilbert, *New Terror, New Wars*, p. 97.   [82] Ibid.

realized, and especially not after 9/11 ... Suicide terrors against the Israelis were bound to succeed in one realm only, and this was the realm of death.[83]

Honderich's example is telling. The sheer absurdity of celebrating Palestinian terror in the post-Clinton era as "terrorism to get freedom and power for a people when it is clear that nothing else will get it for them,"[84] casts a dark shadow on his very notion of "*liberation-terrorism*," which the Palestinian illustration is intended to personify. Even if there were such a thing as "liberating terrorism," which (unlike September 11), could be justified as the *only* available realistic means towards achieving an essentially noble end, Palestinian terrorism is clearly not a case in point. An additional oddity in attempting to justify Palestinian terrorism on the grounds that it rightfully aims to "liberate" Palestinians from Israeli domination, concerns the fact that Arab terrorism against Jews in Palestine began in the 1920s, and was notoriously supported by the Nazis in the 1930s, long before Jewish sovereignty was established over any of the land. The PLO and Fatah organizations, dedicated to the "liberation of Palestine" by terrorist means, were established in 1964 and 1965 respectively, several years before Israel conquered the "occupied territories" from Jordan in 1967.

When contemplating "liberation-terrorism" it is also interesting to consider the paradigmatic case of desperate liberation movements – the internal struggle against Nazism – in which nothing resembling Palestinian terror tactics was ever employed. As former Israeli Prime Minister Benjamin Netanyahu likes to point out, "It is instructive to note, for example, that the French Resistance during World War II did not resort to systematic killing of German women and children, although these were well within reach in occupied France."[85] He goes on to say, "No resistance movement in Nazi-occupied Europe conducted or condoned terrorist attacks against German civilians, attacking military and government targets instead."[86]

Can terrorism ever be justified as essential to liberation? It has sometimes been argued that the type of state terror bombing carried out by allied forces during the Second World War on cities such as Dresden and Hamburg, and later the atomic attacks on Hiroshima and Nagasaki, were justifiable last-resort terrorism of the essential,

---

[83] Berman, *Terror and Liberalism*, pp. 132–3.
[84] Honderich, *After the Terror*, p. 151.
[85] Netanyahu, *Fighting Terrorism*, p. 9.   [86] Netanyahu, *Terrorism*, p. 204.

liberating type. Certainly, many of the bombings meet our strict definition of terrorism and as such many liberals remain unconvinced that
they can be altogether justified. It is possible that in some rare incidents
in which no other form of military strategy would have been effective,
arguments of overriding necessity could conceivably be invoked in their
defense. Clearly, this was not usually the case, and in most instances the
resort to terrorism was based on calculations of utility or on indifference
to civilian life on the enemy side. Possibly, some of the terror bombings,
while unjustifiable, may be retrospectively excusable, considering the
uniquely diabolical nature of the enemy on the European front. This
would still not amount to a justification of terrorism of any kind and I
doubt any useful analogies can be drawn from it.[87]

Finally, to restate the obvious, terrorism, by definition, attacks the
defenseless, the prohibition of which is perhaps the most basic rule of
just-war theory. This violation is not merely conventional, nor is it
based solely on a utilitarian consideration to narrow the overall scope
of suffering in war. Terrorism, as defined in the previous section, defies
a most basic standard of liberal-humanistic morality, at least since Kant
and up to Rawls, which fundamentally forbids the use of human beings
as means to an end only, and commands their treatment as ends in
themselves.[88] Certainly, this imperative would categorically prohibit
the arbitrary use, and intentional killing, of innocents, as mere means
towards attaining practical ends. Perhaps this logic is not purely
Western. Paul Berman cites Sayyid Qutb's understanding of the concept
of Jihad as containing a similar ethical dimension:

> He [Qutb] quoted Mohammed's successor, Abu Bakr, the first Caliph, who
> told his army "Do not kill any women, children or elderly people." Qutb
> quoted the Koran, which says: "Fight for the cause of God those who fight
> against you, but do not commit aggression. God does not love aggressors."
> Qutb thought that ethical commandments were crucial to military victory.
> Writing about Mohammad and his companions, he said, "These principles
> had to be strictly observed, even with those enemies who had persecuted
> them." Jihad did have its rules. It was fastidious.[89]

---

[87] For an illuminating discussion of the Second World War terror bombings, see
Walzer, *Just and Unjust Wars*, pp. 255–68.
[88] See Kant, *Groundwork*, p. 96; John Rawls, *A Theory of Justice*, 9th edn. (Oxford
University Press, 1989), p. 179.
[89] Berman, *Terror and Liberalism*, p. 98.

Be that as it may, among liberals there can be little dispute concerning the moral status of terrorism and terrorists. It is precisely the unequivocal Kantean "thou shalt not" invoked above, prohibiting the arbitrary use of rational beings, which requires Honderich to take great pains towards obscuring the distinction between terrorism and other forms of political violence that do not fall so clearly under this liberal commandment. It is not an incidental feature of his argument that it involves discrediting many of the distinctions that are basic to liberal philosophies, particularly Kantian-based ones.[90] Aside from downplaying the conventional distinction between killing belligerents versus innocent non-combatants, Honderich's disregard for the distinction between civilian casualties incurred in war and terrorist victims entails obscuring the relationship between intentions and consequences, and the difference between deliberate action and unintentional effects.[91] The extent of blame he attributes to the citizens of prosperous nations for the bad lives of inhabitants of developing countries (perhaps with the implication that we had September 11 coming to us), is largely pitted against the traditional moral distinctions between acts and omissions and between perfect and imperfect duties.[92] Rawls's version of liberalism, at least as it appears in *A Theory of Justice*, is reduced by Honderich to no more than "a philosophical celebration of America."[93]

In the end, Honderich's views on terrorism and its causes require him to do away with liberalism, from Kant to Rawls, almost entirely.[94] Quite a high price to pay, one might think, for the defense of suicide bombers. Nevertheless, in this one respect Honderich's intuitions are quite correct: in the end, it must either be terrorism *or* liberalism. Honderich makes his choice, and ultimately we must make ours.

Concluding remarks

Terrorism, unfortunately, is alive and well, but so is its distinctiveness as a particular form of political violence, which can and should be strictly understood and morally condemned. Once again, terrorism is the

---

[90] See, in particular, his section on Liberalism in *After the Terror*, pp. 46–50.
[91] See Honderich, *After the Terror*, p. 103.
[92] Ibid., throughout, specifically on pp. 73–88, 97–9, 103. Many of these distinctions are also called into question by Derrida in connection with terrorism, in Borradori, *Philosophy*, p. 108.
[93] Honderich, *After the Terror*, p. 70.   [94] Ibid., pp. 46–51, 62, 69–73, 81, 90.

intentional random murder of defenseless non-combatants, with the intent of instilling fear of mortal danger amidst a civilian population as a strategy designed to advance political ends. This understanding cannot be "deconstructed," nor can it be inclusively obscured. Terrorism is a particularly morally objectionable form of free riding, as it relies inherently on the moral restraint of others and it is a paradigmatic instance of the ruthless use of individuals as mere means towards an end which they cannot conceivably share. Regardless of its professed cause, terrorism is diametrically opposed to the requirements of liberal morality and can be defended only at the expense of relinquishing the most basic of liberal commitments.

PART II

Freedom, Security, and Rights in a Terrorist Age: Liberal-Democratic Dilemmas

3 | *How terrorism upsets liberty*

As terrorism increasingly penetrates Western democracies, liberals and libertarians are obliged to ask themselves whether contending with it justifies restricting civil liberty and, if so, to what extent. Neither personal security nor individual liberty is ever fully realized – both are a matter of degree – and they are often perceived as being at odds with each other. Hence it has been suggested that we reconsider the existing trade-off between them, or reassess their "rate of exchange." While such questions are sometimes raised by left-leaning liberals, they are in fact particularly acute for liberals on the right, or libertarians, who would normally resist any increase in government intervention. Right-wingers who advocate "hands off" policies on all other occasions now call for an increase in government intervention as regards security measures. Many left-liberals, on the other hand, are reluctant to concede any further power to the state in order to combat terrorism.

This chapter explores the issue of whether increased terrorist threats require a diminution in liberty rights as the price of security. In the US, many of the aggressive measures against terrorism taken by the Bush administration since September 11, such as the Patriot Act and the more recent Military Commissions Act (2006),[1] have stirred considerable debate about striking a new balance between security and liberty. I set out by discussing Jeremy Waldron's analysis of the concept of security, and his reservations about this notion of striking a new balance between security and liberty. I join Waldron in calling into question the applicability of the balance metaphor. Instead, I suggest that when considering a reduction in civil liberties in exchange for greater safety, we should think in terms of a theoretical social contract determining the relation

---

[1] The United States, Military Commissions Act, 2006, Pub. L. No. 109–366, 120 Stat. 2600 (October 17, 2006), enacting Chapter 47A of title 10 of the US Code, Act of Congress (Senate Bill 3930) signed by President George W. Bush on October 17, 2006. Sec. 948a&b. http://frwebgate.access.gpo.gov/ cgi-bin/getdoc.cgi? dbname=109_cong_bills&docid=f:s3930enr.txt.pdf.

between security and liberty under different circumstances. Since, on classical contractarian assumptions, the contract is entered precisely for security reasons, there can be no balance, since personal safety is a prerequisite of liberty. The chapter concludes by discussing what re-adjustments of civil liberties might be acceptable and which would not.

Safety and security

In "Safety and Security," Jeremy Waldron points to the neglect of the concept of security within political theory to date, and goes a long way towards remedying that deficiency.[2] I shall not reiterate Waldron's illuminating analysis here. I shall, however, rely on many of Waldron's insights in a preliminary clarification of the relevant meaning of security for the purposes of considering its relation to the concept of liberty, and the practical suggestions regarding the "balance" or "trade-off" between these two values.

In order to understand what is meant here when discussing security versus liberty, it is first necessary to state what I do not mean. By security, I am not refering, at least for the most part, to the integrity and security of states and their institutions, although admittedly this form of security might be related, and is to some extent necessary, for the sake of citizens being more secure.[3] Nevertheless, following Waldron, I will assume that "when it is said that liberty must be traded off for the sake of security, what is meant by 'security' is *people* being more secure."[4] This is not to say that security concerns only pure physical safety in the narrowest sense, but this core notion of physical integrity and safety stands at the heart of the present discussion. As Waldron states repeatedly, drawing out the deepest insights from the simplest of observations, "nobody wants to be blown up."[5] To this, he suggests, we might add security from material loss, such as loss of property and economic value, and securing one's mode of life,[6] as well as protection from fear, "considered not just as an emotional response to a diminution in actual safety, but as a mental state that is itself partly *constitutive* of insecurity."[7] As Waldron points out in his discussion of security, as well as elsewhere, "That the

---

[2] Jeremy Waldron, "Safety and Security," *Nebraska Law Review* 85, (2006), pp. 301–53.
[3] Ibid., p. 307.   [4] Ibid.   [5] Ibid., pp. 308, 309, 312, 348.
[6] Ibid., pp. 309, 312–13.   [7] Ibid., pp. 309, 313–16.

element of fear is not insignificant is indicated by the word 'terrorism' itself."[8]

Security, Waldron tells us, also connotes an element of assurance, both an assurance of being safe, feeling sure that one is safe rather than merely being objectively safe, as well as an assurance, or guarantee, of enjoying other goods, such as one's civil liberties, securely.[9] In this sense, he explains, security may be best thought of not only as an independent good, but also as a mode in which other goods are enjoyed.[10] To all this, we should add our concern for the safety of others, as part of our own sense of security.[11] When demanding an increase in security, people are often concerned not only for their own safety, but also for that of their children and other loved ones. Insecurity and panic affect the economy, and the general social order can be disrupted by security threats.[12] Citizens' lifestyles and a community's way of life can be disrupted by terrorism, as has been the case in Israel at the height of terrorist bombings.

In what follows, all this should be considered. In discussing security versus liberty, I have in mind first and foremost individual security and personal safety. But the concept of security need not be viewed in the narrowest sense to denote nothing but sheer physical integrity and survival, though this simple understanding remains at its core.

The image of balance

In "Security and Liberty: The Image of Balance," Waldron cautions against a recent trend in political rhetoric which calls for striking a new balance, as it were, between security and liberty in the wake of September 11. Though he refrains from offering conclusive judgments, he points to some serious problems with this common argument, which advocates downgrading civil liberties in view of heightened security threats.[13] For non-utilitarians of the Rawls, Dworkin, or Nozick type, he explains, rights appear practically impervious to social utility arguments of this contemporary sort. If one accords liberty lexical priority over social goods, or regards rights as "trumps" or as side constraints,

[8] Ibid., p. 313. See also Waldron, "Terrorism," pp. 5, 8–9.
[9] Waldron, "Safety and Security," pp. 309, 316–20.   [10] Ibid., pp. 309, 318–20.
[11] Ibid., pp. 320–48.   [12] Ibid., pp. 342–4.
[13] Jeremy Waldron, "Security and Liberty: The Image of Balance," *The Journal of Political Philosophy* 11 (2) (2003), pp. 191–210.

then rights may be overridden only under very special circumstances, primarily when this is necessary to protect the rights of others.[14] On these accounts, security interests can justify a curtailment of liberty if security itself is construed as an individual right, whose protection may at times necessitate overriding liberty rights.[15] No one, after all, conceives of individual rights as altogether absolute. Nevertheless, Waldron points out that even if we concede security the status of a right, the curtailment of liberty demands far weightier and more structured supporting arguments than are commonly supplied by the advocates of striking a new balance between liberty and security in the US, post-September 11. On a practical level, such arguments would have to show that the abridgment of the rights in question would indeed result in a substantial increase in individual security. The need to "do something" for symbolic purposes, or to pacify an outraged public or satisfy psychological distress, cannot justify the curtailment of liberty.[16] On a more theoretical level, proponents of the balancing argument cannot assume that their proposal can be understood straightforwardly in a near-literal sense that implies a simple equation between liberty and security.[17] Arguments favoring an abrogation of rights need to address the special nature of the rights in question and the ordered priorities of moral theory, and to pay special attention to all the intricacies of the various possible relations between one person's rights and those of another.[18]

Beyond this, Waldron draws our attention to two troubling features of the restriction of civil liberties in the name of combating terror. The first concerns the distribution of liberty; the second concerns the traditional liberal fear of government. First: "Though we may talk of balancing *our* liberties against *our* security ... the real diminution in liberty may affect some people more than others."[19] At least as regards the curtailment of procedural rights – those that concern arrests, wire tapping, or investigations – the recent diminution of liberty in the US already applies more to alien residents than to US citizens and permanent residents. Furthermore, any future curtailment of civil liberties as a response to September 11 is bound to affect "members of a fairly visible ethnic group" (Arabs, for

---

[14] Ibid., pp. 196–8.   [15] Ibid., p. 198.   [16] Ibid., pp. 208–10.
[17] Ibid., 192–4, throughout.   [18] Ibid., p. 200.
[19] Ibid., p. 194, my emphasis. On distribution of security, see also Waldron, "Safety and Security," pp. 320–42, esp. 332–40.

example) far more than other US residents.[20] Similarly, in any other
ethnically mixed society the effects of restricting civil rights in the hope
of apprehending more terrorists are likely to be distributed unequally:
"So ... justice requires that we pay special attention to the distributive
character of the changes that are proposed and to the possibility that the
change involves in effect, a proposal to trade off the liberties of the few
against the security of the majority."[21]

A second reason to worry about abdicating any of our civil liberties in
exchange for more security is that reducing liberty means increasing
government power, and this is traditionally a cause for liberal concern:
"The protection of civil liberties is not just a matter of cherishing certain
freedoms that we particularly value. It is also a matter of suspicion of
power, an apprehension that power given to the state is seldom ever
used only for the purposes for which it is given, but is always and
endemically liable to abuse."[22] Liberalism, says Waldron, is born at
least in part of "apprehension about what may be done to us using
the overwhelming means of force available to the state."[23] Following
Judith Sklar, he attributes the origin of this "liberalism of fear" largely
to the political philosophy of John Locke: "It will not do, said Locke,
in justifying strong unconstrained government, to point to the perils
that it might protect us from: 'This is to think that men are so foolish,
that they take care to avoid what mischief may be done them by *pole-
cats*, or *foxes*, but are content, nay think it safety, to be devoured
by lions.'"[24]

Waldron's analytical critique of the "striking a new balance" argument is illuminating and persuasive. I doubt my brief account does
justice to his detailed scrutiny and to all the intricacies of his debate.
His concluding call for care and caution about surrendering civil liberties and about the correlative increase in government power cannot be
disputed by any liberal. I also share Waldron's affinity for the political
philosophy of John Locke and its particular brand of liberalism. As for
resolving the liberty versus security dilemma presented to us by modern
terrorism, however, I strongly suspect that part of the answer lies in the

[20] Waldron, "Security and Liberty," pp. 200–4.   [21] Ibid., p. 194.
[22] Ibid., p. 204.   [23] Ibid., pp. 205–6.
[24] Ibid., pp. 205–6; John Locke, *Two Treatises of Government*, ed. Peter Laslett
(Cambridge University Press, 1960), p. 328.

political philosophy of Thomas Hobbes rather than in the writings of John Locke.[25]

This chapter considers the common suggestion that citizens of liberal democracies, specifically Americans, ought to tolerate a downward readjustment of their civil liberties in the wake of September 11. It concedes Waldron's point that popular talk of striking a new balance between liberty and security is indeed inaccurate. It suggests, however, contra Waldron, that the political position represented by this faulty balancing rhetoric is justified in calling for more security even at the expense of reducing liberty. This chapter suggests that when considering the appropriate relation between security and liberty under various circumstances we should think in terms of a theoretical social contract grounding our liberal societies, and consider the rationale of our theoretical consent to it. Hobbes and Locke in particular are vital here. Both assume that personal security justifies our initial renunciation of liberty in favor of political authority, and both should have something to say about the relationship between the two values later on in political life.[26]

The following section traces Locke's train of thought regarding our initial exchange between liberty and security and invites the reader to bear it in mind when contemplating contemporary dilemmas that may involve similar trade-offs. The main point to remember is that Lockean

---

[25] Hobbes's essential contribution to this issue is certainly acknowledged by Waldron in a later article, where he deals exclusively with the security side of the liberty–security balance. See Waldron, "Safety and Security," pp. 303–5, 309.

[26] The initial concern with personal security makes Locke a better liberal candidate for consulting on contemporary dilemmas concerning the threat of terrorism than other liberal contractarians are (most notably John Rawls). Unlike his contractarian predecessors, Rawls neglects the security issue to an extent that renders his work inapplicable, at least straightforwardly, to the current debate. While it would no doubt be illuminating to hypothesize and speculate as to what a Rawlsian approach to the issue at hand might be, this would be a topic for a very different essay. Nevertheless, I address Rawls's work briefly towards the end of this chapter.

As for other types of liberalism not considered here: non-contractarian, specifically utilitarian, liberalism might admittedly be another avenue to pursue in search of the appropriate liberal response to the security v. liberty dilemma. Notoriously, however, utilitarian thinking consists of weighing a wide array of factual questions concerning the sum total or average happiness for all those concerned. In this case, I believe such an approach would pose an indefinite number of inconclusive, perhaps insurmountable, factual questions. In any event, I leave such questions of utility open to pursuit by those who subscribe to, and are prepared to defend, purely consequentialist moral theories.

liberalism (not only Hobbesean absolutism) is premised on the notion that security and personal safety are prerequisites for freedom. This supplies an additional reason, not provided by Waldron, for his argument that the two cannot logically be balanced against each other, but it is also a reason for rejecting Waldron's normative presumption against restricting liberty in times of danger. If personal safety is a necessary requirement for liberty, it must take priority in the relative ranking of these two goods. Locke never said as much, but this, I suggest, is only because he assumed (rather than argued) that no external threat would ever endanger our natural rights to the extent that massive government does. In so far as he envisioned such dangers, Locke himself would have defended exceeding minimal governmental powers in order to guard against them.

This is where Hobbes comes in. While Hobbes's overall political prescription is anathema to liberalism, his pessimistic description of human nature and the consequences of weak government may have been more realistic than Locke's work. Hobbes's prediction that restricting the sovereign will render him incapable of protecting our right to life may be more relevant to current affairs.

In what follows I ask, somewhat metaphorically, how Lockean liberals ought to respond politically to quasi-Hobbesean situations of war. What is Locke's legacy for dealing with semi-Hobbesean emergencies? Are contemporary liberals who advocate restrictions on liberty essentially Lockeans in Hobbesean shoes? Subsequently, I consider the possibility of justifying more government on Lockean grounds in situations of national security crises, specifically the type of heightened terrorist threat faced by the citizenry of Western democracies and the political choices they currently face vis-à-vis their civil liberties.[27]

The fusion between grave Hobbesean diagnoses and attractive Lockean liberal prescriptions are unraveled in the next three sections. This discussion concludes that advocating limitations on liberty when faced with terrorist threats is not only consistent with liberalism but, in fact, warranted by it. I argue that there is no inconsistency involved in adhering to staunch liberal, or libertarian, views with regard to state

[27] While my interest lies in the current terrorist emergency, these same questions could equally be brought to the fore by other forms of dire peril, such as war or even natural disasters. Some civil liberty issues were raised in the past when liberal democracies faced world wars; for Hobbes, questioning the scope of governmental authority was sparked by witnessing a civil war.

intervention and civil rights under all ordinary circumstances, while supporting more stringent limitations on liberty when faced with terrorist threats or other types of mortal peril. On the contrary: in extreme circumstances this apparent paradox is precisely what liberty requires.

The latter sections of the chapter consider some caveats and inject several reservations. These suggest that whatever the crises, not everything is permissible. As opposed to the "balancing" approach, the liberal foundations of the argument place certain limitations on the type of security measures that can be justified, as well as on their scope.

Government – the less the better

If liberals fear government, why endure any restrictions on our natural liberties in the first place? Locke tells us that we assume the responsibilities involved in civil society in order to protect our property rights (including ownership over ourselves) and gain a degree of stability, which cannot obtain in the state of nature.

Locke's state of nature is not entirely bad. At the outset of his *Second Treatise of Government*, he describes it as a state of liberty and equality between individuals, in which they have two natural rights: the right to preserve themselves and the right to punish others for attempting to kill them or generally threatening their survival.[28] Human beings exercise those rights under the constraint of the law of nature, whereby we are forbidden to harm others. As Locke puts it, "though this be a state of liberty, yet it is not a state of license": people have rights and duties.[29] More specifically, they have rights of ownership not only over themselves but over the things they need to survive: correlatively, others are under a duty not to take those things away from them.[30] As for people's natural moral character, Locke tells us that many of the inhabitants of his "state of nature" are, on the whole, motivated to fulfill their duties towards others, because they are, by nature, peaceful, and foster good-will towards one another.[31]

Under these conditions of liberty, equality, and good will, it appears almost puzzling that people eventually decide to do away with their original state and assume the burdens of political obligations: they do not seem to be doing so badly for themselves as they are. It is no wonder

---

[28] Locke, *Two Treatises*, p. 269.
[29] Ibid., pp. 270–1.   [30] Ibid., Chapter V.   [31] Ibid., p. 280.

that modern philosophers who defend only the most minimal of states turn to Locke for support. If anarchy is almost utopia, there is not much justification for state intervention at all.

But although the state of nature is not by definition a state of war, it is not stable enough for people to be altogether happy in it. For a start, it is likely to degenerate into a state of war, for not everybody is disposed to fulfill their duties.[32] Besides, in the state of nature, it is up to each individual to decide whether their rights are being respected, and to interpret the natural law (which states that they should not harm others): but disagreements on this can be profound, even amongst well-meaning, well-disposed people. We need an impartial judge to interpret the law and mediate between us: a fundamental principle for resolving conflicts is that no one be judged in his/her own quarrel. Finally, we need someone with the appropriate power to enforce the law.[33]

For all these reasons, we decide by contract to form a civil society, in which we know that we will not be threatened in our lives, limbs, and property. Securing our property rights, most definitely including property in ourselves, as it were, is the be-all and end-all of our social covenant. Locke could not have been clearer on this point. He specifically describes the reasons men have for abandoning the state of nature in favor of political society as "the mutual preservation of their lives, liberties, and estates, which I call by the general name 'property'."[34] This logic also dictates the type of civil society that it is rational for us to choose. If securing our natural rights is our goal, it would be patently irrational to constitute a polity that endangered these rights more than they were jeopardized within the state of nature. On these grounds, Locke confronts advocates of absolute monarchy[35] and proposes a system of government in which there are strict limits to what the legislature can do.[36] Essentially, it can only pass laws that respect the law of nature; that is, which ensure that people will not be threatened in their life, limbs, and property (unless of course they transgress those

---

[32] Ibid., Chapter IX, sects. 123, 128, pp. 350, 352.

[33] Ibid., Chapter IX, sects. 124–6, pp. 350–1.

[34] Ibid., sect. 123, p. 350. One might even argue that since Locke's justification for property in external items is a derivative of the self-ownership thesis, securing the right to life and limb takes priority, both logically and normatively, over the former, in his reasoning for constituting a political community.

[35] Ibid., sect. 90, p. 326.   [36] Ibid., sect. 142, p. 363.

laws). Hence our civil liberties, and Locke's famous comment, cited by Waldron, whereby no rational man could agree to their abrogation.[37]

Locke's thinking to this effect notoriously influenced US history, its Declaration of Independence and its Constitution. (It was Locke, needless to say, who first demanded of the legislature that "they must not raise taxes on the property of the people without the consent of the people.")[38] Aside from any other philosophical justifications for a liberal system of government, it is clear that no other form of state could rationally be consented to so long as its alternative is perceived as something like a Lockean state of nature. Only a fool would concede such powers to government that would place him in greater dangers than those posed by the state of nature, which, in Locke's account, is clearly not a state of war.[39] So the social covenant consented to, as it were, by citizens of a truly liberal society is fundamentally (though not exclusively) a Lockean one, grounded on the essential background assumption of a benevolent state of nature. Since the absence of government is not altogether bad (libertarians may at times even find it appealing), there cannot be any justification for too much government.

Beyond the minimal state

Can terrorism alter this judgment? I believe that it can, even if we ought not to regard this change as "striking a new balance" between liberty and security. External peril upsets our prior judgments about the extent of governmental authority when it threatens the liberties we set out to protect. So long as we can do better for our natural rights without government than we can under an excess of it, we would be unreasonable to assume anything beyond the most minimal burdens of political authority. These rational calculations, however, are dependent on the choices we face and their outcome will, inevitably, be different if we presuppose a serious increase in the dangers that lurk outside our political society.

One (hardly original) way of illustrating this point about rational choice and our consent to government is to suggest that there is some type of maximin rule at work here. The members of a hypothetical original state (or the authors of a liberal constitution) may implement

---

[37] Ibid., sect. 93, p. 328.   [38] Ibid., sect. 142, p. 363.
[39] Ibid., sect. 19, p. 280.

this rule with regard to two separate sets of theoretical assumptions resulting in two different reasonable political prescriptions. I will refer to these assumptions as Lockean versus Hobbesian hypotheses.

Under Lockean assumptions, our first (albeit somewhat theoretical) option is to reject any political organization and opt instead to remain outside this framework under the conditions described by Locke. Within this state of nature, we would not benefit from the privileges of civil society. Moreover, the worst outcome of this option would be Locke's prediction that it might eventually degenerate into a state of war. Still, Locke assumed that the gravest dangers of this natural state are still preferable to the worst possible outcome of unconstrained government. Consenting to an unconstrained form of government would be irrational on Locke's account. In his own terms, it amounts to choosing an alternative in which the worst outcome is being devoured by lions in preference to an option whose worst possible outcome is confronting pole-cats or foxes. Consequently, if we are to adopt the alternative in which the worst outcome is superior to the worst outcome of all others, reason prescribes a highly constrained form of government. On Locke's assumptions, it would seem that the worst possible outcome of this option for the individual will not be too severe, as our natural rights are guaranteed by this minimal state.

Assume now that our theoretical rational contractors turn to consider their options under a set of Hobbesean hypotheses. Under this new set of circumstances, remaining in (or returning to) the state of nature (i.e. the absence of government) would involve, inter alia, participating endlessly in a "war of all against all," living one's life in perpetual fear, uncertainty and mistrust of one's fellow man.[40] Restricted government may, on Hobbesean assumptions, result in the sovereign's inability to guarantee our natural rights, understood primarily as the right to survival. In order to avoid this, we could opt for unconstrained government. This, notoriously, was Hobbes's first choice, but its worst outcome remains the very grave and real possibility of excessive state power and its abuse, feared by generations of liberals.

Clearly, the possibility of remaining in (or returning to) a state of nature is considerably less attractive under Hobbesean circumstances than it appeared in Locke's description. Thus, Hobbes himself took the

---

[40] Thomas Hobbes, *Leviathan*, ed. R. Tuck (Cambridge University Press, 1991), Chapter XIII.

view that having no government leaves human beings in a condition
more miserable than that to be suffered under even the worst tyrant.
Hobbes's prediction that restricting the sovereign will render him incapable of protecting our right to life is also very frightening indeed. For
Hobbes, this was the worst-case scenario resulting from opting for
weak government, and he regarded this outcome as both realistic and
inferior to the worst possible outcome of unlimited sovereignty.[41] As
I said, however, this third option remains anathema to liberals.
Nonetheless, any rational contractor faced with a set of Hobbesean
choices will have to consider the wide array of options which lie
between Locke's preference for highly constrained government, on the
one side, and absolute sovereignty, on the other. The same logic which
led Lockean-type contractors to support a minimal state under the first
set of assumptions, will lead them to consider something beyond this
under a set of hypotheses more closely resembling Hobbes's train of
thought.

Life, liberty, and all the rest

No doubt all this is over-dramatized. Certainly, nothing the US or any
other democracy has experienced so far recommends opting for a
Hobbesian-style unconstrained sovereign. The ills of massive government still loom large even in the shadows of Osama bin Laden.
Furthermore, some will no doubt argue that the exercise of extraordinary governmental powers may be justified on Lockean grounds
alone. Consider the special prerogative Locke accords later in the
Second Treatise to the executive to act at his discretion in the public
interest, even at the expense of the legislative body, and at times
outside the rule of law for the sake of security.[42] My illustration is
also somewhat oversimplified, as it does not assess the probabilities of
the various possible results of each option. Furthermore, returning
to the state of nature is, and always was, a very hypothetical option.[43]
Nevertheless, what I described somewhat metaphorically as a move from
Lockean to Hobbesean conditions, represents a shift in circumstances

---

[41] Ibid., Chapters XVII–IXX.
[42] Locke, *Two Treatises*, Chapter XIV.
[43] In the case of terrorism specifically, dismantling certain states would no doubt
alter the situation entirely – this is clearly neither a realistic, nor a desirable,
option.

that Americans began to experience with the collapse of the twin towers. Even if terrorism changes nothing of what we think about liberty and security, it alters the conditions under which we consider our options with respect to them.

I have suggested that a type of Lockean logic lies at the foundation of Americans' civil liberties and that under normal circumstances this reasoning indicates that a highly constrained form of government is preferable to any of its alternatives. Obviously, as pointed out above, a more refined description of our options would show that there is in fact a continuum of choices ranging from minimal government to absolute sovereignty of the Hobbesian type. In reality, American government on September 10 already exceeded the powers accorded to a minimal state. Nonetheless, the first set of circumstances described above crudely represents what a liberal social contract prescribes under the conditions that obtained in the US through September 10, 2001, while the second set of circumstances represents the choices we face in emergency situations, in which minimal government may not be able to contend with external threats. Under circumstances of grave terror, the weakness of government may strikingly begin to result in something like a Hobbesian state of nature rather than a Lockean one, and Locke's constrained sovereign may no longer be capable of guaranteeing our natural rights. This, presumably, is where Locke's suggestion about the prerogative of the executive power is supposed to begin.[44] The authors of *The Federalist Papers* certainly seem to have thought something of the sort. As they state in *The Federalist Papers*, the powers to ensure security

ought to exist without limitation, because it is impossible to foresee or to define the extent and variety of national exigencies, and the correspondent extent and variety of the means which may be necessary to satisfy them. The circumstances that endanger the safety of nations are infinite, and for this reason no constitutional shackles can wisely be imposed on the power to which the care of it is committed.[45]

As for their philosophical progenitors, one need look no further than the latitude Locke left to the executive power:

[44] Locke, *Two Treatises*, Chapter XIV.
[45] Alexander Hamilton in *The Federalist Papers*, no. xxiii: "The Necessity of a Government as Energetic as the One Proposed to the Preservation of the Union." From the *New York Packet*, Tuesday, December 18, 1787. See also Netanyahu, *Fighting Terrorism*, p. 45.

This power to act according to discretion for the public good, without the prescription of the law and sometimes even against it, is that which is called "prerogative"; for since in some governments the law making power is not always in being, and is usually too numerous and so too slow for the dispatch requisite to execution, and because also it is impossible to foresee, and so by law to provide for all accidents and necessities that may concern the public, or to make such laws as will do no harm if they are executed with an inflexible rigor on all occasions and upon all persons that may come in their way, therefore there is a latitude left to the executive power to do many things of choice which the laws do not prescribe.[46]

Clearly, the constitutional arrangements envisaged by the founding generation for the normal workings of American society were quite different from those they intended to apply in situations of grave national danger. We may not, however, wish to go as far as Madison and Hamilton recommended. I have already suggested that there may be a better way of considering our options than simply invoking the old Lockean notion of "prerogative power" which (arguably) justifies bold assertions of executive emergency powers. While Locke's influence on the American constitution is notorious, Hobbes's impact is apparent as well. In particular, Hobbes's justification for political authority as a means of protecting our natural rights (specifically survival), along with his notion of inalienable rights and their specific content, are clearly echoed in the American Constitution as well as in the legal codes of other liberal-democracies. While the rather optimistic picture of human nature and political motivation depicted by John Locke was impressed upon the American Founding Fathers, resulting in their choice of restricted government, Hobbes could not have been totally absent from their minds either. Both Locke and Hobbes are implicitly present in the constitution of the largest Western democracy in the world, and both are invaluable to assessing what measures a liberal social contract would dictate in times of security crises.

One need not be alarmist, and it is admittedly far-fetched to describe the US at present as facing a Hobbesian war of all against all. However, in the extreme case, when terrorism remains unimpeded by the state, the normal workings of society are seriously disrupted. Soon, "there is no place for industry ... no arts; no letters; no society" (though for reasons different than in Hobbes's description); "and which is worst of all,

[46] Locke, *Two Treatises*, Chapter XIV, sects. 160–1, p. 375.

continual fear, and danger of violent death; And the life of man, solitary, poor, nasty, brutish, and short."[47] Needless to say, Hamas and al-Qaida are far from Locke's pole-cats or foxes and, when they are confronted daily, they begin to appear even more frightening than the lions of government. This may not change any mysterious balance between liberty and security, but it certainly changes the worst outcomes of our options, particularly those associated with weak government. It may (or may not) be merely a linguistic curio to point out, as Jacques Derrida did, that in the *Leviathan* Hobbes speaks not only of "fear" but also of "terror."[48]

On September 11, 2001, Americans were introduced to a worst-case scenario that they did not face (or were not aware of) prior to those terror attacks. In terms of the previous section, the worst outcome of maintaining minimal government is no longer a deterioration into a benevolent state of nature, but rather a degeneration into an overall situation of perpetual fear for life and limb in which citizens cannot exercise their most basic liberties. Henry Shue points out, in his discussion of *Basic Rights*, that "If any right is to be exercised except at great risk, physical security must be protected. In the absence of physical security people are unable to use any other rights that society may be said to be protecting without being liable to encounter many of the worst dangers they would encounter if society were not protecting the rights."[49]

This dangerous outcome is no fanciful hypothesis and it does not require a complete return to any theoretical natural state. It has, in fact, already begun to occur in some parts of the globe that are more seriously infected with terror. Where terrorists attack commuter buses, railways, and air travel, freedom of movement is seriously impeded. When places of worship become targets of attack, freedom of religion is diminished. Since terrorists aim to attack large concentrations of people, terrorized citizens will often refrain from exercising their right of assembly. In *Basic Rights*, with no reference to terror, Shue pointed out that personal security is an "inherent necessity" for exercising liberties such as freedom of assembly:

---

[47] Hobbes, *Leviathan*, p. 62.
[48] Borradori, *Philosophy*; Hobbes, *Leviathan*, Chapter IV, Chapter XI.
[49] Henry Shue, *Basic Rights: Subsistence, Affluence and US Foreign Policy* (Princeton University Press, 1980), p. 21.

For it is not that security from beating, for instance, is separate from freedom of peaceful assembly but that it always needs to accompany it. Being secure from beating, if one chooses to hold a meeting, is part of being free to assemble. If one cannot safely assemble, one is not free to assemble. One is, on the contrary, being coerced not to assemble by the threat of the beating.[50]

Security is not merely a means towards enjoying the right to free assembly. It is, Shue tells us, an essential component of such rights.[51]

Likewise, where government is too weak to prevent terrorists from threatening schools, cafes, shopping centers, pedestrian malls, office buildings, and airports, on a daily basis, citizens' choices are severely limited by the necessities of survival. This must be equally true whether the threat to personal security generates from the government or from an external threat.[52] As James Madison once wrote in a letter to Thomas Jefferson, "It is a melancholy reflection that liberty should be equally exposed to danger whether the government have too much or too little power."[53] Furthermore, when a government is no longer able to protect its citizens, the latter slowly begin retrieving their natural rights – citizens increasingly carry arms for protection and they begin once again to view themselves as the best judges for interpreting their natural rights and best suited to protecting them. Moreover, following

---

[50] Ibid., p. 26.   [51] Ibid., p. 27.

[52] In his discussion of Shue's argument, Jeremy Waldron notes that "Shue concentrates on security against threats actually targeted at the enjoyment of one's rights. It is a further question whether his argument applies for security generally. Suppose a person is insecure because of the danger of terrorist attack. Assuming the terrorists simply intend to kill and wound a large number of people (perhaps including him) and do not really care either way about other rights enjoyed or exercised by the potential victims of their attacks. Is it still true that the enjoyment of rights is debilitated by insecurity in that sense? Perhaps, but the argument would be less direct than the argument Shue provides. The argument would be that security in this sense is a condition for rights in-as-much as our hypothetical insecure person needs to be able to concentrate on his exercise of rights and make plans utilizing his rights, and he cannot do this if he is distracted by terror." Waldron, "Safety and Security," p. 319. In the above text, I am attempting such an indirect argument for security as a *sine qua non* for liberty, and I suggest Shue's argument can be relied on in this connection. Furthermore, it is by no means clear that certain forms of terrorism, specifically contemporary Islamist terrorism, are not a threat that directly target rights. Terrorists may, though they need not necessarily, be directly targeting rights, in the sense of targeting a particular, liberal way of life that inherently involves the enjoyment of certain rights.

[53] James Madison, "The Question of a Bill of Rights," letter to Thomas Jefferson, October 17, 1788: www.constitution.org/jm/17881017_bor.htm. See also Netanyahu, *Fighting Terrorism*, p. 45.

the logic of social contract theories, they are justified in doing so, though some will, inevitably, make costly mistakes and harm innocents in the process of attempting self-preservation.

Shue argues that security (along with subsistence) is a basic right, not because its enjoyment would be more satisfying than that of any other right, but because security "is desirable as part of the enjoyment of any other right. No right other than a right to physical security can in fact be enjoyed if a right to physical security is not protected. Being physically secure is a necessary condition for the exercise of any other right, and guarantying physical security must be part of guarantying anything else as a right."[54]

Clearly, personal security is a necessary condition for enjoying any serious degree of liberty, though it is also plainly true, as Jeremy Waldron points out in his discussion of "Safety and Security," that "though Shue's point is no doubt important, it is probably a mistake to think of physical security only as a basic condition for the enjoyment and exercise of rights. People value their safety and physical survival in and of itself."[55] Shue himself does not deny this, though he is making a different point; he says that "Regardless of whether the enjoyment of physical security is also desirable for its own sake, it is desirable as part of the enjoyment of every other right."[56] Waldron is also quite right in observing:

However, even if security is a necessary condition for the enjoyment of rights, it does not necessarily follow that security should have absolute priority. For one thing, a necessary condition for X is worth supplying only if there is a practical possibility of securing sufficient conditions for X; if there is no such possibility, then we should forget about the necessary conditions for X. More importantly, there is something perverse about giving absolute priority to security over rights if security is valued only for the sake of rights. Surely we do not want to devote all our resources and energy to fulfilling a necessary condition for something we value, and nothing at all to the thing that we value.[57]

I shall return to Waldron's first point about the feasibility of securing sufficient conditions for our goals at the beginning of the following section. As for the second point, I am not suggesting here that we entirely rule out any right-based complaints against increases in security, because

---

[54] Shue, *Basic Rights*, pp. 21–2.
[55] Waldron, "Safety and Security," p. 320.   [56] Shue, *Basic Rights*, p. 21.
[57] Waldron, "Safety and Security," pp. 319–20.

security is simply a *sine qua non* for the enjoyment of all other rights. Clearly, considerable thought has to be given to the relationship between these values, rather than simply concluding that security takes absolute priority over liberty, though I also doubt this additional effort ought to be regarded as a plain balance between security and liberty.[58] Things are more complicated than that. Nevertheless, Shue's realistic observation excludes any potential Rawlsian-type arguments whereby, "if security falls into the domain of the principle governing social and economic goods, then a trade-off of liberty against security is simply ruled out."[59] If security is a requirement for freedom, it cannot be perceived as a mere social good; that is, as such an argument would imply, that it is lexically inferior to equal liberty. Moreover, it will not do simply to recognize that liberty and security represent two individual rights, suggesting that they need to be balanced or rebalanced, in order to resolve any tension between them.[60] Security and liberty cannot be weighed against each other in any ordinary way because the former is a prerequisite for the latter. At the very least, "we have to remain open to the possibility that there are substantial, as opposed to purely verbal, internal connections between security (or security of safety) and liberty."[61]

To summarize: Liberals and libertarians adopt Locke's political prescription *inter alia* because they accept his initial assumptions concerning human nature and man's pre-political predicament, the benefits of constrained government and the shortcomings of its alternatives – understood primarily as lack of government on one side, and unlimited sovereignty on the other. But what if anything resembling normal Lockean conditions ceases to obtain? What citizens of post-September 11 America must ask themselves now is indeed *not* how to strike a new balance between liberty and security. Instead, they must ask what is the legacy of their Lockean Founding Fathers for confronting Hobbesian situations? I suggest that citizens of liberal democracies ought to view their underlying social covenant as addressing both "Lockean" and "Hobbesian" scenarios, and prescribing different political solutions for each of the two. We need not (nor can we straightforwardly) rebalance security against liberty in view of unfolding events if we can assume that our original (albeit theoretical)

---

[58] I think I am in agreement with Waldron on both these points. See Waldron, "Security and Liberty," and Waldron, "Safety and Securityo," p. 319.
[59] Waldron, "Security and Liberty," p. 197.   [60] Ibid., pp. 198–9.
[61] Waldron, "Safety and Security," p. 319.

social contract supplies us with emergency regulations, as it were, precisely for this type of eventuality. In a security crisis, we may be justified in opting for more government than we would otherwise consent to, as the only means of protecting our natural rights.

Later on I argued, following Henry Shue, that personal security, or safety, is a prerequisite for liberty, adding credence to the rejection of a simple balance between them, let alone regarding security as a lexically inferior social good in relation to equal liberty. Although security need not take absolute priority over liberty, the two are at the very least internally intertwined in a way that should focus specifically liberal attention on the value of security.

Some caveats

In a security crisis there is no inconsistency involved in a liberal call for less civil liberty. It is justified, however, even if one accepts that security is a necessary requirement for liberty, only on the proviso raised by Waldron, namely, that such restrictions are effective in enhancing security rather than merely reducing public hysteria.[62] Again, "even if security is a necessary condition for the enjoyment of rights, it does not necessarily follow that security should have absolute priority. For one thing, a necessary condition for X is worth supplying only if there is a practical possibility of securing sufficient conditions for X; if there is no such possibility, then we should forget about the necessary conditions for X."[63] Waldron's accompanying analogy here is helpful in illustrating this point: "A necessary condition for me to visit the moon is that I should begin astronaut training right now, but even assuming that my visiting the moon is highly desirable, the necessary condition for it is simply of no interest since *it is not going to happen*."[64]

Skepticism concerning the utility of specific security measures cannot be settled at the level of political theory, and disagreements concerning particular legal proposals will not, therefore, be resolved here. It is instructive, however, to note that other democracies, such as Britain, Germany, France, Japan, and even Canada have had considerable success in combating terrorism by means which would be prohibited

---

[62] Waldron, "Security and Liberty," pp. 198–210.
[63] Waldron, "Safety and Security," pp. 319–20.
[64] Ibid., p. 320, n55; Waldron, "Security and Liberty," pp. 208–9.

in the US.[65] I have in mind primarily more pervasive means of gathering information (essentially those concerning surveillance and investigation) than would be permitted under the American right to privacy and freedoms of speech and religion. Other, more defensive, measures include enhancing both overt and undercover security personnel, close scrutiny of all public buildings and transport, so-called "ethnic profiling," as well as pre-screening passengers before boarding aircraft. All these measures are employed in Israel, for instance, but are strongly resisted by American liberals. Of course, the expediency of such measures is always contestable and success in these matters is a relative term. I also remain hesitant about employing the word "success" with regard to Israel's recent experience with Palestinian terrorism. The level of personal safety in Israel over the past decade cannot be regarded as anything less than a national fiasco. Nevertheless, I doubt that anything resembling the events that took place over America on the morning of September 11, 2001 could have occurred on an Israeli airline, and there is no doubt that Israeli intelligence succeeds in thwarting countless terror attacks on a daily basis.

Waldron, however, is particularly concerned about learning from the British and Israeli models of combating terror. He cautions that following in their footsteps may lead the US down a slippery slope culminating in the eventual abrogation of even the most minimal procedural civil rights, specifically the prohibition on torture. With this concern in mind, he draws his readers' attention to "the depressing precedent of two of our closest allies in the war against terrorism – the United Kingdom and Israel – having resorted in recent memory to methods very close to torture in dealing with their own terrorist emergencies."[66] This last assertion is backed up by an article in the *Guardian* claiming that, as a matter of policy, Israel systematically tortures Palestinians and, moreover, that its government openly admits to this.[67] Later, Waldron criticizes Alan Dershowitz for considering the admissibility of torture under extreme circumstances, say if on September 11 law enforcement officials had "arrested terrorists boarding one of the planes and learned that other planes, then airborne, were heading towards unknown occupied

---

[65] For a detailed account of the means employed in these countries, especially the UK and Germany, and their success in combating terrorism, see John E. Finn, *Constitutions in Crisis: Political Violence and the Rule of Law* (Oxford University Press, 1991); and Netanyahu, *Fighting Terrorism*, pp. 31–7.
[66] Waldron, "Security and Liberty," p. 206.   [67] Ibid., p. 206, n30.

buildings."[68] Aside from the fact that entrusting the government with the power to torture could get entirely out of hand, Waldron remarks critically that "few cases are *just* like this: few have the certainty of Dershowitz's law school classroom formulation or the clean precision of the philosopher's hypothetical."[69]

I will discuss the issue of torture specifically and at length towards the end of this volume with reference to both Israel and the US, as well as to Dershowitz's controversial proposals. For now, suffice it to say that where terrorism ceases to be a unique, cataclysmic event, and instead presents a continuous daily threat, many cases bear a striking resemblance to Dershowitz's classroom hypothesis. These are what Israelis refer to as "ticking bombs" and it is noteworthy that even under such circumstances they cannot be accused, even with some exaggeration, of having gone beyond what Waldron refers to as "methods very close to torture."[70] Moreover, on the account offered here, as opposed to the balancing model, it would be unjustified to surpass these limits and resort to outright torture.

My previous caveat specified that expedience is a necessary condition for suspending civil liberties. It is, however, not a sufficient one. As opposed to the "striking a new balance" argument, the justification offered here for reducing liberty in emergency situations cannot, by its very logic, allow for the suspension of certain basic procedural rights, most specifically the prohibition on torture. This caveat is not based on Waldron's argument against the balancing metaphor and in favor of upholding procedural guarantees, but it serves to strengthen it. The social contract argument presented here suggests a justification for the temporary curtailment of liberty in emergency circumstances and under restrictive conditions (e.g. efficiency), which is quite different to the balancing argument. One distinctly liberal advantage of this account over the "striking a new balance" argument, is that it does not, nor indeed can it, justify the abrogation of certain procedural civil liberties – specifically the right to remain silent under investigation and the related immunity from torture. These rights need not even come into question as they might under the balancing approach or, for instance, if we were to

---

[68] Ibid., p. 206, in reference to Alan Dershowitz *Shouting Fire: Civil Liberties in a Turbulent Age* (New York: Little, Brown, 2002), p. 477.
[69] Waldron, "Security and Liberty," p. 206.   [70] Ibid., p. 206.

rely solely on Locke's idea of "prerogative power" in order to determine the legitimate extent of executive authority under emergency situations.

Earlier I described a terrorized US in terms of a Lockean society faced with a Hobbesian dilemma. I suggested that, if it were to come to this, the Lockean underpinnings of the Americans' social contract, which prescribes a fairly minimal state, would actually dictate a move towards a more powerful form of government. I described this reduction of liberty figuratively, as a shifting position along a theoretical continuum ranging from Locke to Hobbes, as it were. But while a change in circumstances for the worse may justify moving somewhat to the right along this imagined continuum, it cannot justify going altogether off the deep end. A liberal society cannot, even in a national emergency, compromise liberties withheld even by Hobbesean contractors. To do so would undermine the very reasons for entering the social covenant to begin with. I have assumed that government is justified as a means of protecting our natural rights, primarily our property rights – definitely including our rights over ourselves both as an end in itself and as a prerequisite for freedom. Furthermore, more government can be justified if our very survival, and hence our liberties as well, are jeopardized by enhanced external peril. If this is the justification for political authority, as it was for Hobbes and essentially for Locke as well,[71] the sovereign clearly cannot require us to relinquish our natural right to self-preservation without losing the underlying justification for authority.

Hobbes is quite clear on this point. Our contract consists in giving up our natural rights provided that others do the same, but there are certain rights that we simply cannot give up. I cannot, in the original contract, promise to accuse myself, because I would thereby contradict my natural right to self-preservation. Since people contract in order to preserve themselves, it would be inconsistent to ask them to renounce this goal. In Chapter XXI of the *Leviathan*, Hobbes illustrates this idea by identifying two inalienable rights, the abandonment of which is impossible because it would lead people to their destruction. The first of these inalienable rights is the right to remain silent if interrogated by the sovereign.[72] Admittedly, upholding this right with regard to suspected terrorists seriously constricts security forces. Obviously, as Hobbes

---

[71] Locke, *Two Treatises*, sect. 123, p. 350.
[72] The second is the right to resistance, less relevant to the case in hand, described in Hobbes, *Leviathan*, Chapter XXI.

explicitly states, it applies even when the suspect is guilty of the crime.[73] While it need not apply to information regarding the criminal actions of others or their future plans, divulging such information will often be self-incriminating as well.

Unfortunately for Hobbesian contractors, retaining these natural rights will have little practical significance for them. Despite the fact that they cannot relinquish these immunities, their sovereign's powers are not limited by them. While no one is obliged to assist in his own punishment (one might even be entitled to resist) this does not mean that the sovereign cannot punish and kill (or even torture) whenever he deems it necessary. Hobbes's monarch remains unrestricted by his subjects' natural rights because he has no contractual relationship with, and hence no obligation towards, them but is rather in a state of nature in relation to them. Hobbes's subjects contract with one another, not with the sovereign. For all the pre-liberal rhetoric, Hobbes's sovereign retains the natural right to override the subject's natural right to silence. Notwithstanding this, Hobbes in effect contributed these procedural immunities to what eventually emerged as modern liberalism. It is this kind of reasoning about the right to silence that won a staunch proponent of absolute monarchy the title of Father of Liberalism. Aside from the Fifth Amendment in the US, the right to remain silent is also a long-recognized part of English common law[74] (although admittedly the right to silence in UK criminal cases is no longer absolute, as it still is in the US).

The theoretical contractors I have in mind here – certainly the Americans among them – are by nature and philosophical tradition Lockeans rather then Hobbesians. While I have borrowed from Hobbes's description of the absence of government, the different analyses of the natural condition in

---

[73] Ibid.

[74] Ibid., Chapters XIV, XXI. In reality, this right to remain silent has not remained unscathed even within liberal democracies. It was largely repealed by the UK's emergency regulations for Northern Ireland in 1988 on the grounds that the increasing sophistication of members of the IRA in resisting questioning made it more difficult to secure convictions. Consequently, judges were instructed to deduce what they would from the suspect's choice of silence (1991). Note, however, that even in this case the repeal of this immunity was partial, as it obviously did not empower interrogators to coerce self-incriminating speech by resorting to forceful measures of the type Hobbes no doubt had in mind. Relatedly, the immunity from torture and the inadmissibility of confessions obtained by such means was upheld, though in the case of Northern Ireland, the burden of proof regarding allegations of torture was shifted from the security forces to the terrorist suspect (Finn, *Constitutions in Crisis*, p. 102).

Hobbes and Locke are rooted in their different estimations of human nature and, consequently, of what motivates human beings. While external threats may change so as to more closely resemble Hobbes's description rather than Locke's, they do not alter these basic motivations. In short, the contractors I have in mind remain Lockean ones. While they may now have to face quasi-Hobbesian choices as far as external circumstances are concerned, their reasoning remains in line with Locke's political philosophy rather than that of Hobbes. And Locke's subjects do contract with their sovereigns, thus limiting them in a variety of ways. Far from being in a state of nature with regard to their subjects, sovereigns are, in fact, answerable to them. Their powers must be limited by those rights which they cannot relinquish, even on Hobbes's account.

Looking at the issue from a social contract perspective rather than as "striking a new balance" serves to strengthen Waldron's concern for upholding important procedural rights even in times of crisis. Using the logic of social contract theory, there is indeed good cause to pay special attention to those civil liberties that refer "to procedural rights and powers which we think individuals should have when the state detains them or brings charges against them or plans to punish them. These are rights like the right not to be detained without trial, the right to a fair trial process, the right to counsel, etc."[75] Procedural rights represent individual interests that are particularly susceptible to governmental misuse and abuse. Indeed, "Nowhere is this point clearer than in our apprehension about the use of torture."[76] These concerns for procedural rights in general, and for the ban on torture as an extreme illustration thereof, are particularly troubling as regards the 'striking a new balance' model, rightly criticized by Waldron, which might end up weighing in favor of relinquishing many of these rights in exchange for greater security. Once again Waldron gets to the heart of the matter when he observes that "On the face of it, the prohibition against torture should be exactly the sort of thing that gives way in the present atmosphere of adjusting the balance between liberty and security. What we are desperate for in the war against terrorism is information – who is planning what – and torture is supposed to be an effective way of securing information."[77]

[75] Waldron, "Security and Liberty," p. 195.
[76] Ibid., p. 206.   [77] Ibid.

This last observation points to one of the deficiencies of the balancing metaphor, which is that it has no internal liberal limits. One is, in the balancing logic, free to just balance away, as it were, with the possible result of losing very basic procedural rights – like the right to remain silent and immunity from torture, as security needs press down on the other side of the balance. One advantage of consulting the notion of our social contract, as I suggest here, is that it places an internal restriction against going quite so far towards abolishing basic procedural rights. One might assume that any original or hypothetical contractors, contracting for their own self-preservation, would never agree to an arrangement which might place them under torturous investigation.[78]

As opposed to the "striking a new balance" argument (as well as to any straightforward reference to Locke's "prerogative power"), the use of torture is wholly precluded by the justification offered here for curtailing liberty in times of terror. (Chapter 6 offers further, independent, moral reasons for refraining from the use of outright torture.) In a veritable gem of liberalism, Hobbes claims that confessions admitted under torture are flawed since in all likelihood the accused confesses to the crime not because he committed it but in order to avoid physical pain. Whether it is in fact the case that most confessions extracted under torture are unreliable (and with regard to terrorist suspects it may not be), the voluntary abrogation of such measures is entirely ruled out, even for Hobbes, by the logic of contracting in order to protect one's preservation. While such measures may remain available to Hobbes's unrestrained sovereign who bears no contractual obligation towards his subject, they cannot be willingly consented to by Lockean contractors. Limiting the powers of the sovereign so as to exclude the use of certain measures, such as torture and coerced self-incrimination, is absolutely essential despite the impediment it places on combating terror. It is not only a logical cost of even the most minimally Lockean–liberal contractarian justification of government, but also the practical price we must pay for guarding against Inquisition-type judicial systems which were still familiar to Hobbes's generation.

---

[78] As Waldron points out elsewhere, in an entirely different connection, a contractarian approach can at least determine negatively which rules would *not* be agreed to by the parties to a hypothetical original position: "A rule or prohibition is excluded if it could not have been agreed to in advance in good faith by those who are to be subject to it." Jeremy Waldron, "Welfare and Images of Charity," in *Liberal Rights* (Cambridge University Press, 1993), pp. 225–49, esp. pp. 241, 242.

Allowing for the temporary limitation of a degree of liberty under severe circumstances while fervently defending the immunity from torture and the right to withhold self-incriminating evidence, is not only a consistency requirement of the Lockean-type social contract argument employed above. It also comes down to a non-philosophical practical argument about what a liberal citizenry can and cannot endure in times of crisis. As Waldron points out, the civil liberties at stake here are not of a homogenous class; rather, they represent a variety of concerns about the impact of governmental power on individual freedom. Procedural rights that restrict government powers regarding detention, interrogation, trial, and punishment differ from our liberty rights as well as from the more diffuse concern for freedom from government scrutiny.[79]

In layman's terms, it appears reasonable for citizens of liberal democracies to consider tolerating slightly more stringent limitations on some of their liberty rights. Specifically, I have in mind the possible curtailment of liberties such as freedom of expression and religion; the right to bear arms (in the US); and even the right to privacy, if this should prove necessary (and effective) for protecting lives. To use some admittedly extreme, though very concrete, American examples, US citizens could, as citizens of other liberal democracies do, live without the right to possess the weapon of their choice. Perhaps they could forgo the right to possess a grenade launcher, amass an arsenal of ammunition, or form their own militia. Equally, the essence of their free society would not be irrevocably harmed were they (temporarily) denied the right to preach Jihad, issue *fatwas*, or call for the death of Salman Rushdie, all of which they are currently free to do.[80] My guess is that their way of life would survive even if their government supervised flying lessons, or required the licensing of firearms, or if security guards searched their bags and persons for explosives, or if they were forbidden to contribute to Hamas. On the other hand, citizens of liberal democracies cannot be expected to tolerate – indeed they must guard against – the type of oppressive legal measures employed by the darkest of totalitarian regimes. They cannot forgo their right to resist capital punishment or imprisonment, for example, by withholding evidence, nor can they subject themselves to torturous investigations.

[79] Waldron, "Security and Liberty," p. 195.
[80] Netanyahu, *Fighting Terrorism*, p. 42.

The price of liberty

Resisting the use of outright torture and coerced self-incrimination is admittedly only the bare minimum of what need concern us under present circumstances. Detention without trial, relaxed rules of evidence, non-jury trials, arrests, search and seizure without a warrant, and even applying moderate physical force which does not amount to torture in cases of "ticking bombs," are all grave issues that cannot be resolved on Hobbesian grounds. None is as closely linked to the right of self-preservation as are the prohibition against torture and immunity from coerced self-incrimination. All have been legally provided for and implemented in both Israel and the UK, and they are not excluded by the present account so long as they are both necessary for, and reasonably effective in, preserving the lives of innocent citizens.[81]

No expertise on terrorism is necessary in order to estimate that effectively gathering information regarding future attacks will inevitably include monitoring the private movements of individuals and infiltrating groups, some of which will regard themselves as religious. Once having been charged, terrorist suspects also pose a problem for the jury system. As the British discovered when trying IRA members in the 1970s, juries can be intimidated by alleged terrorists: individuals accused of terrorism or involvement therein cannot effectively be judged by their peers, although they need not be tried by lone judges either.[82]

As for detention without trial, although this rings harshly in liberal ears, in the war against terror it is at times essential to establish what certain people are thinking and to find out what they know. As even Waldron acknowledges, "It is not hard to think of scenarios where detention without trial is justified."[83] He worries, however, that "it is hard to think of methods of ensuring that this power is not abused, that it doesn't get out of hand, and that detention does not turn into 'disappearance'."[84] Detention for questioning can, presumably, be restricted to brief periods.[85] It is more alarming to recognize that, when dealing with grave terrorist threats, states may wish to detain suspects in order to

---

[81] On the British Emergency Provisions Act, 1973, for Northern Ireland, as well as on the Prevention of Terrorism Act, 1978, see Finn, *Constitutions in Crisis*, pp. 86–138. For Israel, see Netanyahu, *Fighting Terrorism*, p. 34.
[82] Finn, *Constitutions in Crisis*, p. 99.
[83] Waldron, "Security and Liberty," p. 207.   [84] Ibid., pp. 207–8.
[85] See the UK example: Finn, *Constitutions in Crisis*, pp. 87–9.

prevent them from committing crimes they have not yet set out on, and with which, therefore, they cannot be legally charged. (This is to say, we know they are up to something very deadly, or are likely to be, but we do not quite know what.) Preventative tactics of this kind inevitably conjure up images of a Robespierre-type Committee of Public Safety. Moreover, we have to worry not only about the sinister use of these means to combat political and personal enemies rather than those of the public,[86] but also about honest human error or exaggerated use bred by panic. US citizens, I think, need not be reminded of the dreadful mass internment of Japanese-Americans for the duration of the Second World War. All this is frightening and there is nothing to be said that can render it otherwise.

As opposed to the prohibition on the use of torture, the social contract argument offered above does not preclude detentions as a security measure. The liberal foundations of the argument, however, suggest that if such policies are to be implemented, they must be hedged around by either judicial or parliamentary supervision and, perhaps, preferably both. Even if liberal societies can be justified, on occasion, in detaining individuals without trial, they must include institutional guarantees for narrowing the use of these draconian measures to an essential minimum both in terms of frequency and in terms of their duration. These assurances are practically dictated by the argument offered here, which is grounded essentially on the right to life and liberty.

Government abuse is a very serious concern indeed and it may in fact increase, rather than diminish, in security crises. Advocates of detentions who talk the "striking a new balance" language are rightly accused by Waldron of ignoring such threats: "There is a sort of magical thinking that we are supposed to forget all about such abuses when we evaluate what is being presently proposed from a civil liberties perspective."[87] Justifying enhanced government powers in terms of a social contract, rather than "striking a new balance," avoids precisely this pitfall of forgetting the ills of government and brings out the appropriate relationship between our various concerns. We fear government tremendously – we would be irrational to feel otherwise. Moreover, our apprehensions have not dwindled since September 10 (perhaps they have even increased). However, as of the morning of September 11 there is something that we reasonably fear even more than government, and we have an understanding with each other, as well a contract with

---

[86] Waldron, "Security and Liberty," p. 208.   [87] Ibid.

our sovereign, that represents a rational choice to resist such greater threats, even at the expense of enhancing our pre-existing anxieties.

One additional advantage of constructing the argument about read-justing civil liberties in terms of the social contract, rather than employing the imagery of balance, is that balancing talk implies, as Waldron points out, "that we could make the readjustment in the other direction":[88]

The recalculation after September 11 would then require us not to accept less liberty but to brave a higher risk for the sake of the liberty we cherish. The appropriate change in public policy, then, would be calls to greater courage, rather than diminutions of liberty. Most probably we work at the matter from both ends, and perhaps this is where talk of balance really comes into its own.[89]

Calls for greater public fortitude can be justified when there is absolutely no alternative, but they can also be extremely exasperating when the government that citizens obey and to which they pay taxes is artificially constrained from protecting them. Promises of "blood, toil, tears, and sweat" are intolerable when a government is perfectly capable of preventing this. Earlier, I suggested that when a government is incapable of defending its subjects, the latter might regain their natural rights. Close scrutiny of this proposition alongside the surrounding issues it raises, such as the justification of state authority and civil disobedience, have filled entire volumes, but they are not the subject of this one. Suffice it to say that under the type of liberal theories considered here, the idea of reducing personal security raises serious questions concerning political authority and political obligation. On these accounts, government is endured primarily, if not entirely, in order to enhance and guarantee individual safety – of life and limb, as well as property in external possessions.[90] Demanding that a terrorized public should willingly and bravely face the prospect of gross violations of their natural rights contradicts the rationale for relinquishing their original powers to begin with, and threatens to undermine these liberal justifications for suffering the restrictions of government at all. It is precisely because liberals fear government that they would have to reconsider maintaining it once it had failed to do its job. Of course, security (like liberty) is not an all-or-nothing matter, and it would be patently absurd to suggest simply that any decrease in security, as a result of terrorism or otherwise,

---

[88] Ibid., p. 194.   [89] Ibid.
[90] Locke, *Two Treatises*, sect. 123, p. 350.

removes the central liberal justification for remaining within a political framework. It does seem, however, that for Hobbes, and even Locke, a voluntary downward readjustment of personal safety is out of the question.

Finally, I conceded at the outset that any reduction in liberty in the course of combating contemporary terrorism will not be distributed equally. The price in terms of personal freedom, which may be required in exchange for greater security, will inevitably be much higher for individuals whose outward appearance, ethnic affiliation, and religious denomination accord with our stereotype of terrorists.[91] Hence Waldron's argument that talk of balancing is misleading because it implies that we are weighing everyone's liberty against everyone's security, when in fact we are sacrificing the liberty of the few (minority members) in exchange for greater security for the majority.[92] Resorting to social contract theory rather than the language of balance avoids this self-deception, but it admittedly cannot evade, much less resolve, the issue of justice which surrounds it: in fact it may even intensify it. One distinct feature of social contract theories is that they carry with them a built-in distinction between "insiders" and "outsiders," which lies at the very crux of the moral problem in the current context. As Waldron points out:

The perpetrators of the September 11 attacks were foreigners, members of a foreign organization, and the US government has taken that as grounds for drawing some quite sharp distinctions in its subsequent legislation between the protections accorded to the civil liberties of Americans and the protections accorded to others who are legally in the United States.[93]

George Fletcher makes the same point in criticism of President Bush's executive order setting up military tribunals for the summary trial of suspected terrorists. The order "draws a clear line between citizens and non citizens; only foreigners are subject to the less favorable procedures."[94]

This is extremely troubling, but I cannot see how it can reasonably be avoided altogether, or that it ought to be at any cost. Consider the

---

[91] Waldron, "Security and Liberty," pp. 200–4.   [92] Ibid., pp. 200–1.
[93] Ibid., p. 201. See also Ronald Dworkin, "The Threat to Patriotism," *New York Review of Books*, February 28, 2002.
[94] George Fletcher, *Romantics at War: Glory and Guilt in the Age of Terrorism* (Princeton University Press, 2003), p. 113.

prohibition on ethnic profiling: must airline security in the US choose between the risk involved in equally respecting everyone's privacy and the absurdity of interrogating each and every passenger as severely as they question the dark mid-Eastern gentleman packing a pocket knife in his carry-on luggage? What does avoiding inequality in the course of combating terror actually entail? It can work against introducing additional security measures, as Waldron believes that it does, or it can imply that we ought to apply these measures indiscriminately (say, detain some Christian fundamentalist alongside the Muslim suspects). While the outcome of the first of these prescriptions could be disastrous, the outcome of the second would be unjust, inefficient, not to say outright ridiculous.

I doubt whether Hobbes or Locke has anything interesting to contribute to this issue. As for America's Founding Fathers, they were hardly concerned with racial equality, to say the least. No doubt, the "equal liberty" argument is a moral point well taken, but, followed to its implied conclusions, it runs the risk of resulting either in catastrophe or else in sheer absurdity.

Rawls or Kant might be more helpful in determining what equal concern and respect for persons might require of us, even under emergency circumstances. Perhaps we would do better to consider our prospective security measures in light of the imperative to act only upon such maxims of action as can be willed as universal laws applying to every moral agent.[95] So if we are considering curtailing freedom of speech or of religion, or introducing ethnic profiling or relaxed rules of evidence or administrative detentions, we could avoid questions of equal distribution, and ask instead what we would agree to if we were likely to be particularly vulnerable to such regulations. Much would depend on the specific formulation of the relevant questions and determining their degree of specificity. These might pose an even trickier task than Kant usually presents us with. The questions would have to be general enough to avoid bias, and yet specific enough to include all the relevant information regarding the potential situation. We might think, for example, that terrorism itself is a gross violation of Kantian law, and this judgment could make a difference to the outcome of our ethical deliberation with regard to it. Unfortunately, the suggestion that we apply Kant's universalizability requirement to the formulation of the questions themselves – that is, that we formulate them in a manner we

---

[95] Kant, *Groundwork*, p. 88.

could will, would be applied to such formulations universally – would only leave us with a similar problem.

Certainly, there is something to be said for thinking about civil rights along Kantian lines, as opposed to arguing that they ought simply to be equally distributed. But, while applying Kantian morality might avoid a certain sense of absurdity associated with the equality argument, it might not prevent catastrophe. The difficulty in formulating the appropriate questions could lead to opting for the most general formulation and the strictest application, which would likely prohibit the introduction of any new security measures. Kantian imperatives are not very good at accounting for varying circumstances and Kant himself notoriously believed that his moral code ought to be adhered to not only universally but also absolutely, even at disastrous cost. I doubt very much that this thinking accords with anyone's moral intuitions, much less with the American political tradition. So, while Kant might be consulted on these issues, I doubt anyone but the strictest of Kantians would advise us to slip too far down this slope.[96]

As for Rawls, once again, the insistence on equal liberty under present circumstances has already been addressed. Rawls's neglect of the security issue renders his work rather inapplicable, if not altogether irrelevant, to the current debate. Nevertheless, we might want to ask what limitations on freedom in times of crisis we would consent to if we had to decide while standing behind a Rawlsian veil of ignorance. It is difficult to surmise what the answer to such a question might be since, again, Rawls does not supply us with the appropriate tools for dealing with the security issue. It is nonetheless interesting to note that deliberating the relation between liberty and security behind a theoretical veil of ignorance might actually strengthen the prescription advanced in the last two sections. I have argued that citizens of liberal democracies can accept some curtailment of liberty rights in emergency situations, and should do so in exchange for greater security, but that they cannot tolerate the abolition of the most basic procedural rights, even in times of national crisis. We could not accept certain violations, such as the use of torture, if they were to apply to us, and therefore ought not to tolerate them when they apply to others.

---

[96] Kant's is an ideal moral theory. The age of terrorism presents us with moral dilemmas that surface within a non-optimal setting and requires non-ideal moral theories in order to tackle them.

Concluding remarks

Liberalism is not a death wish, and it ought not to be applied as such. However paradoxical, those who fear government the most must guarantee it sufficient power to effectively protect its citizenry. After all, if it cannot discharge this minimal obligation, why endure its burdens at all? Furthermore, proposals to suspend liberty in order to enhance security need not be regarded problematically as "striking a *new* balance." On the contrary, there is nothing new about this: the implicit provisos for doing so are older than the US Constitution and draw on the same logic and values that gave birth to it. Under circumstances of dire peril, curtailing liberty may be justified as a necessary measure for protecting our natural right to life and, moreover, for the preservation of liberty itself.

Nonetheless, the classical liberal foundations of the argument place clear restrictions on its use. Firstly, they place limits on the type of measure that may legitimately be resorted to; specifically, they forbid the use of torture and uphold immunity from coerced self-incrimination. The frightful abolition of even these rights could be advocated only on purely utilitarian grounds. Secondly, the liberal underpinnings of the present argument imply limitations on the scope and extent of justifiable restrictions. Any potential curtailment of liberty can be justified only if it is reasonably estimated to be both necessary for, and effective in, enhancing public safety.

Notwithstanding these provisions, if my description of the effect of changing circumstances on the limits of justified political authority was at all accurate, then the spread of terrorism and a serious increase in its effects is inevitably destined to upset our liberties almost without recourse.

The following chapter looks at a more specific question regarding procedural rights within liberal democracies. It questions how democracies and their legal systems ought to contend with irregular combatants, terrorists or otherwise, and those suspected of terrorist activity. It is an open question whether those accused of non-military belligerent activity against us ought to be accorded the rights of regular soldiers under international treaties and conventions, or accorded the internal procedural rights granted to civilian criminals under the criminal justice system. Some argue that "terrorists" are entitled to no rights at all. Chapter 4 addresses the complex status of irregular combatants and their rights.

4 | *Combatants – lawful and unlawful*

The September 11 attacks led many Americans to believe that al-Qaida had plunged the US into a new type of war, already familiar to some of the country's closest allies. Subsequent debates over modern terrorism often involve a sort of lamentation for the passing of old-fashioned wars.[1] Paul Gilbert's *New Terror, New Wars* suggests that at least when it came to old wars we knew when they were taking place, who was fighting them, and what they were fighting about. Old-fashioned wars were, by and large, about territory, whereas "new wars" may be more concerned with collective identities and their political recognition, and represent ideological struggle between, say, liberalism and Islamists.[2] Perhaps most significantly, and the greatest source of nostalgia, is that in the past, as Gilbert reminds us, a state of war existed between sovereign states, whereas "new wars" exist "between a state, or a combination of states, on one side, and non state actors on the other."[3] As George Fletcher puts it, we are in "a world beset with nontraditional threats from agents we call 'terrorists'."[4]

This chapter focuses on the new type of agents involved in contemporary armed conflicts and their rights. In the first two chapters of this book I argued that terrorism should be strictly defined as a particular form of political violence. The argument advanced in this chapter does not entail the legal and scholastic controversy over the definition of the term "terrorism" as distinct from other forms of irregular warfare. The thesis defended here is that irregular belligerents, whether "terrorists" or otherwise, are "unlawful combatants" and as such are ineligible either for the immunities guaranteed to soldiers by international conventions of war or for the protections of the criminal justice system. This point about lawless combat in the course of battle is stressed, first as a

---

[1] Fletcher, *Romantics at War*; Gilbert, *New Terror, New Wars*.
[2] Ibid., pp. 7–8. See also Berman, *Terror and Liberalism*.
[3] Gilbert, *New Terror, New Wars*, p. 3.   [4] Fletcher, *Romantics at War*, p. 6.

point of law, but secondly, and more significantly, as a moral position. The next section addresses the historical development of the lawful rules of combat and argues that the distinctions that underlie the laws of war serve the weak as well as the strong and ought to be upheld inter alia for that reason.[5]

There is, at least in theory, a notion of fair play at work in the laws of *jus in bello*, which concerns who may be targeted legitimately in wartime. The laws of *jus in bello* express an, albeit romanticized, perception of war as conducted between equally matched opponents. The following section argues, firstly, that irregular combatants do not play by the rules and, therefore, are not entitled to their protection. At the same time, they remain belligerents, not entitled to the procedural rights granted to criminals in civil law. Second, I argue that the distinction between lawful and unlawful combatants, which specifies those who may legitimately carry out an attack, serves the more basic distinction between combatants and non-combatants. Irregulars, I suggest, do not merely breach the formal reciprocal rules of fair play, their tactics of camouflage and disguise take advantage of the very code they breach. Furthermore, by acquiring a hybrid identity of combatant–civilian, they also blur the more basic moral distinctions between those who may and those who may not be targeted in wartime. Thus, the fundamental vice of irregular combatants is not merely their formal lawlessness, or even unfairness, but rather the threat they pose to the "civilized" conduct of war and the protections it affords to an identifiable defenseless civilian population.

How should irregulars be treated? Two cases of confronting irregular warfare come to mind. The first is Israel's policy of assassinating terrorist leaders, often described disparagingly as "extra-judicial execution," a practice not unknown to the American "war effort."[6]

---

[5] The prohibitions stated in Article 23 of the Hague Convention (October 18, 1907), http://net.lib.byu.edu/~rdh7/wwi/hague.html, are a case in point.

[6] For this type of disparagement see, for example, B'tselem – The Israeli Information Center for Human Rights in the "Occupied Territories," at http://www.btselem. org. For a more scholarly account of this objection, prevalent on the Israeli left, see Michael Gross, "Assassination: Killing in the Shadow of Self-Defence," in J. Irwin (ed.), *War and Virtual War: The Challenges of Communities* (Amsterdam: Rodopi, 2004); Michael Gross, "Fighting by Other Means in the Mid-East: A Critical Analysis of Israel's Assassination Policy," *Political Studies* 51 (2003), pp. 350–68; On some assassinations carried out by the US, see Alan Dershowitz, "Killing Terrorist Chieftains is Legal," *The Jerusalem Post*, April 22, 2004, p. 18.

The second concern is purely American. If Gilbert's description of the uncertainties of *New Terror, New Wars* is telling, the cover photograph of his book by that title is surely worth a thousand words. The photograph depicts a group of detainees captured in Afghanistan and held in the US naval base at Guantanamo Bay, Cuba. Hardly unrelated are the military tribunals provided for in an executive order issued by President Bush in November 2001 concerning the trial of any of the terrorists or al-Qaida members captured in the subsequent war in Afghanistan, and the more recent Military Commissions Act, 2006.[7] Like Israel's assassinations, these new extra-judicial measures met with fierce criticism in left-leaning circles,[8] although they were not unanimously criticized by liberals.[9] Section three analyzes these two contemporary debates and argues that the belligerents in both cases are legitimately regarded as unlawful, and duly denied the rights of soldiers.

Once captured and disarmed, however, irregular combatants, even the terrorists among them, must be guaranteed some minimal standard of humanitarian treatment, which ought to be specified and guaranteed by the international community. There are certain things, I suggest towards the end of this chapter, like outright torture, that we may not do to any other person, regardless of their actions.

A history of lawlessness in combat

In the months after September 11 a small band of conservative lawyers within the Bush administration staked out a forward-leaning legal position regarding the unfolding war in Afghanistan. It was, these lawyers said, a conflict against a vast, outlawed, international enemy, in which the rules of war, international treaties, and even the Geneva Convention did not apply. At first, the administration avoided taking any clear official stand on these issues, although the emergent approach

---

[7] Military Commissions Act, 2006.
[8] For example, Dworkin, "The Threat to Patriotism"; Waldron, "Security and Liberty," pp. 191–210; Fletcher, *Romantics at War*, pp. 112–16.
[9] See, for example, Fletcher, *Romantics at War*, pp. 115–16, where he criticizes Laurence Tribe and Cass Sunstein for publicly supporting this deviation from constitutional practice.

appears to have been from the start that America's enemies in this war were "unlawful" combatants, without rights.[10] More recently, the Military Commissions Act, 2006 codified the legal definition of the term "unlawful combatant," and invested the President with broad discretion to determine whether a person may be designated an unlawful enemy combatant. The Act authorizes the executive to conduct military tribunals of "unlawful enemy combatants" and to hold them indefinitely without judicial review.[11] Testimony coerced through humiliating and degrading treatment would be admissible at these tribunals.[12]

After September 11, 2001, many Americans agreed that al-Qaida could not be fought according to traditional rules. The relevant rules, those agreed on at the Hague and Geneva conventions, stipulate the conditions under which combatants are entitled to the war rights of soldiers, specifically the right to prisoner-of-war (POW) status when captured.[13] Crucially, prisoners of war can refuse to answer questions beyond name, rank, and serial number, and are guaranteed basic levels of humane treatment.[14] On the assumption that they are not personally responsible for atrocities or other war crimes, they are immune from any personal culpability and criminal proceedings.[15] The legal criteria

---

[10] See, for example, John Barry *et al.*, "The Roots of Torture – The road to Abu Ghraib began after 9/11, when Washington wrote new rules to fight a new kind of war: A *Newsweek* investigation," *Newsweek*, May 24, 2004. Fletcher, *Romantics at War*, pp. 112–13, also suggests a link between the Bush administration's legal approach and the concept of "unlawful combatants." Nevertheless, Fletcher stresses that the defense regulations from February 28, 2003, regarding the military tribunals – originally authorized by President Bush on November 13, 2001 to try any terrorists or al-Qaida member captured in the ongoing war – make no explicit claims about "unlawful combatants."

[11] Military Commissions Act, 2006.

[12] Military Commissions Act, 2006, 948b.

[13] Hague Convention (October 18, 1907), Annex to the Convention, Section I, "On Belligerents," Chapter II, "Prisoners of War"; Geneva Convention relative to the Treatment of Prisoners of War, adopted on August 12, 1949.

[14] Ibid., on humane treatment, Art. 4 and throughout. On questioning and information, see Art. 9; Geneva Convention relative to the Treatment of Prisoners of War, 1949 (www.unhchr.ch/html/menu3/b/91.htm), esp. Part III – Captivity, Section I – Beginning of Captivity, Art. 17.

[15] Geneva Convention, Art. 99.

for attaining the war rights of soldiers appear simple and clear-cut. According to the Hague Convention of 1907, in order to be entitled to POW status fighters must wear "a fixed distinctive sign visible at a distance" and must "carry their arms openly."[16] Two further important conditions are that the combatants in question must form part of a "chain of command" and that they themselves obey the customs and the laws of war. These provisos were intended primarily to distinguish between soldiers on the one hand and spies or saboteurs, and perhaps also guerrilla fighters in civilian clothes, on the other.[17] The law remained relatively silent, however, regarding this latter category: what, if any, are the rights and immunities of combatants who do not abide by these terms, that is, who do not abide by the rules of war, who wear no insignia and carry their arms in secret? The US Military Commissions Act, 2006 makes use of the conditions originally stipulated by international conventions specifically for attaining POW status, and explicitly distinguishes "unlawful enemy combatants" from those who are "lawful," defining the latter exclusively as belligerents who belong to an army or militia associated with a state, wear identifiable uniforms of insignia, carry their arms openly, and abide by the law of war.[18]

In *Romantics at War*, George Fletcher supplies a detailed description of a 1942 case in which eight German would-be spies were captured on US territory shortly after they entered it and before carrying out any part of their mission. Fletcher looks carefully at the landmark US Supreme Court opinion in which Justice Harlan Stone took on the task of retroactively explaining and excusing the swift trial and execution of six of these German infiltrators without due process of law. Crucially, Justice Stone labeled these Germans "unlawful combatants," observing that they had buried their uniforms on arrival and did not bear arms openly. Although at the time of their capture they had not yet

---

[16] Hague Convention (1907), Annex to the Convention, Section I, "On Belligerents," Chapter I, "The Qualifications of Belligerents," Art. 1; Geneva Convention, Part I – General Provisions, Art. 4. See also, Fletcher, *Romantics at War*, p. 106; Walzer, *Just and Unjust Wars*, p. 182.

[17] Hague Convention, Annex, Section I, Chapter I, Art. 1. Geneva Convention, Part I, Art. 4. See also Fletcher, *Romantics at War*, p. 106; Walzer, *Just and Unjust Wars*, p. 182.

[18] Military Commissions Act, 2006, 948a (1) and (2).

carried out any acts of sabotage and espionage, Stone argued that in view of their "lawlessness," stemming from their civilian appearance, they were "subject to trial and punishment by military tribunals for acts which render their belligerency unlawful."[19] Fletcher's in-depth legal analysis of the case is insightful in recognizing the judicial opinion that followed it as the theoretical precedent for President Bush's controversial makeshift military tribunals. He claims that Chief Justice Stone, writing this after-the-fact opinion, was in fact the first to use the term "unlawful combatant," which is never explicitly employed either in the Hague Convention or elsewhere in international law,[20] although Stone had argued that his opinion represented "universal agreement and practice."[21]

Arguing for the rights of insurrectionists, Palestinian historian Karma Nabulsi rejects the stark distinctions drawn by modern laws of war between civilians and combatants and the derivative distinction between lawful and unlawful combatants.[22] Her rejection is closely linked to a more general disdain for the traditional dichotomy drawn between *jus ad bellum* and *jus in bello*, which she regards as artificial, suggesting that considerations of morality apply with equal force to both the origins and the conduct of war.[23]

Nabulsi states, unarguably, that the distinction between types of combatants was ultimately never resolved in international law:[24] "In the traditional laws of war, only professional soldiers were granted belligerent status ... Accordingly, all civilians who participated in hostilities were considered outlaws."[25] This was precisely US Supreme Court Justice Stone's point when he spoke of "universal agreement and practice" in his opinion on the case of the eight German saboteurs.[26] But according to Nabulsi this "agreement and practice" regarding so-called lawless combatants was not entirely universal: "In

---

[19] Fletcher, *Romantics at War*, p. 107.
[20] Ibid. This fascinating and relevant case is discussed and analyzed by Fletcher at length on pp. 96–112.
[21] Ibid., p. 107. See, for example, Nabulsi's description of the treatment of irregulars during the Napoleonic wars in *Traditions of War*, p. 32.
[22] Nabulsi, *Traditions of War*.
[23] Ibid., p. 242. This view is phrased in terms of "The Republican Tradition of War," pp. 177–240, which Nabulsi primarily describes rather than defends but with which she clearly identifies.
[24] Ibid., pp. 15–18, 241.   [25] Ibid.
[26] See Fletcher, *Romantics at War*, p. 107.

contrast, those contesting the legal norm [at Geneva in 1949] argued that all citizens who bore arms for the nation were legitimate combatants. Equally controversial was the issue of prisoners of war. Small countries sought to have all armed defenders protected from reprisals if captured (as professional soldiers already were)."[27]

Throughout her fascinating project, Nabulsi traces this failure to reach an internationally agreed distinction, between those who may legitimately partake in combat and those who may not, to the existence of three incommensurable traditions of war: martial, Grotian, and republican. The latter two are described as representing irreconcilable political philosophies and derivative views on legitimate warfare, specifically concerning resistance to occupation.[28] Furthermore, Nabulsi argues that these ideologies of war, far from being purely theoretical, represent different political agendas: "Martialism constituted the political philosophy of occupying armies."[29] And its underlying ideology is described as the glorification of struggle as the highest activity of man, romanticizing war and violence, worshipping power as an end in itself, and believing in the superiority of certain races and peoples.[30]

While martialism had relatively little impact on international law, Nabulsi argues that the influential Grotian tradition, whose objective was to codify war, turned out to be equally objectionable as it too effectively served the powerful and favored the strong.[31] Crucially, Nabulsi suggests that the Grotian emphasis on the distinction between *jus in bello* and *jus ad bellum*, and the very attempt to codify and regulate war with reference solely to the former, is at the heart of the distinction between lawful and lawless combatants that she contests. She argues adamantly throughout her work that the distinction which legitimizes combatants only of regular armies – thus favoring the strong and powerful – is part and parcel of the reluctance to look beyond the conduct of war into the justness of wars themselves, specifically wars for national liberation carried out by conquered peoples.[32]

As for its style, the Grotian tradition, like contemporary international law, is formalistic and legalistic, allegedly aspiring to "neutrality" or

---

[27] Nabulsi, *Traditions of War*, p. 17.
[28] The final three chapters, which form the main body of her work, describe these conflicting traditions at great length and in great detail: ibid., pp. 80–240.
[29] Ibid., p. 76.   [30] Ibid., pp. 126–7.   [31] Ibid., p. 175.
[32] This argument is presented at the outset of Nabulsi's book, ibid., p. 1.

"objectivity" towards the reasons for combat. Relatedly, it adopts a form of (false) moral relativism with respect to conflicting national ideologies, attempting solely to regulate the conduct of armed conflict rather than delving into its source.[33] Hence the distinction between the laws of war (*jus in bello*) and the principles of just war (*jus ad bellum*), and the near exclusion of the latter issue from modern laws of war. In style as well as in substance, then, this apparently "neutral" standpoint, she claims, in fact structurally favors the rights of states and their standing conventional armies over all insurgent groups and their individual participants:

At the heart of the nineteenth – and early twentieth – century Grotian system was an essential dichotomy between the rights of states and armies on the one hand, and the position of ordinary members of society on the other. The important values of their tradition were law, order, power, and the sovereignty of the state. As the Grotian tradition was "index-linked" to legitimate power, its central ambition was to limit the rights of belligerency to a particular class of participant (the soldier) and to exclude all others from the right to become actively involved in political violence in times of war. [34]

Finally, the failure of international law to explicitly resolve the issue of lawless combat is attributed by the author to the conflict between this dominant Grotian approach and contesting ideological frameworks.[35] Nabulsi's final chapter depicts "The Republican Tradition of War," which she traces back largely to the political philosophy of Jean Jacques Rousseau but also to the ideas and practices of other eighteenth-century figures such as Pasquale Paoli in Corsica and Tadeusz Kosciuszko in Poland.[36] While ultimately less influential than the Grotian ideology, the doctrinal positions of this republican tradition of war were also "present in force at all the relevant conferences: Brussels in 1874, the Hague in 1899 and 1907, and Geneva in 1949."[37] Consequently, the delegates at each of these conferences were never able to reach an agreement concerning lawless combat, which remains unresolved within international law.

While Nabulsi's analysis of this third tradition is historically descriptive, she clearly favors its positions from a normative standpoint. The values attributed to republican war, as she describes it, are indeed admirable: "liberty and equality, individual and national self-reliance,

[33] Ibid., pp. 128, 142, 156, 166, 167, 170, 171, 176.   [34] Ibid., p. 157.
[35] Ibid., p. 242.   [36] Ibid., pp. 77, 177–240.   [37] Ibid., p. 178.

patriotism and public-spiritedness" and, last but not least, "a notion of just war *combined* with justice in war."[38] Nabulsi goes on to explain that "[T]he republican paradigm ... blended just war and justice in war."[39] As opposed to the Hobbesean–Grotian worship of order, republicans, typified by Rousseau, are committed above all to liberty, both individual and collective, and to a related concept of equality rather than to peace at any price:[40] "Central to this view was that citizens could not be detached from the defense of the state."[41] Republicans, most notably Rousseau, are described as rejecting the basic distinction between civilians and combatants and the derivative distinction between lawful and unlawful forms of combat. The justice of the war and its liberating nature is, for republicans, essentially tied to the issue of just actors in war.

This difference between Grotians and republicans grounds the author's explanation of the inability of representatives of the various traditions to settle the issue of lawful combat:

At a deeper level, the argument over the distinctions between combatant and non-combatant was rooted in conflicting notions of human nature and the good life. For the Grotians, the Hobbesean imperative of purchasing peace at any price – be it collaboration or even slavery – was natural to the condition of man. Occupation was therefore something to be endured, or at best observed from the (hopefully) distant spheres of public life. In the republican vision, occupation was an affront to both individual and collective freedom; it was a pervasive and invasive phenomenon from which no retrenchment was possible.[42]

Despite the presence of this conflicting approach, Nabulsi concludes that the result of the predominantly Grotian influence on international law is a body of *jus in bello*, which places serious limitations on the conduct of war and the character of the participants therein, irrespective of the justness of their goal.[43] The Grotian system and the body of international law to which it gave rise are thus accused of inherently favoring states and armies and upholding the status quo and the interests of the powerful at the expense of occupied peoples. The age-old distinction between *jus ad bellum* and *jus in bello*, along with the subsequent marking to distinguish combatants from civilians and the

---

[38] Ibid., pp. 77, 224, my emphasis.   [39] Ibid., p. 240.
[40] Ibid., pp. 192, 193, 240.   [41] Ibid., p. 192.   [42] Ibid., p. 240.
[43] Ibid., p. 175.

derivative, non-codified, discrimination between lawful and unlawful combatants, are presented as inherent in this sinister scheme of things. The outcome is taken to be a built-in legal slant in favor of states and their standing armies, even when waging unjust wars, over irregulars who defy *jus in bello*, even if engaged in a just struggle, say for national independence.

Despite the legal lacuna, the distinction between the lawful and the unlawful combatant is widely accepted, and the reasoning behind the notion of unlawfulness in combat can be traced back to international agreement and practice, as was pointed out by Justice Stone. Nabulsi rejects this distinction on the grounds that it serves the interests of larger and stronger nations, specifically those of occupying powers, at the expense of occupied peoples.[44]

The philosophy of lawlessness in combat

Nabulsi's discussion is historical and political rather than philosophical in the strict sense, and nowhere does she propound or defend normative arguments to be contended with. While she rejects a variety of well-entrenched distinctions within international law or convention, she does little more to discredit them than to repeatedly restate the accusation that they favor the strong and powerful at the expense of the oppressed. From a philosophical perspective, Nabulsi traces the specific concept of justness in war that has underlain international law back to the Hobbesean–Grotian aspiration for peace and order above all (even at the expense of liberty).[45] As befits a good work of history (rather than philosophy), she concentrates on the questionable origins of the international laws and practices that she rejects – the biased and self-interested motivations involved in their enactment – as well as critically describing the historical figures responsible for modern laws of war. Nonetheless, her thesis is partly normative rather than purely descriptive, alleging that the laws of war inherently favor the stronger party by adopting a form of false moral relativism towards conflicting national ideologies and attempting solely to regulate the conduct of armed conflict rather than delving into its source.[46]

---

[44] This is the gist of Nabulsi's argument throughout.
[45] Nabulsi, *Traditions of War*, Chapter 5, e.g. pp. 163, 172.
[46] Ibid., pp. 128, 142, 156, 166, 167, 170–1, 176, 242.

More recently, Jeff McMahan's "The Ethics of Killing in War" also challenges the distinction drawn by the traditional theory of war between principles governing the resort of war (*jus ad bellum*) and those governing the conduct of war (*jus in bello*).[47] Not unlike Nabulsi, he too proceeds to question the related combatant–non-combatants dichotomy upheld by the rules of war.[48] McMahan argues that at the deepest moral level, considerations governing the justness of the war and those governing its conduct necessarily converge and are not independent of one another. Contra Walzer, McMahan denies the possibility of a war meeting the requirements of *jus in bello* while violating those of *jus ad bellum*. Morally speaking, he argues one cannot fight "justly" in an unjust war (though one can fight a just war unjustly).[49] Ideally, McMahan aspires to place greater responsibility on the individual soldier for his participation in any given war.[50] As for the traditional distinction between combatants and civilians, his thesis explicitly implies that in a just war, "it can be permissible, on occasion, to attack and even to kill non-combatants."[51] Moreover, this license is not presented as a case of overriding the rule about non-combatants' immunity; rather, McMahan argues that civilians may at times be legitimate targets because non-combatants are in some cases morally responsible for wronging the enemy and therefore liable to force or violence in war.[52]

This, however, is as far as the similarity between McMahan and Nabulsi goes. Ultimately, McMahan distinguishes between "the deep morality of war" on the one hand, and the laws of war on the other. On the deeper, purely moral, level he argues that one cannot separate considerations of *jus ad bellum* and *jus in bello*, nor can one free soldiers or civilians from responsibility for partaking in unjust wars. Crucially, however, he observes that "it is entirely clear that the laws of war

---

[47] Jeff McMahan, "The Ethics of Killing in War," *Ethics* 114 (4) July 2004, pp. 693–733.

[48] Ibid., p. 2; VIII, pp. 38–43.

[49] Ibid., V, pp. 18–29. In summary, McMahan argues that unjust wars, by definition, can never fulfill the *jus in bello* requirement of proportionality, so that unjust wars will always, by their very nature, defy the laws that govern the conduct of battle as well. Consequently, according to McMahan (and specifically contra Walzer), "an unjust war cannot be fought in strict accordance with the rules."

[50] Ibid., IV, pp. 10–18; VII, pp. 34–8.

[51] Ibid., VIII, p. 42.   [52] Ibid., VIII, pp. 38–43.

must diverge significantly from the deep morality of war ... Perhaps most obviously, the fact that most combatants believe that their cause is just, means that the laws of war must be neutral between just combatants and unjust combatants, as the traditional theory insists that the requirements of *jus in bello* are."[53]

Why make any distinctions regarding the means of war rather than empowering the just side to enlist all measures that help it to gain its desired end? The rationale behind the moral distinction between civilians and soldiers and the subsequent differentiation between the causes of war and who may be targeted within it, as well as between types of combatants, does not rest on the questionable proposition that morality, in war or otherwise, is a relative matter. Moral relativism (true or false) has nothing to do with it. The distinctions in question rest purely on the empirical, and indisputable, observation that warring parties have contesting views of justice which they each hold to represent objective truth. The convictions of one side may be objectively correct while the other side is engaged in an unjust act of aggression based on an erroneous creed. Often, each combatant has some justice on its side, and in many cases particular issues of justice may be less discernible in absolute terms. The distinction between the principles of just war and the laws of war does not deny an objective answer to the question of *jus ad bellum*. It represents a good moral reason for concentrating on the laws of war so long as the question of the war's justness is still being violently contested.[54]

If Nabulsi's normative argument has one moment of truth, this concerns the notion of *levée en masse*.[55] When discussing the Vietnam War, Walzer argues that in those cases in which an insurgent movement definitively wins the "hearts and minds" of a people, judgments of *ad bellum* and *in bello* seem to converge. According to Walzer, when an invading army faces a resistance movement that enjoys sincere popular support, the anti-guerrilla forces will necessarily fight an unjust war because such a war cannot be fought justly – the anti-insurgents are at

---

[53] Ibid., p. 730.

[54] As McMahan observes, what is most important is that "wars, when inevitable, should be fought as decently and with as little harm to the innocent as possible," ibid., p. 732.

[55] I am grateful to Michael Walzer for pointing this out to me. See Nabulsi's references to *levée en masse*, *Traditions of War*, pp. 17, 46, 49, 53–4, 168, 173, 235.

war with an entire people, not with an army or a movement.[56] Similar arguments are popular among the Israeli left with regard to Israel's presence in the territories conquered from Jordan in 1967. While such arguments might facilitate Nabulsi's political agenda, they can hardly uphold her theoretical stance on justice in war. Note that Walzer's reasoning for regarding this type of anti-guerrilla warfare as immoral rests entirely on its inability to uphold the distinction between combatants and civilians, which he, unlike Nabulsi, regards as vital. If Nabulsi rejects this traditional distinction to begin with, she can hardly return to enlist it as ammunition against combating popular insurrections.

As for Walzer's argument, it suggests that popular support for a violent uprising renders its opposition unjust. Walzer assumes that *levée en masse* lends the guerrilla struggle a form of democratic legitimacy, which consequently places a moral barrier on combating it. While Walzer's argument may apply in the case of Vietnam, it is doubtful whether the use of force against all popular movements is always *ipso facto* unjust. Popular support is sometimes granted to morally dubious leaders, at times to oppressive and aggressive organizations, and often to terrorists. While popular will and self-determination of peoples is undoubtedly an important moral consideration in evaluating political movements and their causes, it is less clear that "democratic" support for a belligerent movement should automatically render its opposition unjust or bestow legitimacy on its irregular combatants.

There is, in any event, no legal basis for the proposition that wars against popular guerrillas are necessarily unjustified or that widespread support for irregulars endows them with belligerent status. As Walzer himself admits, "the military handbooks neither pose nor answer such questions."[57] As for international law, the legal exceptions to the rules made on behalf of irregular combatants in the case of *levée en masse* are very restrictive. According to Walzer, the provisions requiring combatants to wear distinctive dress and reveal their weapons in order to qualify for the war rights of soldiers "are often suspended, particularly in the interesting case of a popular uprising to repel invasion or resist foreign tyranny. When the people rise *en masse* they are not required to put on uniforms. Nor will they carry their arms openly, if they fight, as they usually do, from ambush: hiding themselves they can hardly be

---

[56] Walzer, *Just and Unjust Wars*, p. 187.   [57] Ibid.

expected to display their weapons."[58] Walzer cites Francis Lieber, who believes that captured fighters in such cases ought to be treated as prisoners of war.[59] According to the Hague convention, however, the only qualification that is suspended in the case of *levée en masse* is the requirement to "have a fixed distinctive emblem recognizable at a distance."[60] And even this liberty to fight in civilian dress is limited both temporally and spatially. It applies only to popular insurrections launched at the moment of invasion and carried out on territories not yet subject to occupation.[61] Even under these restrictive circumstances, the law (unlike Walzer) does not free any combatants from the require-ment to display their weapons openly if they wish to qualify as "belli-gerents," entitled to POW status if captured.[62] Moreover, Walzer himself, like the Hague convention, does not release irregulars engaged in a popular uprising from the obligation to respect the customs and laws of war, and specifically the requirement to refrain from targeting civilians.[63]

When discussing the criteria specified in the Hague conventions (1907) for attaining POW status, George Fletcher explains the distinc-tion between types of combatants by associating it with the more basic protection accorded to civilians in wartime: "To understand the posi-tion of the Hague Convention we must consider the reasons for the distinction between combatants and noncombatants. This distinction ultimately serves the interests of civilians by separating them, in principle,

---

[58] Ibid., p. 183.   [59] Ibid.

[60] Hague Convention, Annex to the Convention, Section I, "On Belligerents," Chapter I, "The Qualifications of Belligerents," Art. 2. See also Nabulsi, *Traditions of War*, p. 17.

[61] Hague Convention, Annex to the Convention, Section I, "On Belligerents," Chapter I, "The Qualifications of Belligerents," Art. 2; my emphasis. The reference to Art. 1 refers to the requirement to wear a distinctive emblem.

[62] Ibid.

[63] See Walzer, *Just and Unjust Wars*, Chapter 11: "Guerrilla Warfare," pp. 176–96; Chapter 12: "Terrorism," pp. 197–206. The logic of Walzer's illuminating three-ply distinction between guerrilla warfare, political assassination, and terrorism suggests that he might have us distinguish between illegal combatants who nonetheless discriminate between civilians and soldiers and those who do not. While Walzer's distinction between guerrillas and terrorists is invaluable, I think it ought not to come into play at this early stage of defining the category of lawless combatants, which is a legal status rather than a moral appraisal of their specific deeds and causes.

from the field of battle."[64] While Nabulsi argues that states adopted these distinctions purely in order to pacify conquered populations and prevent them from resisting oppression, she also admits that regularizing armies and distinguishing between combatants and civilians could be more sympathetically construed as directed against some possible interests of the military, most crucially by preventing armies from slaughtering civilians.[65] Walzer takes this line in defending the distinction between the rights of soldiers and those of irregulars, laid down, at least implicitly, by the Hague and Geneva Conventions. The distinction between soldiers and guerrillas, he argues, is morally valid even in situations of unjust occupation faced with admirable resistance, in view of the protection it accords to civilian populations (rather than their oppressors). This also explains why the license to refrain from distinctive dress granted to irregulars at the time of foreign invasion does not apply to irregulars in occupied territories.[66] As Walzer puts it later, distinguishing between soldiers and civilians by means of external insignia is essential in order to protect civilians from attack: "soldiers must feel safe among civilians if civilians are ever to be safe from soldiers."[67]

In fact, Nabulsi acknowledges at the outset that her opposition to the distinction between lawful versus unlawful combatants strikes at the very basis of humanitarian laws of war as it entails the rejection of the more basic distinction between combatants and civilians.[68] Like Fletcher and Walzer, she associates this controversial distinction with the more basic separation within the modern laws of war between combatants and non-combatants, which lies at the core of humanitarian laws of war. Yet she believes these principles ought to be disregarded in view of their bias against irregular insurgents.

Defending the basic distinction between combatants and civilians in wartime is well entrenched within international law, as is emphasized by various scholars.[69] At the most minimal level of justification, this fundamental distinction represents the morally worthy aspiration to minimize the suffering inevitably involved in the hellishness of war

---

[64] Fletcher, *Romantics at War*, p. 107.   [65] Nabulsi, *Traditions of War*, p. 163.
[66] Walzer, *Just and Unjust Wars*, p. 178.
[67] Ibid., p. 182.   [68] Nabulsi, *Traditions of War*, p. 1.
[69] Walzer, *Just and Unjust Wars*; Fletcher, *Romantics at War*. For the legal distinction and protections accorded to civilians in wartime, see Protocol I – Addition to the Geneva Conventions, 1977, Part IV: Civilian Population. Even Nabulsi admits this rationale while criticizing the distinction, *Traditions of War*, p. 1.

and of preventing wars from becoming total. While Nabulsi admits that her rejection of lawlessness in combat challenges the more basic distinction between civilians and soldiers, I doubt that even she would accord armies the right to ignore non-combatant immunities altogether; she certainly never presents any argument to this effect. As for the more controversial, derivative, distinction, Fletcher continues his explanation of the criteria specified at the Hague convention for attaining POW status and other war rights (over and above the aspiration to distinguish clearly between civilians and soldiers) as follows:

there is also at play a subtle principle of reciprocity between combatants ... When two soldiers from opposing armies encounter each other on the front lines, they each acquire a privilege and expose themselves to an additional risk. The privilege is to be able to kill the opponent at will, whether the opponent is attacking, at rest, or even sleeping. The risk however is reciprocal: each side is in danger of being killed just because each is wearing a certain uniform. Those who refuse to wear a uniform or a "distinctive emblem recognizable at a distance" do not expose themselves to this reciprocal risk. They claim the right to be aggressors in wartime without paying the price, and this they may not do ... The unlawfulness derives from the deliberate refusal to share in the risks of warfare.[70]

Describing guerrilla warfare, Walzer makes some similar points, tying the legal criteria for attaining war rights to the protection of civilian populations and stressing the notion of reciprocity. According to Walzer, regardless of the justness of their cause, guerrillas in civilian disguise generate a moral hazard by subverting the most fundamental rules of war, whose purpose is to protect the civilian population by specifying for each individual a single identity: either soldier or civilian. He cites *The British Manual of Military Law*, which makes the point with special clarity: "both these classes have distinct privileges, duties and disabilities ... an individual must definitely choose to belong to one class or the other, and shall not be permitted to enjoy the privileges of both."[71]

The upshot of both Fletcher and Walzer's comments seems to be that irregulars in civilian camouflage are doubly at fault. First, they threaten the well-being of the surrounding population by blurring the distinction between soldier and civilian. As Walzer puts it, if the partisans do not

---

[70] Fletcher, *Romantics at War*, p. 108.   [71] Walzer, *Just and Unjust Wars*, p. 179.

maintain the distinction of soldiers and civilians, why should the occupying forces do so?[72] Guerrillas in disguise invite their enemy to subvert war conventions: "By refusing to accept a single identity, they seek to make it impossible for their enemies to accord to combatants and non-combatants their 'distinct privileges and disabilities'."[73]

Furthermore, disguised partisans defy the rules of "fair play," by attempting to gain the advantages of both statuses. According to Walzer, "The key moral issue, which the law gets at only imperfectly, does not have to do with distinctive dress or visible weapons, but with the use of civilian clothing as a ruse and a disguise. (The case is the same with the wearing of civilian clothing as with the wearing of enemy uniforms.)"[74] This "feigning of civilian, non-combatant status" is regarded by international law as an incident of "perfidy," explicitly prohibited by the 1977 Protocol Addition to the Geneva Conventions (Protocol I).[75] The crucial point with civilian disguise, as Walzer describes it, is "the kind and degree of deceit involved: the same sort of deceit that is involved when a public official or party leader is shot down by some political enemy who has taken on the appearance of a friend and supporter or of a harmless passer-by."[76] Walzer readily admits that such incidents may be justified in terms of their cause. Nonetheless, "assassins cannot claim the protections of the rules of war; they are engaged in a different activity."[77] The same applies to disguised guerrillas, as it does to a variety of other hostile acts, such as espionage and sabotage carried out in disguise behind enemy lines, which Fletcher also mentions apropos lawless combatants.[78] As far as the secret agents of conventional armies are concerned, Walzer tells us, "It is widely agreed that such agents possess no war rights, even if their cause is just. They know the risks their efforts entail, and I see no reason to describe the risks of guerrillas engaged in similar projects any differently."[79]

---

[72] Ibid., p. 179.   [73] Ibid., p. 180.   [74] Ibid., p. 183.

[75] Protocol Additional to the Geneva Conventions of August 12, 1949, and relating to the Protection of Victims of International Armed Conflicts (Protocol I), June 8, 1977, Part III: Methods and Means of Warfare – Combatants and prisoner-of-war status, Section I – Methods and means of warfare, Art. 37 – prohibition of perfidy (c) the feigning of civilian, non-combatant, status.

[76] Walzer, *Just and Unjust Wars*, p. 183.   [77] Ibid.

[78] Ibid.; Fletcher, *Romantics at War*, pp. 92–116: the 1942 case of the eight German saboteurs which he insightfully ties to the issue of unlawful combatants.

[79] Walzer, *Just and Unjust Wars*, pp. 183–4.

Aside from the danger they pose to non-combatant immunity, then, unidentified combatants are also involved in a related type of dubious rule-breaking: an attempt to enjoy the benefits of a certain situation without engaging in its burdens – the risks and hazards involved in overt and identified warfare. As long as irregulars do not resort to murder and terrorization of the civilian population at large, they are not "terrorists" in the strict sense. Chapter 2 argued that the tactic of terrorism proper constitutes the worst form of free riding as it intrinsically depends on its opponents upholding the combatant–non-combatant distinction, which the terrorists themselves directly defy. Lesser forms of irregular warfare, such as guerrilla tactics, do not directly violate the norms of non-combatant immunity upheld by their conventional adversaries. Nonetheless, even irregulars who are not outright terrorists in the strictest sense, do not play quite fairly as they violate the conventional code of war and, therefore, they ought not to benefit from its advantages. Thus, even when irregulars have just cause, and even where they refrain from targeting innocent civilians, they are not legally eligible for the protection of international conventions and the war rights of soldiers specified in them, nor should they be.[80] This is so, obviously with greater force, as far as actual terrorists are concerned.

Whether irregulars resort to terror tactics or not, the type of deceit that involves civilian attire and concealed weaponry is related to the fundamental distinction between combatants and civilians because the rules it flouts are those specifically designed to protect the surrounding population. Hence the dual charge leveled by Fletcher and Walzer against non-reciprocal behavior and defying the fundamental distinction between combatants and non-combatants, thus endangering the immunity of the latter. Irregulars in civilian disguise do not abide by the rules of war and are therefore ineligible for its protection. The disguised irregular is no ordinary rule-breaker whose moral transgression consists solely of unfair play, or gaining an undeserved advantage. Worse still is that, in contrast to the spies and saboteurs of conventional armies that penetrate foreign soil, disguised guerrillas or partisans fighting on their own terrain (however justifiably) blur the distinction between soldier and civilian and threaten to draw their stronger adversary into a conflict that makes no such distinction. They specifically defy those rules that lie at the very heart of humanitarian conventions and are vital to the

---

[80] Ibid., p. 182.

well-being of civilians and, above all, to the welfare of the members of the weaker population. While the soldier–civilian dichotomy and the derivative distinction between lawful and unlawful combatants might be convenient for occupying armies, it is absolutely essential for the protection of defeated populations. Such distinctions ought not to be dismissed, particularly by those who have the latter's interests at heart, even in exchange for a temporary strategic advantage. Those who are concerned with the interests of the weak and vulnerable as opposed to those of the strong and powerful might, on reflection, consider embracing the restrictions of *jus in bello* rather than rejecting them.[81]

Admittedly, it could still be argued that in some particular circumstances it might be worthwhile for the civilian population to assume the risk involved in irregular warfare. Recall Walzer's argument whereby it may at times be justified to resort to perfidy.[82] This would depend on the kind of aggression or oppression that is the *casus belli*, and on the chances of successfully opposing this aggression, weighed against the risk of enemy retaliation. In the case of a cruel and long-oppressing regime (or an occupying force), it is not at all unlikely that the chances of liberation would make it worth endangering the well-being of the civilians in one's own collective. This point is readily conceded. Walzer admits that some instances of irregular warfare, most notably the partisan struggle against the Nazis, were justified – in spite of the danger it posed to the surrounding population. Nevertheless, the point remains that belligerents involved in such activity must assume the accompanying risks for themselves, just as they assume the dangers to their civilian population. However noble in the particular incident, partisans are unprotected by international laws of war, which are designed to deter irregular tactics in general and with the good cause of narrowing the violence and protecting civilians.[83] In the case of the noble partisan, we would be justified in applauding his behavior, without reproaching his opponent (who may be reprehensible on other accounts) for denying him the rights of a regular soldier.

Aside from rightfully denying even the most laudable of partisans the rights of soldiers, it is also doubtful whether such irregular endeavors could ever be successful in opposing truly oppressive regimes. The partisan struggle against Hitler's Germany is again a case in point.

---

[81] The prohibitions stated in Art. 23 of the Hague Convention are a case in point.
[82] Walzer, *Just and Unjust Wars*, p. 183.   [83] Ibid., p. 182.

The short-term success of resistance operations relied on the rules of war themselves (e.g. a surprise attack by belligerents disguised as unarmed French farmers relied on the assumption that conquered people in civilian clothing do not pose a military threat). In the long term, the very fact that the Nazis defied many of the rules of war, particularly those regarding non-combatant immunity, rendered the partisan struggle militarily insignificant. It is hard to believe that even under extreme circumstances the suspension of any limitations on war and military reprisals in the name of a just cause, even national independence, would result, overall, in serving the party with the lesser artillery.

To summarize: The rationale behind the distinctions examined here – both the basics and their derivatives – is the morally worthy humanitarian aspiration to protect the defenseless, alongside the utilitarian objective of narrowing the cycle of violence in the course of combat by singling out a certain class of agent, namely, soldiers who are exclusively susceptible to attack.[84] I suggested that the controversial distinction between lawful and unlawful combatants ultimately serves the weaker party better than any morally credible alternative. None of the parties – neither the meek nor the mighty – can legitimately pick and choose among these distinctions, demanding their protections without assuming their burdens. Since selective application of the rules of war (or any other principle) is not a morally viable option, all parties (the weaker side in particular) are better off assuming the burdens and limitations which derive from these distinctions, alongside their protections, rather than rejecting them both. I suggested that certain types of irregular combatants most often dubbed "terrorists" are in fact guilty of "free riding" in the following sense: they seek to gain the protections

---

[84] The basic distinction of *jus in bello* is between combatants and non-combatants. Its explanation is a source of scholarly debate. Walzer, *Just and Unjust Wars*, Chapter 9, argues that non-combatants are, in an important sense, innocent and are therefore entitled to a type of moral immunity to which soldiers are not entitled. Richard Norman, *Ethics, Killing, and War* (Cambridge University Press, 1995), Chapter 5, argues that there is no difference in blameworthiness between soldiers and civilians, but that killing civilians expresses a particular disrespect for human life. The combatant–non-combatant distinction, Norman argues, is intended to reduce the dehumanization and depersonalization that characterizes war in general. George I. Mavrodes, "Conventions and the Morality of War," *Philosophy and Public Affairs* 4 (1975), pp. 117–31 p. 117, argues that the distinction has no intrinsic basis and is purely conventional. The basis for the distinction, according to Mavrodes, is the mutual interest of the warring parties to narrow the cycle of violence by limiting their ability to fight.

offered by these distinctions for themselves and their populations without assuming the responsibilities that inherently go with them. It is precisely this option that must be categorically denied by the international community and its legal system if we are to retain any type of limitations in wartime.

Twin troubles: America's detainees and Israel's assassinations

International law and practice effectively leave irregular combatants virtually unprotected, though their "unlawful" identity is not in itself a criminal offense. As George Fletcher points out, the very notion of lawless combat invokes a legal status rather than a crime. Fletcher makes this point by drawing our attention to the jurisprudential distinction drawn by H.L.A. Hart in the early 1960s between a rule defining a crime (such as spying) and a norm generating the possibility of achieving a legal status (becoming a lawful combatant):

The basic difference is that the violation of the first kind of rule generates liability and punishment. The breach of the second kind simply means the actor does not secure the legal results she desires. For example, she tries to become a licensed pharmacist and fails. She tries to write a valid will and fails. She tries to enjoy the privileges of being a combatant and fails.[85]

While the hybrid identity of combatant–civilian is not in itself a prosecutable offense, many of the specific acts of war attributed to irregulars are prosecutable as "war crimes," perhaps as "terrorism." Two familiar examples are the events of September 11 and the Palestinian attacks on civilians in Israel. The targeting of non-combatants in the course of an armed conflict has long been recognized as a war crime by the Geneva Conventions, and more recently by the Rome Statute.[86] Needless to say, murder is prohibited by both American and Israeli law. It is equally obvious that the pilots of September 11, like the suicide bombers in Israel, did not abide by the requirements of the Hague Convention. They did not show up for the flight in military

---

[85] Fletcher, *Romantics at War*, p. 109.
[86] Ibid., p. 57; Walzer, *Just and Unjust Wars*, pp. 136–7; See also, Protocol I, Additions to the Geneva Conventions, 1977, Part IV: Civilian Populations, Chapter II: Civilians and Civilian Population, Art. 51: Protection of the Civilian Population, 2. "Acts or threats of violence the primary purpose of which is to spread terror among the civilian population are prohibited."

dress and they naturally kept their weapons, such as they were, concealed. These omissions do not in themselves constitute a crime; nonetheless, it is precisely this non-compliance, rather than their fiendish deeds, which are at the crux of the terrorist's unprotected status. Furthermore, unlike the case of unlicensed pharmacists or invalid wills, the practical consequences of a combatant's legal incapacity will at times be more severe than those associated with any specific crime.

On November 13, 2001 President Bush issued an executive order authorizing military tribunals to try any of the terrorists or the al-Qaida members who might be captured in the ongoing war in Afghanistan: "The Tribunals Bush had in mind … would be staffed by military officers subject to command influence, the proceedings would be in secret, and they could use any evidence they thought relevant. Of course, there would be no jury. The judges could decide by a two-thirds vote to impose the death penalty." There would be no appeal, accept by the President or the Secretary of Defense.[87] It is likely that this form of prosecution lies in store for the detainees of Guantanamo Bay, whom the Bush administration has, not implausibly, categorized as "unlawful combatants."[88] Recently, the Bush administration suffered a legal defeat on this front when the US High Court accepted an appeal filed on behalf of Salim Ahmed Hamdan, challenging the tribunal's procedures against terror suspects. President Bush had declared Hamdan an "enemy combatant," a status that would make him ineligible for the privileges accorded to prisoners of war.[89] More recently, however, and in the wake of the Supreme Court's decision on *Hamdan* v. *Rumsfeld*,[90] Congress enacted the Military Commissions Act, 2006, mentioned earlier, which states that its purpose is to "establish procedures governing the use of military commissions to try alien unlawful enemy combatants engaged in hostilities against the United States for violations of the

[87] Fletcher, *Romantics at War*, pp. 112–13.
[88] At present there is one such trial in the works, involving three defendants. See *Washington Post*, July 9, 2004.
[89] 34-year-old Hamdan, alleged to have been al-Qaida leader Osama bin Laden's personal driver and bodyguard, was captured in Afghanistan in November 2001 and has since been held by the US in Guantanamo Bay.
[90] *Hamdan* v. *Rumsfeld*, 126 S. ct. 2749 (2006), see: www.supremecourtus.gov/opinions/05pdf/05–184.pdf.

law of war and other offenses triable by military commission."[91] It authorizes the president to establish such military commissions.[92] The rights guaranteed by the Third Geneva Convention to *lawful* military combatants are expressly denied to *unlawful* military combatants for the purposes of this Act by Section 948b.[93]

Two distinct concerns regarding the treatment of irregulars are at stake here. The first concerns the justness of the tribunals; the second concerns the humanity of the preceding detention. Perhaps the most deplorable aspect of the detention is its lack of transparency. As things stand, the American public remains virtually uninformed about the current fate of those irregulars held indefinitely by the US military in Cuba. Recent reports about the treatment of conventional soldiers in Abu Ghraib prison, Iraq, cannot but invoke nightmarish speculations concerning the fate of "unlawful" militants from America's previous campaign.

Regarding the tribunals, Fletcher points out that one particularly disturbing aspect concerns this notion of "unlawful combatants." The people who would be subject to summary trials are "either members of Al Qaeda, someone who engaged in or assisted international terrorism against the US, or anyone who has harbored an Al Qaeda member or an international terrorist."[94] However, as Fletcher points out:

There is no way of knowing who is a member of this network without first making a judgment about who is guilty of an act of terrorism – and that is precisely the question at stake in the summary proceedings before the military tribunal. The circularity of using "terrorism" twice – first as the criterion of

---

[91] Military Commissions Act, 2006, Sect. 948a.
[92] Military Commissions Act, 2006, Sect. 948b.   [93] Ibid.
[94] Fletcher, *Romantics at War*, p. 113. Later, the Military Commissions Act, 2006, Sect. 948a (1) (A), singles out unlawful combatants as follows: "(i) a person who has engaged in hostilities or who has purposefully and materially supported hostilities against the United States or its co-belligerents who is not a lawful enemy combatant (including a person who is part of the Taliban, al Qaeda, or associated forces)," or "(ii) a person who, before, on, or after the date of the enactment of the Military Commissions Act of 2006, has been determined to be an unlawful enemy combatant by a Combatant Status Review Tribunal or another competent tribunal established under the authority of the President or the Secretary of Defense."

jurisdiction and second as the definition of the crime – should make one wonder if justice is possible in tribunals so defined.[95]

One can only guess at the reasoning behind this alleged circularity. The notion of illegal combatants is indeed vital to its logic. Bush's lawyers seem to have attributed a different meaning to the term "terrorism" in each of its uses. In the first instance, the term is invoked in order to convey a certain inferior status on the accused – namely, that of an unprotected "lawless combatant." In the second instance, the term "terrorism" is used to describe a list of prosecutable crimes – belonging to certain illegal organizations or taking part in the killing of civilians. The criterion for jurisdiction is based on the status attributed to irregular combatants – the assumption that they are by virtue of their omissions entitled neither to the immunities of soldiers nor to the rights accorded by law to civilian criminals. Later, the term "terrorism" refers to a specific crime: not the failure to wear a uniform or carry one's arms in the open, but specified criminal activity such as assisting al-Qaida or aiding and abetting the murder of Americans. There are perhaps two distinct meanings of "terrorism" at work here: the lawless status of terrorists as unprotected "unlawful combatants," which renders them subject to summary trial, and "terrorism" as a crime for which they are to be judged at these trials.

This understanding may not get the Bush administration entirely off the hook. The allegation of circular terminology is, as I understand Fletcher's critique, not primarily a logical flaw but rather a moral one. Bearing in mind both the President's original executive order of November 2001 and the more recent Military Commissions Act, 2006, Fletcher's allegation of logical circularity may not be entirely accurate. The term "unlawful enemy combatant" is indeed employed twice. The 2001 "unlawful combatants" order uses the term first in connection with the identification of a class of people who, upon suspicion of being unlawful combatants, are to be subject to a certain procedure; and, secondly, it uses that phrase to refer to what the procedure will try to prove. This is not circular at all, anymore than it is circular to say that those suspected of murder will be charged in a special court that will then adjudicate to see whether the suspicion of murder can be proved.[96] However, Fletcher's substantial worry about

---

[95] Fletcher, *Romantics at War*, p. 114.
[96] I am grateful to Jeremy Waldron for this point.

the tribunals remains one of identifying the class of individuals subject to this inferior brand of justice – that is, al-Qaida members – rather than any foreigner whom the Bush administration regards as suspicious.[97] Even if one accepts the administration's legal assessment whereby "unlawful combatants" may be denied due process of law and tried with fewer procedural guarantees, these procedures should at least be employed in order to guarantee that the individual brought before the tribunal is indeed an "unlawful combatant."

Earlier in 2001 – before the planes hit New York and Washington and President Bush ordered his tribunals – Palestinian attacks on civilians in Israel had escalated. The previous year had seen Israel's hasty withdrawal from Lebanon, the collapse of the Camp David accords, and the Palestinian rejection of the Clinton–Barak offer. This had triggered the second Palestinian uprising – the '*Al-Aqsa Intifada*' – which began in September 2000. In response, Israel reinstituted an old tactic of assassinating mid- to upper-level Palestinian militants. Between September 29, 2000 and the end of 2005, Israeli military forces assassinated over 187 Palestinians accused of leading terrorist activity.[98]

Many moral, legal, and practical arguments have been put forward in condemnation of Israel's assassination policy, all of which deserve close scrutiny. It had been dubbed "extra-judicial execution"[99] and even equated with the terrorism it purports to combat.[100] Others question whether we ought to entrust military and political personnel with making such crucial decisions, or whether the practice, even if justified, ought to be placed under judicial review. Some, who are less opposed in principle to this strategy, nonetheless point accusingly at the civilian casualties incurred in the course of such operations. Others question the policy's effectiveness as a means of combating terrorism, concluding that it is merely a form of revenge or retaliation rather than of self-defense. As such, it is also suggested, these operations quicken rather than reduce the cycle of violence and bloodshed. All these arguments will be discussed at length in the following chapter. Legally speaking, however, it is unclear, for all the rhetoric, that targeting irregular combatants, whether terrorists or otherwise, is in any sense illegal or

---

[97] Fletcher, *Romantics at War*, pp. 113–14.
[98] B'tselem – The Israeli Information Center for Human Rights in the "Occupied Territories": www.btselem.org.
[99] This is the term used in B'tselem, and is prevalent among the Israeli left.
[100] For example, Honderich, *After the Terror*, p. 151. Chomsky, *9–11*, p. 72.

that the rules of war contain any basic principles that should render this practice unlawful. In a recent landmark decision, the Israeli High Court ruled that such assassinations do not violate international law.[101]

Clearly, the underlying principle of Israel's assassination policy and its Supreme Court's ruling on this practice is the familiar distinction between lawful and unlawful combatants. Israeli Supreme Court Justice Barak states explicitly his judgment of this point, citing both the Second World War Quirin case, which Fletcher discusses, as well as the recent US *Hamdi* v. *Rumsfeld*.[102] I suggest that terrorists, or guerrillas, operate within the military rather than the civil sphere and are therefore not entitled to the protection of the due process of law. On Justice Barak's account, "unlawful combatants" remain civilians, but nonetheless lose their civilian immunity from attack when they unlawfully take a direct part in hostilities.[103]

As for international conventions, Protocol I added to the Geneva Convention, regarding the protection of civilian populations, states clearly that "(3) Civilians shall enjoy the protection afforded by this section, unless and for such time as they take a direct part in hostilities."[104] The controversial term here as far as Israel's assassinations are concerned is the phrase "direct part." There are those who would argue that some of Israel's targets (most notably Sheik Ahmed Yassin) did not take a "direct part" in hostilities, and were therefore "civilians" protected by international law. In its decision on targeted assassination, the Israeli High Court defined the notion of direct participation in a relatively

---

[101] HCJ 769/02 [Dec. 11, 2005], available at: http://elyon1.court.gov.il/Files_ENG/02/690/007/a34/02007690.a34.pdf.

[102] HCJ 769/02, Para. 25. Justice A. Barak citing: Ex Parte Quirin 317 US 1 30 (1942); and *Hamdi* v. *Rumsfeld*, 542 US 507 (2004). See also Para. 31 on "unlawful combatants."

[103] Barak, HCJ 769/02.

[104] Protocol I added to the Geneva Conventions, 1977, Chapter II: Civilians and Civilian Population: Art. 51: Protection of the Civilian Population. For the Israeli Court's discussion of the term "direct part in hostilities" and the relatively wide interpretation accorded to that term within this decision, see HCJ 769/02. As Vice President of the Israeli Supreme Court, Justice E. Rivlin, points out there in agreement with Justice Barak, Barak's interpretation of "unlawful combatants" as civilians (rather than combatants) who unlawfully take a direct part in hostilities, amounts to the same conclusions as reached by those who define "unlawful combatants" as a third category added to the traditional combatant–civilian distinction. Barak simply reaches the same outcome via a different avenue, shying away from explicitly introducing "unlawful combatant" status as a third category of the laws of war. He does in fact employ the term "unlawful combatants" time and time again within his opinion.

broad manner, so as to include not only those terrorists who actively attack civilians, but also those who decide upon the attacks and send out the attackers. According to Justice Barak in that decision, those taking a "direct part" in hostilities include not only those bearing arms before, during or after an attack, but also those providing services to "unlawful combatants" and those participating voluntarily in the armed struggle as human shields, though not including those civilians who are forced into such situations by the terrorists.[105]

In fact, all of Israel's targets, without exception (and including Yassin), were directly involved in the militant struggle against Israel, either by instigating, or organizing, planning, personally inciting, actively recruiting for, or carrying out, attacks against Israeli civilians, as well as soldiers. They themselves would be the last to deny this. On no account can they be considered simply as civilian criminals, or as any type of protected "persons taking no active part in the hostilities"; indeed, they do not claim this status.[106]

On the other hand, as irregulars who do not uphold the war conventions, terrorists, or guerrillas, are equally not entitled to the war rights of soldiers.[107] Thus, Israel assumes, they are never immune from attack, not even in their homes or in their beds. Like soldiers, they may be killed during armed conflict at any time, whether armed or unarmed, whether posing a grievous threat or idly standing by.[108] Unlike regular soldiers,

---

[105] HCJ 769/02, Paras. 34–7, esp. Paras. 35–6. See also Kristen E. Eichensehr, "On Target? The Israeli Supreme Court and the Expansion of Targeted Killings," *Yale Law Journal*, June 2007, 116 (8), pp. 1873, 1875–6. Criticizing the Israeli Supreme Court ruling.

[106] The phrase "Persons taking no active part in the hostilities," referring to a protected status, is taken from the Geneva Convention of 1949 and includes civilians as well as prisoners of war who have laid down their arms. See the Geneva Convention, Part I: General Provisions, Art. 3 (1).

[107] For the qualifications for attaining these rights, such as POW status, specifically the accumulative requirements to abide by the rules of war, wear identifying dress, and carry one's arms openly, see the Hague Convention, Annex to the Convention, Section I, "On Belligerents," Chapter I, "The Qualifications of Belligerents," Art. 1. Geneva Conventions Part I: General Provisions, Art. 4. See also Fletcher, *Romantics at War*, p. 106; Walzer, *Just and Unjust Wars*, p. 182.

[108] On the broad notion of self-defense in wartime and on the many contexts in which it is legal to kill enemy soldiers, see Fletcher, *Romantics at War*, p. 107; Walzer, *Just and Unjust Wars*, pp. 139–42; Dershowitz, "Killing Terrorist Chieftains"; Daniel Statman, "Targeted Killing," *Theoretical Inquiries in Law* 5 (2004), pp. 179–98, esp. p. 195.

however, they may also be killed in purely civilian settings. Aside from their unprotected legal status, the moral rationale for this license concerns the lack of reciprocal rule-keeping discussed in the previous section. Irregulars do not expose themselves to conventional risks, nor do they themselves uphold any conventions concerning the appropriate contexts for combat. The terrorist will not recoil from combating the enemy in unconventional settings. There seems, therefore, to be little, if any, moral reason to uphold conventions regarding optimal battle settings in the case of irregulars who do not themselves abide by these rules.

In contrast to the problem of accurately identifying al-Qaida members, Israel faces virtually no practical or moral difficulty identifying those responsible for the violent strikes against it. There is rarely, if ever, any doubt as to the culpability of the pursued targets, as the terrorist chieftains and the organizations they represent are always proud to publicly accept responsibility for the atrocities they plan and execute. Yassin, Rantisi, Yahiya Ayyash, Raed Karmi, and Salah Shhada are all cases in point. Transparency is also not an issue in these cases. It is possible to withhold information regarding the conditions under which prisoners are detained, even the identity of the specific detainees, but one can hardly conceal the assassination of a prominent figure. While some operations may be carried out covertly, no secrecy surrounds their consequences.

When defending Israel's assassination policy, Daniel Statman illuminates this distinction between regular military officers and belligerents who do not abide by the reciprocal conventions of war. Statman refers to the common moral and legal view according to which the killing of enemy combatants in wartime is allowed even if they are not posing a direct and imminent threat.[109] However, he admits, it is illegal to target enemy commanders in civilian settings (say, when vacationing at a hotel), suggesting that while Israel may target combatants in military settings, it may not do so in civilian contexts. He then proceeds to deny that such legal conventions apply to irregular belligerents.

Why is it legitimate to kill an enemy officer in his office or on the way to it but illegitimate to kill him in a hotel?[110] How does the change in

---

[109] On this license to kill soldiers, see Fletcher, *Romantics at War*, pp. 107–8; Walzer, *Just and Unjust Wars*, p. 142.
[110] Statman, "Targeted Killing," p. 195.

location serve to provide moral immunity to a person who might otherwise be legitimately killed under our broad understanding of self-defense in wartime?[111] Statman explains this distinction as grounded purely in convention, but he nonetheless attributes weighty moral significance to such conventions as they contribute to reducing the killing, the harm and the destruction of war.[112] Fletcher's *Romantics at War* suggests a slightly different explanation of the significance of changing location. A soldier in uniform, Fletcher explains, assumes a collective identity as an enemy agent, which renders him threatening to the other side and thus vulnerable to attack.[113] On the other hand, Fletcher's thesis suggests that, while vacationing, the same individual resumes his civilian identity and as such cannot be targeted personally. Either way, it is clear that such distinctions are conventional in nature; conventional in the sense of requiring some form of artificial construction (such as the notion of "collective identity"). It is equally apparent, however, that the rules of war are morally grounded in the aspiration to minimize suffering by confining the fighting to a distinct class of individuals – namely, soldiers – and protecting civilian populations from direct attack.

How do these rules apply to irregular combatants who do not abide by them? Recall Fletcher's characterization of unlawfulness in combat as arising from the deliberate refusal to share in the reciprocal risks involved in warfare – that is, identifying oneself as vulnerable to attack by wearing a uniform and carrying one's arms openly.[114] David Sussman expresses a similar intuition when he argues in his recent article explaining "What's Wrong with Torture?" that it is nonetheless morally reasonable to require a captured terrorist to divulge information that will thwart his cause. The terrorist, Sussman argues, disregards the laws of war and thereby forfeits the conventional right of soldiers to surrender without compromising their cause. While a regular captured combatant retains the right to withhold evidence that would obstruct his country's goal, we need not respect the terrorist's reluctance to compromise his sense of integrity, camaraderie and objectives:

The terrorist disregards the principle of just combat, striking at his enemies' loved ones simply because they are dear to him. The terrorist makes no effort

---

[111] Ibid., p. 195.   [112] Ibid., p. 196.
[113] Fletcher, *Romantics at War*, pp. 107–8.   [114] Ibid., p. 108.

to distinguish himself from civilians and other non-combatants, forcing his foe into the terrible choice of either waging war against innocents or failing to protect himself and those near to him. Given as the terrorist attacks his enemy's own integrity this way, it is hard to see how he is entitled to terms of surrender that do not require him to in any way compromise his cause. Plausibly, such terms should be reserved for combatants who accept certain risks (by wearing uniforms, living apart from civilian populations, and so on).[115]

The targets of Israel's assassinations, as well as America's non-conventional enemies, are guilty of a further breach of morally significant conventions. While this need not be true of all unlawful combatants, the irregular organizations confronted by Israel and the US do not refrain from attacking soldiers in civilian settings or even from targeting civilians directly. Should the very rules of war they thwart nonetheless apply to them? I believe the complicated reality of the matter is that some should and some should not.

What the rules don't say and what they should say

We saw that the prohibition against targeting combatants in civilian locations is the product of convention, though one with a morally significant rationale; that is, a desire to limit the amount of suffering in wartime. Israel's policy of assassinating the self-professed commanders and instigators of irregular warfare in non-conventional settings can indeed be criticized for violating this convention. However, as Statman points out:

like all conventions, the moral force of this convention is contingent on its being followed by all sides. Hence, if one side violates the convention, the other is no longer committed to adhering to it. In this regard, rules based on convention differ from rules founded on strict moral grounds, which are obligatory regardless of what the other side does. Since the killing of children is subject to such a strict moral prohibition, it is forbidden even if the enemy takes such a horrendous course of action. But killing officers in their homes (during war) is not, in itself, morally worse than killing them in their headquarters; therefore, if one of the sides violates this convention, it loses its moral force.[116]

---

[115] David Sussman, "What's Wrong with Torture?" *Philosophy and Public Affairs*, 33 (1), (2005), pp. 1–33, esp. p. 18.
[116] Statman, "Targeted Killing," p. 196.

The convention against targeting combatants in civilian settings may be useful in reducing the horrors of war and as such morally worthy, even if it is not intrinsically valid. The case is much the same with some other, though admittedly not all, conventions of war. Clearly, it is wrong to state that all conventions require mutuality, and I doubt Statman intended to imply that they do. The conventions which constitute the rules of armed conflict need not be of this type. They may require only that sufficient others follow them in order to make them morally significant; and that moral significance does not go away merely because one's opponent then violates them in some particular conflict.[117] On the other hand, some conventional rules of war appear to make sense only if they are adhered to mutually, or multilaterally. Some conventional norms appear to be merely mutually agreed-upon rules of the game, albeit morally worthy ones. In such cases – that are admittedly difficult to discern and starkly distinguished from the more inherently moral type of conventions – mutuality would appear to be an essential requirement. Jeff McMahan suggests another useful example: "It is not obvious, for example, that poison gas is inherently more objectionable morally than artillery, provided that its use is confined to the battlefield; yet the convention that prohibits its use is widely obeyed, mainly because we all sense that it would be worse for everyone, ourselves included, were the taboo to be breached."[118] According to Statman,

Conventions, however, require mutuality; otherwise, the side adhering to them would simply be yielding to the side that refuses to follow them. Since groups like Al-Qaeda, the Tanzim and the Hamas, have no regard whatsoever for the conventions of war, the party fighting against them is released from these conventions too, though not from the strict moral rules of conduct.[119]

McMahan makes the same point about the limited binding force of conventions: "it is widely accepted that the violation of a convention by one side tends to release the other side from its commitment to respect the convention."[120]

Again, Statman and McMahan's point about the mutuality requirement of conventions is certainly not true of all the conventions that

---

[117] I am grateful to Jeremy Waldron for pointing this out to me.
[118] McMahan, "The Ethics of Killing in War," p. 732.
[119] Statman, "Targeted Killing," p. 196.
[120] McMahan, "The Ethics of Killing in War," p. 732.

constitute the rules of armed conflict. At most, as McMahan puts the point carefully, "violation of a convention by one side *tends* to release the other side from its commitment."[121] It is, for example, untrue of the international convention against the use of torture that will be discussed in the final two chapters of this book.[122] It is evidently untrue, to take another obvious example, of the prohibition on genocide.

Statman's distinction between rules based on convention and those founded on strict moral grounds may be too sharp, but it does nonetheless contain an insight that is crucial to the issue at hand. Although not all the rules of armed conflict found in international conventions require mutuality, some may. Statman's distinction implies that those conventional rules which do not rest on independent, inherently moral reasons, but are rather merely (albeit morally useful) rules of the game, as it were, do not apply in the absence of mutuality. As a matter of empirical fact, both types of rules to which Statman refers – those based purely on convention and those based on strict moral grounds – can be found within international conventions. However, the point is that the former require mutuality in order to retain their moral force while the latter do not.

The previous sections showed that while no distinction between lawful and unlawful combatants is explicitly laid down within international law, the status of lawless combatantcy can be deduced negatively from the positive definition of soldiers eligible for POW status under the Hague Convention of 1907 and the Geneva Convention of 1949. This, it has been noted, was precisely the move made in the Military Commissions Act, 2006, which defines enemy combatants as unlawful if they do not belong to a certain type of organization, do not wear identifying insignia, carry their arms openly or abide by the rules of war.[123] The last section suggested that combatants who bear no external insignia and carry their arms in secret fail to achieve a particular

---

[121] McMahan, "The Ethics of Killing," p. 732, my emphasis.

[122] For the absolute legal ban on torture in international conventions, regardless of mutuality, see the International Covenant on Civil and Political Rights, adopted December 16, 1966. See: www.ohchr.org/english/law/ccpr.htm, Art. 7 and 4(2). And also, the United Nations Convention against Torture and Other Inhuman or Degrading Treatment or Punishment, Part I, Art. 2. Adopted by the General Assembly on December 1975 [resolution 3452 (xxx)]. www.hrweb.org/legal/cat.html. See also Jeremy Waldron, "Torture and Positive Law," *Columbia Law Review*, 105 (6), pp. 1681–750, p. 1688.

[123] Military Commissions Act, 2006, Sect. 948a (1) and (2).

legal status – that of a soldier – and are therefore ineligible for the specific privileges that accompany this legal status. The breach of certain norms, specifically wearing uniforms and carrying arms openly, as well as generally abiding by the rules and customs of war, means that the combatant in question does not secure the legal immunities granted to those who fulfill these requirements. This person defies certain conventions and therefore cannot enjoy the specific privileges accorded by them to those who abide by their norms.[124] Those particular conventions of war – those requiring uniforms, unconcealed weapons, and so on – appear to be just the type of conventional rule that Statman and McMahan have in mind when arguing for a reciprocal, or mutual, relationship. Clearly, even according to the Hague and Geneva Conventions, non-compliance on one side – in this case, refusal to share in the risks of covert warfare – frees the other party from some, though not all, of its commitments (e.g. granting POW rights). Apparently, as far as those rules of war that are purely conventional in nature are concerned, they do not apply to combatants who fail to abide by their specifications.

Admittedly, it is difficult to propose precise guidelines for distinguishing between norms based on convention and those international conventions which are also founded on strict moral grounds. As far as the rules of war are concerned, we saw that this distinction is not always a stark one. Even purely conventional rules of war will sometimes have a strong moral rationale, such as the aspiration of limiting modern warfare. Nonetheless, it seems clear that some distinction along these lines is necessary and that some relatively easy cases can be agreed upon. Statman's example of the prohibition on targeting high-ranking combatants in resort hotels is a case in point. There is no doubt about the legitimacy of the target or the license to kill him off-guard or even in his sleep; nonetheless, we have good reasons for contracting to refrain from targeting combatants in certain contexts, but these reasons are nullified if the agreement is not mutually adhered to. The same is true, for instance, of the use of mustard gas on the battlefield. As McMahan points out, there is no independent moral reason to believe that it is morally worse to use gas (on the battlefield) than bullets. The agreement to refrain from its use is grounded in the morally praiseworthy aspiration, as well as our self-interest, to reduce the amount of overall

[124] Fletcher, *Romantics at War*, p. 109.

suffering in wartime. It is reasonable to assume, however, that if one side were to violate this convention, the other side would be released from its contractual commitment to respect it.[125]

The same logic applies to attaining POW status if captured. While these rules are presumably grounded in a morally significant concern for the humane treatment of prisoners, the specific rights accorded by the Hague and Geneva Conventions assume a mutual relationship and the undertaking of reciprocal risks. They do not apply legally to those who do not live up to their stipulated standards, nor can they be demanded on moral grounds by those who do not share in the burdens associated with upholding these norms.

The case is different with those norms, also agreed upon in international conventions, that refer more directly to strict moral prohibitions and defend basic human rights. Consider the crime of gassing civilians in extermination camps, as opposed to releasing lethal gases on the battlefield. If, during the Second World War, either of the warring parties had reverted to using poison gas against soldiers, the other side would have presumably been justified in retaliating in kind, as all sides did in the First World War, in the absence of an agreement to refrain from doing so. On the other hand, the Allied forces would not have been justified in avenging the horrors of the Nazi death camps by setting up their own gas chambers for German ex-patriots in the United States. In keeping with this logic, Protocol I, added to the Geneva Convention in 1977, does not release states from their legal obligation to respect civilians and civilian populations, even if these obligations are violated by their adversaries.[126] Correspondingly, Statman's example of targeting children is a point well taken. Even when states, or terrorists, blatantly defy such rules, their opponents may not retaliate in kind.[127] This is also true of a variety of human rights violations, such as the use of outright torture, and, I would venture to add, seclusion and the long-term detention of individuals who have not freely assumed responsibility for the actions attributed to them or been publicly proven guilty. The latter is most directly related to the basic moral prohibition on punishing the innocent, while the former reflects a basic moral commitment to

---

[125] McMahan, "The Ethics of Killing," p. 732.
[126] Protocol I, Additional to the Geneva Conventions (1977), Part IV, Section II, Article 51, # 8.
[127] Statman, "Targeted Killing," p. 196.

uphold a bare minimum of humane treatment of individuals as such, whatever their crime. The absolute immunity against torturous treatment is discussed at length in Chapters 6 and 7.[128] Once again, however, the task of specifying a wholly conclusive and definitive list of basic human rights that ought to be upheld in wartime regardless of the enemy's course of action is beyond the scope of this book. Notwithstanding this, I suggest that while combatants who are not soldiers cannot reasonably demand the right to be targeted only on the battlefield, or to reveal only their name rank and serial number when captured, they ought to retain a minimum of basic human rights that are not merely the product of convention.

Concluding remarks

The distinction between lawful and unlawful combatants is inherently tied to the more basic differentiation between combatants and civilians and is essential for protecting the latter. As such, it is a morally worthy distinction, which ought to be specified in law and upheld in practice rather than remaining in a permanent state of legal limbo. International law ought to explicitly recognize the distinction between combatants who play by the rules of war and share in its risks, and those who disregard them. Essentially, this involves specifying, rather than merely implying, the criteria for lawful behavior in combat and the benefits that attach to it, along with those benefits withheld from combatants who do not abide by the rules. On the most practical level, it comes down to drawing the appropriate conclusions regarding the rights of irregulars, and lack thereof, in battle and in its aftermath.

In doing so, international lawyers should pay special attention to the distinction between the rights and privileges stemming from convention only, and those conventions of war which are based on strict moral grounds. Although this chapter does not put forward any particular policy or proposal regarding all aspects of the treatment of irregulars, it does suggest that the rights founded purely in convention presuppose

---

[128] For the absolute prohibition on torture in international law see the International Covenant on Civil and Political Rights and the United Nations Convention against Torture and Other Inhuman or Degrading Treatment or Punishment, Part I, Art. 2.

mutuality and should, therefore, be accorded only to those combatants who abide by them. On the other hand, certain basic human rights must be accorded to all human beings as such, regardless of mutuality or the suspect's legal status or alleged crime. As Israeli Supreme Court Justice Aharon Barak put this in his aforementioned ruling on targeted killing: "Needless to say, unlawful combatants are not beyond the law. They are not 'outlaws.' God created them as well in his image; their dignity as well is to be honored; they as well enjoy and are entitled to protection, even if most minimal, by customary international law."[129] Such are, I would add for example, not only the right of a captured combatant not to be subjected to grievous physical pain and pressure, but also the right to receive proper food, medical and dental care, to be kept in a humane environment, as well as to avoid false imprisonment, or endless concealed incarceration. Consequently, while the lawless status of irregular combatants ought to be legally distinguished from their lawful counterparts, this distinction will not necessarily bear the precise significance that some self-interested state leaders wish to accord to it, nor should it always supply them with the licenses they seek to acquire.

[129] HCJ 769/02 [2005].

PART III

Fighting Terrorism

5 | Targeting terror

The dramatic increase in Islamist terrorist activity throughout the world and in Arab terrorist activity in Israel throughout the last few years has placed the issue of combating terrorism at the forefront of moral philosophy (or should do). Curiously, as Western states wage "war on terror," Israel finds itself increasingly under attack for its policy of assassinating terrorist leaders. It has been argued that Israel's "targeted killing" policy violates international standards of legitimate warfare. In the extreme, it has been claimed that this practice is on a moral par with the terrorist activity it purports to combat.[1]

Indeed, targeted killing is most closely related to the practice of political assassination, with which it shares certain basic features. Certainly, it has more affinity with assassination, in name as well as deed, than with either conventional warfare or terrorist activity. This chapter deals exclusively with the targeted killing of terrorists rather than any other type of state-sanctioned assassination. Once again, terrorism is understood here, following Michael Walzer, as a particular form of political violence: the intentional random murder of defenseless non-combatants, many of whom are innocent even by the assailants' own standards (infants, children, the elderly and infirm, and foreign nationals), with the intent of spreading fear of mortal danger amidst a civilian population as a strategy designed to advance political ends.[2] A brief comparison between political assassination and targeted killing suggests that the similarities and differences between them highlight the appropriate attitude towards anti-terrorist assassination policies.

---

[1] Honderich, *After the Terror*, p. 151; Chomsky, *9–11*, p. 72.

[2] Walzer, *Just and Unjust Wars*, pp. 197, 203. This definition of terrorism is admittedly controversial, as discussed at length in Chapters 1 and 2. Those who contest Walzer's classic definition, however, argue for a wider, rather than more restrictive, definition that would necessarily include the one offered here.

What's wrong with killing bad guys?

To the pre-analytical mind of laymen (particularly those who grew up on Hollywood movies) the idea of "killing the bad guys," so to speak, seems intuitively rather a good thing. What is it about targeted killing that leads us to question this view? Surely, it is not the pacifist stand-point. The controversy over targeted killing makes sense only outside the pacifist arena. For the pacifist, fighting and killing are always, and unconditionally, wrong. The present discussion is warranted only if we start with the non-pacifist view whereby it is sometimes morally justified to fight and kill other people.[3]

I have argued that there ought to be little disagreement among Western liberals concerning the immorality of terrorists and their abhorrent deeds.[4] I assume here, further, that there is usually little doubt as to the culpability of the pursued targets. Normally, the perpetrators themselves accept responsibility (as opposed to guilt) – bin Laden or Hamas, to cite extreme examples. Typical Palestinian targets, for example, have included: Ibrahim Bani Odeh, a well-known bomb maker; Fatah leader Hussein Abayyat; Yahiya Ayyash, assassinated in Gaza in 1996; Tanzim leader Raed Karmi; Mahmoud Abu Hanoud, a high-ranking Hamas commander assassinated in November 2001; Hamas leader Salah Shhada, assassinated in July 2002; Hamas's Sheik Ahmed Yassin, and his successor, Dr. Abdel Aziz Rantisi.

I will focus on the argument most characteristic of the opposition to assassination policies, namely, that the targeted killing of arch-terrorists is not the morally appropriate response to their actions. Such claims typically run along the following three lines. First, the assassination of terrorist leaders is illegal; that is, it violates international law. Secondly, it is an immoral measure, as it constitutes extra-judicial execution. According to this view, either terrorists ought to be captured and tried or, at the very least (when this is impractical), decisions concerning their assassination ought to be placed under judicial scrutiny and supervision. Thirdly, it is sometimes claimed that targeted killing is an ineffective

---

[3] Daniel Statman, "Jus in Bello and the Intifada," in Tomas Kapitan (ed.), *Philosophical Perspectives on the Israeli–Palestinian Conflict* (Armonk, NY: Sharpe, 1997), pp. 133–56.

[4] There are admittedly exceptions to this putative consensus, for example, Honderich, *After the Terror* – this, I have argued, is at least partly due to Honderich's dissent from liberal morality, pp. 46–51 and *passim*.

means of combating terror as it only strengthens the commitment of the victims' co-nationals to engage in belligerent activity against the assassins and their compatriots, and erodes the prospects of peace. Furthermore, assassination is both inexpedient, as well as immoral, in a further respect: while its professed aim is to target a specific culprit, it often causes grave harm – whether negligently or inevitably – to innocent bystanders.

This chapter focuses on the moral aspects of targeted killing. It argues that controversies about the expediency of such policies, far from being distinctly pragmatic are, to a large extent, part and parcel of the normative issue. As for international law, I have already pointed to the legal lacuna regarding irregular combatants. Positive international law is, by all accounts, less than clear on the specific issue of targeting terrorists.[5] Nevertheless, law and morality are sufficiently intertwined to warrant occasional reference to existing law and conventions of war within a moral analysis of targeted killing. International law is clear on other, related, wartime issues, such as who may and may not be killed in combat. Clear-cut conventions often reflect shared moral values and intuitions, which can shed light on the controversial issue to hand. Finally, our ethical conclusions ultimately shape our views on the appropriate legal attitude towards targeted killing. I return to this point towards the end of the chapter.

Limited wars and targeted killing

Specific opposition to targeted killing does not arise from within pacifist circles. The background hypothesis which underlies opposition to assassination policies is that soldiers, albeit within certain constraints, may legitimately kill and be killed in war in the name of self-defense.[6] The condemnation of targeted assassinations, then, necessarily hinges

---

[5] See Gross, "Assassination," p. 2; Gross, "Fighting by Others Means," pp. 350–68, 354; Gad Barzilai, "Islands of Silence: Democracies Kill?" paper presented at the annual meeting of the Law and Society Association, Budapest (2000), pp. 4, 5, 14.

[6] Ibid., p. 4: "killings of soldiers by soldiers during wartime are permissible." Gross, "Assassination," p. 4: "If one has a right to kill in self-defense during wartime, why not a corollary right to assassination?" See also Israeli High Court discussion of targeted assassination: "In general, combatants and military objectives are legitimate targets for attack. Their lives and bodies are endangered by the combat. They can be killed and wounded." HCJ 769/02 [2005], Para. 23.

in the first place on a normative distinction between killing enemy soldiers, on one hand, and targeting terrorists, on the other.

The routine way of determining those who may and may not be killed in war is to distinguish between combatants (uniformed soldiers as well as irregular belligerents) and innocent, unarmed civilians. Clearly, the combatant/non-combatant distinction, which renders immunity to the latter, cannot facilitate arguments against assassinating terrorist leaders. By their own admission, terrorists are not civilians. They controversially regard themselves as freedom fighters or guerrilla warriors, but never claim to be unengaged in combat. On the contrary, terrorist leaders and the organizations they represent are always proud to publicly accept responsibility for the atrocities they plan and execute.

Alternatively, it might still be argued that while targets of assassination policies are by all accounts non-civilians, they are targeted in civilian settings (at their desks, in their cars, or even in their beds) and this fact distinguishes their killing from legitimate combat on the battlefield. While this is slightly more plausible than the previous argument, it is ultimately destined to the same fate. First, killing combatants in irregular settings may, under normal circumstances, fall short of an officer and gentleman's ideal, but it does not breach any international laws or normative conventions: "Soldiers may be killed in self-defense under circumstances that far outstrip those that constrain ordinary self-defense. Any soldier may be killed during armed conflict at any time whether armed or unarmed, whether posing a grievous threat or idly standing by."[7]

As Walzer puts it, "It is not against the rules of war as we currently understand them to kill soldiers who look funny, who are taking a bath, holding up their pants, reveling in the sun, smoking a cigarette."[8] No doubt we feel uneasy about killing soldiers in such circumstances, as Walzer clearly does, but there is no rule against doing so. In the case of arch-terrorists, it is unclear that we should even experience unease about targeting them in unexpected contexts; for example, in their office or on their way to it.

---

[7] Gross, "Assassination," p. 5. See also Fletcher, *Romantics at War*, pp. 107–8. The same point is made by Daniel Statman, "The Morality of Assassination: A Response to Gross," *Political Studies* 51 (4) pp. 1–33; Statman, "Targeted Killing," p. 195.

[8] Walzer, *Just and Unjust Wars*, p. 142.

Admittedly, conventional soldiers may not be killed in civilian locations (e.g. when on leave or on vacation). This, as we saw at the end of the previous chapter, is the product of convention, though one with a morally significant rationale, that of limiting the cycle of violence in wartime to the battlefield and its immediate vicinity. Terrorists are often assassinated in their homes, or hideaway. Sheik Ahmed Yassin was assassinated on his way out of a mosque. Following Statman, I questioned whether terrorists who do not uphold conventional rules are entitled to their protection. Unlike rules founded on strict moral grounds, such as the prohibition against killing children or gassing civilians, which are obligatory regardless of what the other side does, conventional prohibitions (even ones with a moral rational) depend on mutuality. Killing combatants in their homes (during an ongoing armed conflict) is not, in itself, morally worse than killing them in their headquarters; therefore, if one of the sides violates this convention, it loses its moral force.[9]

More importantly, in the case of terrorism, it is doubtful whether there is a front line or conventional battlefield to be considered. When a soldier relinquishes an opportunity to shoot his opponent while the latter is relaxing behind enemy lines, he retains the realistic prospect of confronting him, and his indistinguishable comrades, in a more conventional context when the battle resumes. Terrorist leaders on the run, however, do not ordinarily expose themselves to such risks. Unlike the case of the soldier who may honorably spare his enemy when engaged in non-belligerent activity, only to confront him again on tomorrow's battlefield, the opportunity to combat terrorism on the conventional front line will, by definition, never arise at all. There seems, therefore, to be little, if any, moral reason to uphold unwritten codes concerning optimal battle settings (which do not apply officially even to conventional soldiers) or even those limiting combat to non-civilian settings, in the case of terrorists.

One further argument against assassination points to the anonymity of soldiers, as opposed to the personalized identity of particular named terrorists, as grounds for a morally relevant distinction between the two cases. Soldiers, it is argued, lose their right to life, not as individuals, but only as representatives of an enemy political entity. They are vulnerable to acts of aggression as a result of their collective and anonymous identity that supersedes (or is at least combined with) their individual one, rather

---

[9] Statman, "Targeted Killing," p. 196.

than to any particular grievance held against them.[10] Moreover, as
named private individuals, most soldiers are innocent of personal
crimes or responsibility for the wars in which they participate.[11] Their
vulnerability stems solely from their role as military agents of their
political communities.[12] It is only as such that they constitute morally
legitimate targets.[13] As Rousseau pointed out, war is "something
that occurs not between man and man, but between states. The individuals who become involved in it are enemies only by accident."[14] In
contrast, terrorist leaders are pursued individually and targeted by name.
Removing the anonymity from the personal identity of the enemy–victim,
it is argued, dramatically transforms the morality of war. Accordingly,
the adoption of an assassination policy changes the moral landscape, so
to speak, and re-imports into the battlefield the same moral rules that
govern relationships between individuals, in particular the rules governing the use of lethal means.[15] Consequently, failing to work through
conventional legal channels in order to punish arch-terrorists, resorting
instead to unregulated brute force, is regarded as both illegal and
immoral, as it would be in any criminal case.[16]

As opposed to the first two modes of distinguishing between targeted
terrorists and soldiers, the present argument succeeds in identifying a
morally relevant difference between killing soldiers in battle and assassinating arch-terrorists. It is, however, arguable whether this distinction
strengthens the case against targeted killings or in fact facilitates the
assassins' case. It suggests, counter-intuitively, that the killing of innocent
soldiers in battle is morally preferable to the targeted killing of particular

---

[10] For example, Noam Zohar, "Collective War and Individualistic Ethics: Against
the Conscription of Self-Defence," *Political Theory* 21 (1993), pp. 606–22.
Gross, "Assassination," takes anonymity to be the main feature which sets
soldiers apart from named targets of assassination.

[11] See Walzer, *Just and Unjust Wars*, p. 138. As Paul Gilbert, *New Terror, New Wars*,
p. 14, has recently put it, the requirements for *jus ad bellum* – for having the right
to go to war to begin with – are constraints placed on statesmen and political leaders
rather than soldiers. Soldiers are responsible only for their own conduct in wartime.

[12] Gross, "Assassination," p. 22.

[13] For an interesting account of the collective identity of the soldier, and of its limits,
see Fletcher, *Romantics at War*, esp. pp. 5, 54–5, 92–6.

[14] Jean Jacques Rousseau, *The Social Contract and Discourses* (London and
Vermont: Everyman, 1993), Chapter 4.

[15] This is one of the general lines of argument raised by Gross, "Assassination," esp.
pp. 6–8.

[16] This objection is commonplace among the Israeli left.

offenders who readily admit their responsibility for the actions attributed to them.

Why should we accept that killing anonymous soldiers because they represent "the enemy" is legitimate (on grounds related to the liberal notion of self-defense), whereas targeting particular, named culprits in the course of a war against terrorism is morally abhorrent? Daniel Statman argues plausibly that targeting terrorists in the course of war does not constitute "named killing" in any morally problematic sense, such as "killing somebody simply because he is who he is, regardless of any contingent features he has or actions he committed."[17] Just as soldiers are legitimate targets because of the role they play as agents of a community at war and the threat they pose to the other side, particular terrorists are targeted not because of who they are, but because of the specific strategic role they play in the armed conflict.[18] Furthermore, while soldiers are not personally responsible for the instigation of, or for the means employed in, the armed conflicts in which they are engaged (aside from their own personal conduct), terrorist leaders share direct responsibility for both. Moreover, this special responsibility is one they acquire voluntarily. As opposed to conscripted soldiers, arch-terrorists are motivated volunteers.

This is not to deny that re-personalizing the situation (naming the victims) transposes our normative evaluation of killing. It suggests only that in the case of killing terrorists, this transformation strengthens the assassins' moral case rather than that of their victims. Admittedly, while soldiers may kill in war in the name of self-defense, regardless of the material and moral innocence of their opponent–victims, once the victims are named they may be killed only if materially and morally non-innocent.[19] Killing of the first type – regardless of guilt – is legitimate self-defense only so long as anonymity is preserved and the victims are killed solely as agents of a threatening enemy power.[20] The anonymity factor (the fact that soldiers are depersonalized in war) helps explain why it is legitimate to kill anonymous soldiers regardless of their moral and material innocence, whereas it is forbidden to kill particular innocent individuals.

Moral opposition to assassination based on this distinction, however, is valid only so long as the victims *are* morally and materially innocent,

---

[17] Statman, "Targeted Killing," p. 190.   [18] Ibid.
[19] Gross, "Assassination," pp. 9, 10.   [20] Ibid., p. 13.

which terrorists never are.[21] The distinction between personalized individuals and amorphous soldiers can only explain why, in military
circumstances, it may be legitimate to kill certain innocent human
beings even when they do not pose any immediate threat, despite the
fact that under normal circumstances it is entirely illegitimate to do so.
The anonymity factor cannot possibly explain why it should be legitimate to kill innocent anonymous combatants but illegitimate to kill
identified *guilty* combatants. At most, it paves the way towards arguing
that in war, as in civilian life, when a culprit is identified, he or she ought
to be lawfully tried and sentenced.[22]

As for this "due process" argument, it seems almost redundant to arti-
culate the distinction between terrorist leaders and civilian criminals.
Terrorists clearly operate within the military, rather than the civil, sphere.
Aside from the obviously warlike character of the activity in which terrorist
leaders are engaged, and for which they are pursued by their assassins, they
themselves do not deny the military nature of their deeds; indeed, they take
pride in it. More often than not, they bear militaristic titles of command.
Some even wear military-style uniforms or identifying dress, though they
remain irregulars, unprotected by the rules of war.[23] On no account can
they be considered civilian criminals, nor do they claim this status.

In a recent article on "Israel's Policy of Targeted Killing," Steven
David argues that the best moral justification for Israel's targeted killing
policy is retribution.[24] I doubt this is the case. Notwithstanding the
distinction between terrorists and civilian criminals, there is a strong
argument to be made against *punishing* terrorists by assassination in
defiance of due process. While David may be justified in suggesting that
terrorists deserve to suffer punishments which are proportional to their
crimes, one could still argue here that if a particular person is suspected
of a crime – whether civilian or military – and however grave it might
be, they ought to be brought to trial, though this is not always practic-
able. The legal option is usually resisted by armed forces on the grounds
that arresting terrorists can be extremely costly in terms of human life.[25]

---

[21] Ibid., p. 11, where he appears to acknowledge this fact.
[22] Gross takes up this argument in "Fighting by Other Means," pp. 350–68, 352–4.
[23] Walzer, *Just and Unjust Wars*, p. 181; Barzilai, "Islands of Silence," p. 10.
[24] Steven R. David, "Israel's Policy of Targeted Killing," *Ethics and International
      Affairs* 17 (1) (2003), pp. 111–26, p. 111.
[25] Gross, "Fighting by Other Means," p. 353.

As opposed to targeted killing, it will usually require ground forces to infiltrate hostile populations. As Israel's Supreme Court noted in its ruling on targeted assassinations: "Arrest, investigation, and trial are not means which can always be used. At times the possibility does not exist whatsoever; at times it involves a risk so great to the lives of the soldiers, that it is not required."[26] Additionally, trying terrorists in accordance with basic procedures of criminal law may create an unusual, and at times insurmountable, obstacle to indicting them.[27] Proving specific identity, affiliation and direct responsibility in accordance with strict legal procedures can prove particularly problematic when dealing with underground organizations. Gathering evidence, often available only on enemy territory, and enlisting witnesses to testify against terrorist suspects, will often be extraordinarily difficult and raise overwhelming hardship in proving guilt beyond reasonable doubt. These considerations, however, cannot, in and of themselves, justify discarding the rule of law. Indeed, similar considerations may at times obtain for police in criminal cases as well, and they cannot altogether outweigh considerations of procedural justice.[28]

Undeniably, a strong objection to purely *punitive* assassinations can be constructed along these lines. As Michael Gross points out, "At first glance, punitive assassination is nothing more than 'extra-judicial execution'. Like torture, it is unequivocally banned by UN conventions without regard for 'a state of war or threat of war, internal political instability or any other public emergency'."[29] Furthermore, offenders need not be civilian criminals in order to warrant the protections of due process: "the closest analogy to terrorists are war criminals, that is, participants in an armed conflict who violate humanitarian law. War criminals are judged by other states, usually the victors. But the point is that they are judged; a suspected war criminal cannot be summarily executed but must be captured and tried."[30] Gross attempts to bypass this prohibition on

---

[26] HCJ 769/02 [2005], Para. 40.
[27] Barzilai, "Islands of Silence," pp. 8–9: "arresting people in the territories, bringing them before courts in Israel, and indicting them, would have posed on the prosecution and the Israeli courts a great deal of burden of proof, as used in criminal procedures, and the need to respect basic procedures of due process of law ... Military courts in Israel have been subjected to the same legal procedures as civil courts."
[28] Gross, "Fighting by Other Means," p. 353.
[29] Gross, "Assassination," pp. 11–12.   [30] Ibid., pp. 12–13.

"extra-judicial execution" in the case of international terrorists, by suggesting that

Terrorists who admit their roles or whose criminal acts can be ascertained by other forms of evidence might be tried in absentia and executed. But this is no longer assassination, nor is it extra-judicial execution but the only sort of due process possible when hostile states harbor terrorists. Punishment in this way does what assassination can't: it circumvents the condition of anonymity that permits killing during war and allows named killing of specific individuals.[31]

Trying terrorists *in absentia* prior to their "execution" does, in a sense, re-import due process back on to the scene. Absentee trials would place targeted killing under the direct and close scrutiny of the judicial system, primarily the US and Israeli supreme courts. However, as far as punitive assassination is concerned, this solution remains fraught with difficulty. Obviously, this procedure would be unacceptable to the victims themselves and their compatriots, and as far as they are concerned these operations would remain essentially "extra-judicial" as there would be no *fair* trial involved. When dealing with terrorist groups, this perceived injustice might instigate acts of retribution just as assassinations not preceded by legal trials are said to do. Judging terrorists *in absentia* is also unlikely to circumvent international opposition of the type aimed at assassination operations, and with good reason. Absentee judgments raise issues concerning adequate defense (on the assumption that a defense lawyer would be appointed in the absence of the accused) as well as the principled belief that criminals, of whatever type, ought to be bodily *brought* to trial. Construing targeting killing as executing a death sentence is somewhat cynical in view of the fact that the penalty is decreed by the enemy's court in the absence of the accused. It also leaves open possible objections along the lines raised in opposition to the death penalty in general.

Such objections may relate to, for instance, the possibility of wrongful conviction and the irreversibility of capital punishment. In the case of targeted killing, even when a terrorist himself admits responsibility for the crimes attributed to him, as is often the case, there is always a danger of mistaking an innocent man for the appropriate target and killing the wrong person by mistake. This is far from a frequent occurrence, but it has been known to happen. In January 1974, Israel's Mossad attempted

[31] Ibid., p. 13.

to target Ali Hassan Salameh, the mastermind of the massacre at the 1972 Olympics, but instead mistakenly killed a Moroccan waiter, Ahmed Boushiki, in Lillehammer, Norway.[32] Moreover, even when a target is accurately identified, military agents can accidentally hit the wrong man. Trials matter, even in wartime, *inter alia* as a means of avoiding mistakes and preventing harm to innocents, as far as is humanely possible. However, trials are not required in order to carry out military operations, despite the regrettable fact that such operations often harm civilians and at times mis-identify the appropriate target. The fact that some targeted assassinations have been off the mark does not de-legitimize them, any more than mistaken targets in conventional military attacks de-legitimize conventional warfare.

One tragically memorable wartime mistake of this kind occurred in 1944 when the RAF set out to bomb Gestapo headquarters in Copenhagen, Denmark, but accidentally hit a hospital, killing scores of children.[33] I doubt this tragic mistake would lead anyone to doubt that bombing enemy headquarters is a legitimate act of war.[34] Rare mistakes in identifying a military target do not render acts of war unjustifiable.

The appropriate rebuttal to the "due process" argument is clearly acknowledged by Gross, and it concerns the direct character of prevention: "Assassinating terrorists, however, is not the same as punishing terrorists for prior misdeeds. Defensive assassination targets individuals in order to prevent imminent harm."[35] Targeted killing is not primarily a form of punishment. Purely punitive, or vengeful, action cannot be construed as self-preservation or self-defense, or defended along these lines. Punishment, even in the face of the most diabolical crimes against humanity, ought optimally to be pursued by due process of law, as it was, for the most part, regarding Nazi criminals in the aftermath of the Second World War. Assassinating terrorists, however, is rarely purely

---

[32] Aside from the identity issue, this case also involved the violation of a third party's sovereignty in peacetime, which I would be more than reluctant to defend. In contrast, this chapter defends a policy of targeted killing in the course of an ongoing militant struggle.

[33] Netanyahu, *Fighting Terrorism*, p. xxi; Netanyahu, *Terrorism*, p. 9.

[34] Another argument against the death penalty warns against a state's legal system killing "in cold blood." This type of opposition to the death penalty cannot apply within military contexts in which states' killing is considered legitimate and is in any case a daily matter of fact.

[35] Gross, "Assassination," p. 11.

punitive or vengeful. Certainly it ought never to be so. It is essentially neither capital nor any other form of punishment. It is centrally motivated, *inter alia*, by the prevention of further terrorist strikes rather than by merely the desire to punish for past deeds.[36] Prior offenses serve to a large extent as an indication of future intentions rather than as sufficient justification for penal action. Israel's Supreme Court ruling was clear on this point: "a civilian taking a direct part in hostilities one single time, or sporadically, who later detaches himself from that activity, is a civilian who, starting from the time he detached himself from that activity, is entitled to protection from attack. He is not to be attacked for the hostilities which he committed in the past."[37]

Assassination cannot be defended as an alternative to a judicial process of trying and sentencing offenders. That is indeed a job for a court of law rather than an army. However, targeted killing in the course of an ongoing low-intensity war of attrition against terrorist groups is primarily a form of combat rather than pure punishment or revenge; as such, it need not comply with the procedural requirements for trying those accused of crimes committed in the past. Targeting arch-terrorists within the context of an ongoing struggle is employed as part of a wider attempt to weed out terrorism; that is, to repulse rather than punish terrorists and harboring states. Undeniably, this objective is at times accompanied by other motives, such as personal or national vengeance, pacifying collective outrage, or punishment. This, however, is equally true of many acts of conventional warfare sincerely undertaken in self-defense. Defensive wars are often accompanied by feelings of rage, vengefulness or penal intent, none of which is taken as de-legitimizing their defensive justification.

In view of the mortal peril posed by terrorists, pursuing and assassinating militantly active self-professed terrorist leaders, with the clear intent of impeding further incursions, is a preventive measure of self-defense, whatever the emotions or politics which accompany this goal happen to be. Certainly, pre-emptive anti-terrorist strikes, including those which involve assassination, ought to be looked upon as acts of

---

[36] Barzilai, "Islands of Silence," pp. 7–8, critically scans Israel's targeted killing operations, stating clearly that, in all cases, efficiency – i.e. the prevention of further terror attacks – was a primary consideration in carrying out all such operations.

[37] HCJ 769/02 [2005], Para. 39.

self-preservation, at least to the extent that killing off-duty innocent soldiers in conventional wars can be regarded as such.

The normative status of terrorist targets is neither on a par with the status of conventional soldiers nor comparable with that of civilian criminals. While it is difficult to specify precise limits for distinguishing between irregular combat and some forms of criminal activity, such as organized crime, I think it is safe to say that the type of organization discussed here – those dedicated to an ongoing violent struggle with Israel or the US – are not civilian criminal organizations. In these cases, at least, Fletcher and Waldron are right, that "when it comes to terrorism, we know it when we see it."[38]

As for military status, we saw that the relevant rules, those agreed on at the Hague and Geneva conventions, supply little guidance about how to proceed against terrorists.[39] The Hague and Geneva conventions, one may recall, stipulate the conditions under which combatants are entitled to the war rights of soldiers, specifically the right to prisoner of war (POW) status when captured. According to the Hague Convention of 1907, in order to be entitled to POW status, fighters must wear a "fixed distinctive emblem recognizable at a distance" and must "carry arms openly."[40] The category of those who do not abide by these rules remains something of a "no man's land," in that it is not clear what rules, if any, apply. Irregulars who operate within para-military organizations (whether terrorists or otherwise) and confront states, clearly function within a military context. Nonetheless, they do not live up to the criteria specified in the war conventions – they conceal their weapons and disguise themselves as civilians – and thus fail to secure the status and protections accorded by the rules of war.

Precisely this vagueness in international law, as well as the terrorists' failing to live up to its requirements, led Israeli Supreme Court Justice Aharon Barak to shy away from directly defining Palestinian terrorists as "combatants" as opposed to "civilians." In his judgment on targeted

---

[38] Waldron, "Terrorism," pp. 5–35, esp. p. 6; Fletcher, "The Problem of Defining Terrorism," p. 2.

[39] Fletcher, *Romantics at War*, p. 95.

[40] Hague Convention, Annex to the Convention, Section I, "On Belligerents," Chapter I, "The Qualifications of Belligerents," Art. 1. See also Fletcher, *Romantics at War*, p. 106; Walzer, *Just and Unjust Wars*, p. 182. Two further requirements of combatants specified in this article of the Hague Convention are that they form part of a chain of command and abide by the rules and customs of war.

assassination, Justice Barak preferred to reach the "unlawful combatant" definition via a slightly different avenue. Rather than regarding terrorists as combatants acting unlawfully, Barak insists that according to existing (rather than desirable) international law, terrorists or irregulars do not by their belligerent actions lose their civilian status. However, as civilians who illegally participate directly in the hostilities, they lose the protections accorded to civilians in wartime, and are therefore, as Barak puts it: "Civilians who are Unlawful combatants."[41] Here's how he does it:

The basic approach is thus as follows: a civilian – that is, a person who does not fall into the category of combatant – must refrain from directly participating in hostilities ... A civilian who violates that law and commits acts of combat does not lose his status as a civilian, but as long as he is taking a direct part in hostilities he does not enjoy – during that time – the protection granted to a civilian. He is subject to the risks of attack like those to which a combatant is subject, without enjoying the rights of a combatant, e.g. those granted to a prisoner of war. True, his status is that of a civilian, and he does not lose that status while he is directly participating in hostilities. However, he is a civilian performing the function of a combatant. As long as he performs that function, he is subject to the risks which that function entails and ceases to enjoy the protection granted to a civilian from attack ... That is the law regarding *unlawful combatants*. As long as he preserves his status as a civilian – that is, as long as he does not become part of the army – but takes part in combat, he ceases to enjoy the protection granted to the civilian, and is subject to the risks of attack just like a combatant, without enjoying the rights of a combatant as a prisoner of war. Indeed, terrorists who take part in hostilities are not entitled to the protection granted to civilians. True, terrorists participating in hostilities do not cease to be civilians, but by their acts they deny themselves the aspect of their civilian status which grants them protection from military attack. Nor do they enjoy the rights of combatants, e.g. the status of prisoners of war.[42]

---

[41] HCJ 769/02 [2005], Para. 28.
[42] HCJ 769/02, Para. 31. Emphasis on *unlawful combatants*, added. See also Paras. 27–31 for Barak's characterization of "civilians who are unlawful combatants". Recall that according to Protocol I added to the Geneva Conventions, 1977, Chapter II: Civilians and Civilian Population: Art. 51(3) states clearly that: "(3) Civilians shall enjoy the protection afforded by this section, unless and for such time as they take a direct part in hostilities." The Israeli court discusses the term "direct part in hostilities" at length in Para. 32038 of HCJ 769/02 [2005].

I argued that terrorists, or irregulars, are unlawful combatants to whom no conventional rules apply. On the account offered in the previous chapter, while no distinction between lawful and unlawful combatants is explicitly laid down within international law, the status of lawless combatants can be deduced negatively from the positive definition of soldiers eligible for POW status under the Hague Convention of 1907.

Is terrorism analogous with war crimes? In so far as it is, assassination policies can be justified as a form of self-defense so long as (and only to the extent that) it is seriously directed at preventing future violations of humanitarian law within an ongoing struggle, rather than merely punishing prior transgressions.

Judicial review

In Israel, the power to authorize targeted killings lies ultimately in the hands of the Prime Minister and the Defense Minister. A certain lack of clarity surrounds the procedures that lead up to the final order, and certainly they are not specified in law, but some general details are familiar to the Israeli public. In each instance, the Prime Minister is expected to secure his Defense Minister's formal consent to any particular operation. In practice, while the balance of power between the Prime Minister and the Defense Minister leans towards the former, the significant role played by the Defense Minister and the military in this decision-making process must not be underestimated. In most, if not all, cases, the Defense Minister is personally involved in the decision, as are the Chief of Staff, the Commander of the Air Force, and other military commanders in charge of planning, as well as high-ranking military intelligence officers. Often, the Prime Minister will consult other members of Cabinet, although not necessarily the government as a whole. At times, a proposed targeting operation will be brought to a vote, though this too is often held in a restricted forum of selected ministers. Such decisions are said to rely heavily on military intelligence and expertise and give considerable, even decisive, weight to the advice and opinions of high-ranking officers. In some cases, the executive decision authorizes the killing of a specific target, leaving the military in charge of the specific time and place. More sensitive cases (like the assassination of Sheik Ahmed Yassin) appear to require an additional last-minute authorization from the Prime Minister.

In view of this questionable decision-making procedure, one further argument calls for the judicial supervision of this administrative power. It does not necessarily assert that terrorists must under all circumstances be brought to trial but, rather, cautions against placing the authority to assassinate in the hands of a small group of practically unaccountable members of the executive. This argument applies to both punitive and preventative action and is perhaps best stated by analogy, not with punishing criminals or with killing soldiers, but with the proper attitude and course of action that ought to be adopted towards serial criminals. Why, for instance, do we not want to have police death squads? The answer has nothing to do with violating the rights of serial "bad guys." They may have no entitlement not to be killed as a preventive measure (given plausible background assumptions concerning their unquestionable guilt and certain qualifications). The point is rather that we do not trust the police to make the necessary decisions in all cases. This is a kind of secondary argument against targeted killing (which does not make it any weaker): even if in some cases there is nothing wrong with the killing itself, we want institutional guarantees against abuse and the like. Similar considerations to those which prevent us from supporting police death squads may apply in the case of assassinating terrorists as well. The problem is not their right to life, but rather that we might not have enough confidence in military and political personnel to entrust them with making such crucial decisions. This line of thought is, first, a very good general argument against absolute power and its effects, but it also represents a plausible suspicion in the relevant cases.[43]

This is possibly the most serious worry concerning government-instigated targeted killing and probably the most difficult to contend with. Nevertheless, it can also be dealt with; certainly, it is often outweighed. While potential abuse is admittedly a strong reason to avoid making targeted killings legal, it is doubtful whether it is a conclusive argument against their moral permissibility in all, or even most, cases which involve terrorism. At most, it suggests that such operations ought to be placed under some type of judicial (i.e. non-military and non-political) scrutiny and supervision. This is the position adopted by Israeli jurist Gad Barzilai.[44] Admittedly, while judicial oversight might remove the

---

[43] I am most grateful to David Enoch for raising this objection and formulating it with such precision, as well as for the successful accompanying analogy.

[44] Barzilai, "Islands of Silence," p. 10.

accusation of "extra-judicial execution" in the literal sense, the process would continue to be suspect and would nonetheless remain "execution without trial," at least without trial by due process. Still, legal constraints would prevent decisions being taken on life and death issues solely by an exclusive group that may abuse its power or make fatal mistakes. Generals may be dominated by militaristic conceptions. Politicians may be insincere, or misuse their power to advance partisan political ends, rather than having security-oriented goals, under the guise of preventing terror attacks on civilian populations. Targeted killing might also be misused by politicians in order to pacify an outraged terrorized public, or adopted out of sheer vindictiveness. Naturally, any *national* judicial body would never be entirely clear of such suspicions. Judges, like politicians and military personnel, may be influenced by public opinion. Judges are not infallible, and they are potentially biased in favor of their nation's cause. The Supreme Court in the US, and increasingly in Israel, is itself a politicized institution.[45] Notwithstanding these observations, placing decisions concerning targeted killings under judicial supervision would presumably mitigate the dangers of misuse and introduce some level of accountability and transparency. In the case of targeting particular terrorists, the rationale of procedural restrictions, along with the concerns they are designed to circumvent, would, however, presumably be outweighed by concern for innocent human life in those cases in which the danger posed by the potential target is imminent. In such cases, the fear of abuse warranting judicial review would be superseded by the emergency situation (with the proviso that the executive body must be retrospectively accountable for showing good cause for its belief that the threat was indeed imminent and could be removed only by assassination). It is also plausible to argue that certain types of operational considerations (e.g. an isolated opportunity to strike down a life-threatening terrorist in a particular place at an immediate point in time), would justify an unauthorized assassination that could be judicially scrutinized only retrospectively.

Most targeted killings, admittedly, are not carried out in the face of immediate danger, nor do operational difficulties always entail immediate action. A direct appeal to "self-defense" as warrant for targeting wanted terrorists may still be justified even where the threat is less than outright and present, so long as the danger is nonetheless clear and

---

[45] See, for instance, Barzilai's implied criticism of Israel's February 2002 Supreme Court decision not to interfere in IDF's targeted killing policy, "Islands of Silence," p. 5.

imminent.[46] The right to life can reasonably be invoked as a prevailing consideration, not only in the classic case of intercepting a "ticking bomb," but also where the potential target is more than likely to instigate or command an attack in the near future. In such cases, where the confronted threat falls short of immediacy, proposed assassinations could reasonably be required to undergo (swift) judicial scrutiny designed to establish whether their objectives were truly defensive rather than purely punitive, vengeful, or otherwise politically motivated.

It is interesting to note here that Israel is particularly alert to the dangers of non-supervised attacks in cases which involve potential harm to civilians. In its most recent confrontation with Hizbullah in Lebanon, Israel made use of legally trained officers to supervise Israel's bombardment. This placed at least some legal, though not judicial, supervision and restriction on the carrying out of administrative power in wartime. Throughout the attacks on Hizbullah within civilian areas in Lebanon, each individual target, as well as the type of weapon to be used, was reviewed by an IDF expert in humanitarian law.[47]

Be that as it may, it is important to note that imposing specifically judicial restrictions on anti-terrorist operations, however feasible and

---

[46] See Barzilai's example of legitimate elimination, "Islands of Silence," p. 6, n2, which implies that the danger need not be absolutely immediate, as in the case of a so-called ticking bomb, but must be imminent, as in the case of an active terrorist commander who continues to instigate dangerous terrorist attacks.

[47] UN General Assembly, Report by Philip Alston, UN Special Rapporteur, October 2, 2006: http://mineaction.org/downloads/Emine%20Policy%20Pages/ Human%20Rights%20Council%20Docs/Israel%20Lebanon%20Special %20Rapporteurs%20Report%20on%20Res.%2060%20251.pdf. Paragraph 35: "Both for principled and pragmatic reasons, Israel set certain limits on the conduct of its hostilities with Hezbollah. The mission was informed by IDF representatives that Israel followed its practice of drawing up lists of potential targets, with each individual target, as well as the type of weapon to be used, being reviewed by an IDF expert in humanitarian law."

In such cases, apparently, the procedure is as follows: When a commander in the field or near the field identifies a target which he wants attacked, a target from which he is taking fire, or from which he sees rockets being fired, or which intelligence gives him info on Hezbollah presence; he radios details to Jerusalem, at which time legal officials in IDF HQ or Ministry of Defense scrutinize request in terms of international humanitarian law and give approval or not. That decision is subsequently communicated back to field commander in (hopefully) a timely manner.

I am very grateful to Jeremy Waldron for drawing my attention to this UN report.

justified in the abstract, would place targeted killing out of step with all other forms of military action, for reasons that remain curious. Military and political personnel are normally authorized to make a wide range of on-the-spot decisions which include, for instance, waging war, embarking on particular battles, and a vast array of tactical and strategic decisions made and carried out within belligerent situations. These decisions are also rarely carried out under circumstances of immediate and dire peril. Any such decision, which is free of judicial review, will usually affect the lives of numerous individuals, most of whom are innocent. The unsupervised authority vested in generals and politicians in all such situations is subject to potential abuse and misuse in a variety of ways not dissimilar to those which raise concerns vis-à-vis targeting terrorists, and on a far larger scale. Nevertheless, in the name of "national security" or personal safety, we resign ourselves to these negative side effects and remain satisfied with retaining only the power to punish gross moral digressions in military decision making and action (such as massacres or other extreme violations of human rights), if they are uncovered. It is puzzling that the lives of terrorists in particular warrant calls for extraordinary judicial protection which is not imposed on other types of military action in which the lives of innumerable innocent individuals are at stake. If there is nothing about terrorists that warrants preferential treatment, as I argued in the last section, then there is also no justification for placing decisions concerning their targeting under judicial review, which is not imposed on any other type of military decisions.

In the following section I argue that the targeted killing of terrorists is closely akin in its outward form to the revolutionary tactic of political assassination, but that it is not tantamount to it. Both are types of extrajudicial killing and they have been condemningly compared.[48] While targeted killing shares key normative features with acts of political assassination, I argue that when it is employed in the process of combating terror it exhibits additional moral qualities that serve to distinguish between these two types of assassination in favor of its anti-terrorist form.

Political assassination

As we saw in Chapter 2, Michael Walzer's *Just and Unjust Wars* supplies a detailed analysis of revolutionary political assassination, which

---

[48] Barzilai, "Islands of Silence," pp. 2–3.

Walzer sharply distinguishes from both guerrilla warfare and from terrorism, which is strictly defined. Recall that according to Walzer, assassination is clearly distinguishable from the type of random murder which usually characterizes contemporary terrorist strikes, as it necessarily involves "the drawing of a line that we will have little difficulty recognizing as the political parallel of the line that marks off combatants from non-combatants."[49] When acting in the capacity of assassins, revolutionaries draw a moral distinction,

> between people who can and people who cannot be killed. The first category is not composed of men and women bearing arms, immediately threatening by virtue of their military training and commitment. It is composed instead of officials, the political agents of regimes, thought to be oppressive. Such people are of course protected by the war convention and by positive international law. Characteristically (and not foolishly), lawyers have frowned on assassination, and political officials have been assigned to the class of non-military persons, who are never the legitimate objects of attack. But this assignment only partially represents our common moral judgments. For we judge the assassin by his victim, and when the victim is Hitler-like in character, we are likely to praise the assassin's work, though we still do not call him a soldier.[50]

On the other hand, where the judgments of particular political assassins differ from our own, the "political assassins are simply murderers, exactly like the killers of ordinary citizens. The case is not the same with soldiers, who are not judges politically at all and who are called murderers only when they kill noncombatants."[51] Unlike soldiers, then, our moral assessment of political assassins necessarily hinges on a (possibly biased) moral evaluation of the justice of their cause.

What are the normative implications of the comparison between political assassination and state policies of targeting terrorist leaders? Comparative scrutiny of the two lethal cases suggests that targeted killing shares certain morally favorable aspects with the phenomenon of political assassination without partaking of its normative shortcomings.

Walzer argues that the strength of political assassination as a revolutionary tactic stems from the parallel between the "soldier versus citizens" distinction, upheld by conventions of war, and the political "officials versus citizens" distinction, upheld by revolutionary assassins.[52] Conventional laws of war, the "political codes" of assassins and state-initiated targeted

---

[49] Walzer, *Just and Unjust Wars*, p. 198.   [50] Ibid., pp. 199–200.
[51] Ibid., pp. 200–1.   [52] Ibid., p. 200.

killings all share the following feature celebrated by Walzer: they all *aim* at their victims and refrain from targeting certain categories of people whom they regard as immune from attack. None kills indiscriminately and, for all three, private citizens retain their right to life. Political assassination and targeted killing are also similar in the following respect which, as opposed to the above, sets them apart from conventional warfare: they aim specifically at those who are perceived as guilty rather than targeting anonymous groups of soldiers functioning as representatives of the enemy power. We saw that this distinguishing feature serves as a source of opposition to assassination. I argue, however, that with regard to terrorists, personal identity and guilt point to assassination having the moral advantage over the anonymous killing of innocent soldiers. Walzer's paradox, whereby we "might even feel easier about killing officials than about killing soldiers, since the state rarely conscripts its political, as it does its military agents,"[53] applies with far greater force in the case of targeted terrorists.

Although officials choose their officialdom as a career, while soldiers are often conscripted recruits, we rarely feel at ease with political assassination. This moral discomfort in the face of political assassination stems largely from two of its distinct features, identified by Walzer, which do not obtain in the case of killing soldiers. First, soldiers target other soldiers, while revolutionary assassins target non-military personnel – civilian officials and political representatives of the regimes they regard as oppressive, who stand clearly under the protection of war conventions and international law.[54] Secondly, soldiers and officials differ significantly in this respect: "The threatening character of the soldier's activity is a matter of fact; the unjust or oppressive character of the official's activity is a matter of political judgment. For this reason the political code has never attained the same status as the war convention. Nor can assassins claim any rights, even on the basis of the strictest adherence to its principles."[55] These two characteristic aspects of political assassination mitigate any intuitive (albeit paradoxical) ease with the assassination of particular individuals as opposed to wholesale killing on the battlefield. Neither disturbing feature, however, exists in the case of targeted killing policies aimed exclusively at terrorists.

[53] Ibid., p. 200. [54] Ibid., pp. 199–200.
[55] Ibid., p. 200.

In the first place, while political assassination is carried out against
civilian officials who are protected by war conventions and international
law, targeted terrorists are, by their own admission, not only combatants
but belligerent leaders: they are the instigators, organizers, and commanders of an armed struggle. So, like officials but unlike soldiers, they
are willing volunteers rather than conscripted recruits. Unlike officials,
however, the role they have chosen to take on is a militant, rather than
civilian, one.

The second morally problematic aspect of political assassination,
which sets it apart from killing soldiers (whether on or off the battlefield), is also far less bothersome in the context of combating terrorism.
As opposed to assessing the actions of ordinary soldiers, which are
threatening by nature (though not necessarily immediately so), our
moral assessment of a political assassination requires taking a substantive stand on the political struggle engaged in by the revolutionaries.
The unjust or oppressive character of the assassinated official's activity
is, as Walzer states, "a matter of political judgment" rather than one
that poses a direct and unquestionable threat.[56] So, while we judge
soldiers' actions as acts of self-defense in the face of indisputable
danger (so long as they kill other soldiers), "we judge the assassin by
his victim."[57] Killing combatants in war is understood as self-defense
within the context of a threatening situation and is not judged politically. It is therefore permissible to kill enemy soldiers regardless of the
identities of those who kill or are killed and of our normative evaluation
of the battle itself or the war of which it is a part.[58] In contrast, the justice
of political assassination, which does not confront a direct threat, is
always context-dependent. As Walzer puts it, "when the victim is Hitler-
like in character, we are likely to praise the assassin's work, though we
still do not call him a soldier."[59] Since most political assassinations are

---

[56] Ibid., pp. 200–1.   [57] Ibid., p. 200.

[58] For example, we do not hold soldiers of the Third Reich personally responsible
   for killing other soldiers on the Russian front, despite the fact that they were
   engaged in an unjustifiable war of aggression. It should perhaps be noted that Jeff
   McMahan recently argued to the contrary regarding soldiers' culpability for their
   actual participation in unjust wars. Jeff McMahan, "Just Cause for War," *Ethics
   and International Affairs* 19 (3) (December 2005). While noteworthy, I doubt it
   has any bearing on the limited issue at hand.

[59] Walzer, *Just and Unjust Wars*, p. 199.

not morally clear-cut, "Hitler-like" cases, we justifiably deny political assassination the status of legitimate combat accorded internationally to wartime killing.

However, when the targets of assassination policies are arch-terrorists rather than civil officials, the situation regains the threatening nature that characterizes and legitimizes killing soldiers in war. While targeted terrorists may not always pose an immediate threat to life or limb (although they often do), they always pose a clear and direct danger, at least to the degree posed by soldiers when they are caught off-guard. It is quite implausible to regard the threat posed by terrorist instigators, organizers, and commanders, in charge of planning, ordering, and carrying out strikes against civilians, as less obvious and imminent than the threat posed by a soldier while showering, relaxing, sunbathing, or lighting a cigarette.[60]

Furthermore, Walzer's observation that the moral evaluation of any particular assassination hinges on a substantive judgment of the victim's role (the degree of its oppressive or unjust nature), as well as of the political context, does not apply with equal force in the case of terrorism. In contrast to political assassination, the moral evaluation of targeted terrorists requires no case-by-case political judgment of the victim and his cause. Terrorists are targeted for the means they employ in the course of their struggle rather than for the ends they serve. Judging the assassin by his victim requires only taking a stand against terrorism as an illegitimate form of combat, while all other specific political debates over substantive issues are left open by this basic moral stance. One can condemn terrorism and still support Palestinians in their struggle to pry additional concessions from Israel. One can feel sympathy for developing nations and attribute a large part of their plight to Western economic exploitation and other global policies, without condemning President Bush's pursuit of bin Laden.

Admittedly, the condemnation of terrorism, regardless of its root cause, is in itself a moral and political judgment. It is one which we saw Ted Honderich and others clearly reject.[61] Nonetheless, judging terrorists and their assassins requires a far more basic moral judgment than the complex political one involved in evaluating individual

---

[60] Walzer, *Just and Unjust Wars*, p. 142.   [61] Honderich, *After the Terror*, passim.

instances of political assassination.[62] It involves taking a moral stand on terrorist tactics rather than on the political cause they serve. Unlike that of civil officials, the unjust or oppressive character of the terrorist's activity is not a matter of political judgment in the narrow sense. It does not require an evaluation of conflicting political demands or a renunciation of the terrorists' cause, which one may even support. Assessing the oppressive character of a terrorist's activity (as opposed to that of a civil official) involves political judgment only to the extent that it requires taking a moral stand against the deliberate, indiscriminate, random killing of non-combatants. Here the assassins' judgment of their victim is, or should be, widely shared by liberals. As I argued in Chapter 2, terrorism by definition defies a basic standard of Western morality which fundamentally forbids the intentional killing of innocent civilians and the arbitrary use of innocent lives as a mere means towards attaining political ends.[63] To the extent that we judge assassins by their victims, as Walzer suggests, it is questionable whether we can consistently oppose terrorism and simultaneously renounce the assassins' judgment in these instances.

For all these reasons it is difficult to confront state policies which target arch-terrorists solely on moral grounds without adopting an ethical approach which defends terrorism and terrorists outright. To this extent Ted Honderich's controversial *After the Terror* is quite correct, as well as refreshingly candid, and in fact more consistent than much of the contemporary opposition to killing terrorists. One cannot condemn the US and Israel's "war on terror" on purely moral grounds (as opposed to questioning its expediency in reducing terrorism)

---

[62] For an explanation (rather than an analogy) of what I take to be a basic moral judgment as opposed to a complex political one, think of the only plausible liberal verdict on Nazism. The condemnation seems straightforward and unavoidable enough to be dubbed "basic." It is independent of complex political questions on which liberals could reasonably differ, such as whether the Germans were in fact wronged at Versailles; whether they were indeed unduly suffering, as Hitler claimed; or whether they had any justifiable grievances against their Slavic neighbors to the East. Perhaps, as in the present case, it could be argued that some of their specific grievances against the Jews were justified – though I sincerely doubt this. The point is that, within liberalism, no moral debate whatsoever could arise about some of the Nazis' goals (say, conquering the world and exterminating entire groups of people), and no complex political judgment was required for assessing the means they employed.

[63] For the most obvious moral imperative which would clearly forbid this, see Kant, *Groundwork*, p. 96.

without justifying terrorism itself.[64] The justification of terrorism, in turn, can be attempted, as indeed it is by Honderich, only at the expense of rejecting much of modern Western thought and liberal morality.[65]

I will not reiterate the wrong involved in deliberately terrorizing civilians. Those who support terrorists will naturally oppose their assassination.[66] The present inquiry is directed at the common liberal conviction that condemns terrorism but questions, or categorically denounces, the targeted killing of its perpetrators. It remains to be seen whether pragmatic arguments can come to the aid of those who denounce terrorists but condemn their assassination in the same breath.

Efficiency arguments

The ethical controversy over targeted killing is rarely conducted, regardless of its estimated expediency. In the public political arena, both sides of the debate habitually enlist "military expertise" and empirical assessments of utility, which coincide with, and reinforce, their respective normative positions. Moral condemnation of targeted killing often goes hand in hand with the objection that such strikes are ineffective. Pragmatic assertions play a double role within the anti-assassination stance. They pose both independent grounds for rejecting assassination as well as supplementing non-utilitarian arguments against it. Specifically, opponents suggest that assassinations merely solicit acts of retaliation, and consequently that they ultimately escalate rather than diminish the level of conflict. Assassination, it is argued, deepens hostility and mistrust, which jeopardizes the chances of attaining peace between the warring parties,

---

[64] Honderich, *After the Terror*, passim, esp. pp. 115–51. As we saw in Chapter 2, Honderich explicitly justifies Palestinian terrorism against Israel (p. 150), and therefore naturally opposes any militant steps taken by Israel in response. His principled opposition to Israel's "war on terror" is consistently based on his justification of terrorism itself.

[65] Ibid., in general, but esp. pp. 46–51, 62, 81, 90. See my Chapter 2: Recall that Honderich's views involve discrediting many distinctions that are basic to these liberal philosophies, such as the relationship between intentions and consequences; deliberate action and unintentional effects; killing belligerents and killing innocent non-combatants; acts and omissions; and perfect and imperfect duties. Honderich, *After the Terror*, passim, but see esp. pp. 73–88, 97–9, 103. Many of these classic distinctions are also called into question in connection with terrorism by Derrida, in Borradori, *Philosophy*, p. 108.

[66] This is clear enough in Honderich's condemnation of Israel, *After the Terror*, p. 151.

thus not only enhancing but also prolonging the conflict.[67] Aside from the antagonism caused by the assassination itself, such operations often result in a non-negligible degree of collateral damage to the surrounding community. Targeted killing is thus regarded as inexpedient – as an ineffective means of reducing hostility – as well as immoral, because it often exceeds its target and kills innocent bystanders.

Correspondingly, proponents of targeting terrorists habitually cite evidence of its alleged expediency. Clearly, they admit, assassination does not annihilate terrorism in one fell swoop. No one argues that it presents an overall solution to terrorism. Those who support it believe, however, that assassinating terrorists is a successful means of reducing terrorist hostility, at least in the long run, as it acts both as a deterrent (rather than punishment) and as an impediment in the face of terrorist organizations and their leaders.[68] When taking the long-term consequences into account, proponents of assassination estimate that:

Such killings will weaken the terror organizations, cause demoralization among their members, force them to restrict their movements, and so on. The personal charisma or professional skills of the leaders and key figures of certain organizations are crucial to the success of their organizations, something that is especially true with regard to terror organizations that operate underground and with no clear institutional structure. It is reasonable to believe that killing such individuals will gradually make it harder for the terror machinery to function.[69]

Assessing the efficiency of assassination policies involves evaluating not only their long-term (rather than merely immediate) effects but also their psychological impact. It is a reasonable observation that terrorist leaders, as opposed to low-ranking terrorist perpetrators, do not always wish to die for their cause. They often conceal themselves in the midst of civilian populations and reposition themselves constantly when faced with personal danger. The consistent and vivid threat posed by their

---

[67] For example, Gross, "Fighting by Other Means," pp. 356–8; Gross, "Assassination," pp. 2–4, 10–11. These anti-assassination arguments are commonly voiced in the political sphere.

[68] See, for example, Benjamin Netanyahu's address to the US Congress on September 20, 2001, in Netanyahu, *Fighting Terrorism*, p. xxiii: "To win this war we must fight on many fronts. The most obvious one is direct military action against the terrorists themselves. Israel's policy of preemptively striking at those who seek to murder its people is, I believe, better understood today and requires no further elaboration."

[69] Statman, "Targeted Killing," p. 192; Statman, "The Morality of Assassination," p. 6.

enemy, which is waiting to pluck them out of any place, perhaps when they least expect it, presents a considerable emotional and practical obstacle. Wanted arch-terrorists do not go about their business as usual. Instead, they move around incessantly, hoping to confound their enemy, presumably at considerable cost to their missions and public image. Arresting such terrorists, as an alternative to attempting their assassination, is operationally difficult and costly in human life, and is unlikely to meet with the co-operation of local authorities. As Gross points out, "governments headed by the Palestinian authority or Taliban do not readily extradite suspected terrorists."[70] Since terrorists are combatants, and irregular ones at that, it is unwarranted to demand that any nation pay the high costs involved in apprehending them. Left to their own devices, however, there is every probability that terrorists will resume their activities. The threat of assassination is also intended to play a part in the calculations of state leaders harboring terrorists and supporting their organizations. Heads of state rarely aspire to become international outlaws on the run. For them in particular, the threat of assassination ought to serve as a considerable deterrent to sanctioning terrorism and supporting terrorist groups.

The counter-argument, once again, concerns the potential costs of assassination policies. Particular assassinations are sometimes followed by further terrorist attacks (which may or may not have been carried out otherwise) and which are always described by their instigators as retaliation for the assassination of their brethren. Whether these strikes are indeed the outcome of any particular assassination is always an issue of contention. While policy-makers often deny this, opponents of assassination view subsequent terror attacks as proof of the policy's failure and of the role they attribute to assassination in the continued cycle of violence.[71] In the long run, they argue, assassination (alongside the collateral damage that often accompanies it) contributes to feelings of mistrust, humiliation, and festering resentment within the victim's community, which in turn damage prospects for attaining an eventual peaceful resolution to the hostilities.[72] These objections represent two

---

[70] Gross, "Assassination," p. 12.

[71] For example Gross, "Fighting by Other Means," pp. 356–7. For Gross, such feelings of resentment on the part of the targets' compatriots are tied to the perfidious and treacherous means, particularly the use of local collaborators, often employed by the assassin-state (most notably Israel).

[72] For example, ibid., p. 359.

types of more general utilitarian consideration for fighting limited wars
and excluding certain forms of combat. These are concerned "not only
with reducing the total amount of suffering, but also with holding open
the possibility of peace and the resumption of pre-war activities ... And
if that is to be possible, the war must be fought, as Sidgwick says, so as
to avoid 'the danger of provoking reprisals and of causing bitterness
that will long outlast' the fighting."[73] Some opponents of targeted killing admit, however, that judging its efficiency is extremely problematic:
"Thwarted attacks remain unobserved, and counterfactuals – attacks
that would have been launched had there never been a firm assassination
policy – are difficult to gauge."[74] It is difficult for anyone to establish
absolutely the facts of the matter concerning the utility of targeting
individual terrorists. The factual argument about the expediency of
assassinating terrorists clearly cannot be resolved by philosophers, but
it cannot be avoided either. This severely complicates the moral issue, as it
requires tackling it without resolving the practical questions to everyone's
satisfaction.[75] It is worth pointing out, however, as Daniel Statman does,
that "Morally speaking, war is a risky business. Still, on just war theory,
one is allowed to use lethal measures if there are good reasons to believe
they will be efficient in self-defense."[76] So, according to just-war theory,
we need not be absolutely sure that the strategy we employ is beneficial to
our self-defense; we need only employ it in good faith on the assumption
that it is, and show good cause for this belief.

Furthermore, in the absence of wholly conclusive factual evidence as
to its efficiency, targeted killing has at least one definite consequentialist
benefit: namely, it carries with it a far lower risk of immoral results than
any other available military strategy. On the assumption that we must
take some course of militant action against terrorism, assassination is,
at the very least, our "best shot." From any moral perspective which
takes utility into account, this advantage is not negligible. As Statman

---

[73] Walzer, *Just and Unjust Wars*, p. 132 (with reference to Henry Sidgwick, *The Elements of Politics*, London: Macmillan, 2000, p. 264).

[74] Gross, "Fighting by Other Means," p. 357; Gross, "Assassination," p. 3.

[75] It is no news that the vagueness of the future accounts for a plurality of opinions, even among those who might agree in principle. See Berlin, *The Crooked Timber of Humanity*, pp. 1–19, esp. pp. 12, 14, 17. This is one isolated point with which even Ted Honderich might agree. See Honderich, *After the Terror*, pp. 144–5, 146: "What makes it hard to see the right thing is not so much seeing ... the moral truth. What makes it hard is seeing how the world will turn out."

[76] Statman, "The Morality of Assassination," p. 7.

comments, "while assassination does involve some moral risk, it also has a chance of achieving better results from a moral point of view."[77] Even Gross observes that:

In an age when low intensity war is increasingly replacing conventional armed conflict, pinpoint attacks against combatants are preferred to indiscriminate assaults on mixed populations of civilians and soldiers, assassination should be particularly attractive ... For policy makers fearful of extensive civilian casualties, tactics like assassination or "targeted killing" exert a certain appeal if they can avoid the widespread devastation associated with conventional war.[78]

Later, Gross acknowledges that nations fighting terrorists who intentionally target non-combatants "are faced with very difficult questions of appropriate response. The stronger power cannot, in good conscience, target non-combatants on the other side ... In this context, assassination has much to offer. It avoids the pitfalls of disproportionality, nondiscrimination (by targeting only the terror suspect) and the fear of violating noncombatant immunity."[79] On the assumption that it achieves at least some of its goals, assassination is preferable to other forms of combat because it succeeds to a large extent (though admittedly not entirely) in sparing civilian lives. It never deliberately targets the innocent.

Admittedly, as in any other assault on military targets in war, a certain degree of unintentional collateral damage to civilians must be expected. This is, in fact, particularly complicated by the aforementioned fact that terrorists habitually choose to conceal themselves in the midst of civilian populations. Civilian fatalities are regrettably predictable when, as is often the case, targeting operations are attempted from the air. Such fatalities, which have been the source of condemnation by human rights groups can, however, be justified by appealing to the Doctrine of Double Effect, which permits the performance of certain acts of war even though they are likely to have evil consequences – specifically, the killing of non-combatants.[80] At the very least, the stringency of the prohibition on killing non-combatants in wartime does not apply to unintended effects. As Michael Walzer puts this: "There are, after all, unintended deaths and legitimate military operations, and the absolute rule against attacking

---

[77] Statman, "The Morality of Assassination," p. 7; see also Statman, "Targeted Killing," p. 193.
[78] Gross, "Assassination," p. 1.   [79] Ibid., pp. 1, 13.
[80] On the Doctrine of Double Effect see Walzer, *Just and Unjust Wars*, pp. 151–9; and pp. 257, 277, 280, 283, 317, 321.

civilians does not apply."[81] Such indirect consequences of war can be justified, under certain circumstances, in so far as they are incurred only as a sincerely unintended by-product of an assault on a morally legitimate target (e.g. enemy soldiers, military supplies, etc.), and that this target was aimed at narrowly, in an attempt to avoid negative consequences. Furthermore, the harm done to civilians must be proportionate to military achievements; that is, the negative consequences of the operation must be balanced by its contribution to the overall military goal.[82] Finally, we might, as Michael Walzer suggests, wish to be more zealous in defending civilians and add the further requirement that the attacker must take care to minimize civilian casualties, if possible, even at some risk to his own soldiers. In keeping with this additional proviso, Walzer defines his more stringent version of the principle of double effect as follows: "The intention of the actor is good, that is, he aims narrowly at the acceptable effect; the evil effect is not one of his ends, nor is it a means to his ends, and, aware of the evil involved, he seeks to minimize it, accepting costs to himself."[83] But as even Walzer recognizes, "there is a limit to the risks that we require ... War necessarily places civilians in danger; that is another aspect of its hellishness."[84]

I argued in the former sections that avowed terrorists are legitimate wartime targets. Furthermore, I argued in this section that there are reasonable, albeit inconclusive, grounds for the belief that targeting terrorists is conducive to self-defense. Certainly, incurring civilian casualties does not set these operations apart from most other acts of war, such as bombing military targets, or destroying military supplies or ammunition reserves. On the contrary, targeted killing fulfills the requirement of aiming narrowly at an acceptable target, to the very highest degree. Achieving the direct effect (i.e. hitting the target and no one else), is clearly the agent's single intent. Targeted killing is not unique, nor is it de-legitimized by the fact that it results in civilian casualties.

Moreover, targeted killing cannot be accused of inflicting a degree of harm to civilians that is disproportionate in relation to the operation's military objective. The danger posed by an assassination (or a

---

[81] Walzer, *Just and Unjust Wars*, p. 156.   [82] Ibid., pp. 153–5.
[83] Ibid., p. 155.   [84] Ibid., p. 156.

succession of assassinations) to members of the surrounding community, is necessarily smaller than the risk faced by non-combatants caught in the midst of any conventional type of military operation. Civilians are placed at far lower risk when an enemy air force aims at a relatively pinpointed target within a very definite and confined area, than they are by any conventional act of aviation warfare, such as the classic case of the bombing of an ammunition factory in an enemy town. This is not a point of logic, or merely an estimate or observation. When contemplating the requirement to minimize civilian risk, as well as the notion of proportionality, consider the figures put forward by B'tselem – The Israeli Information Center for Human Rights in the "Occupied Territories" (an organization not noted for underestimating the number of civilian fatalities caused by Israel):

In the course of the Al-Aqsa Intifada (between Sept 29 2000 and December 2003), at least 126 Palestinians were "extra judicially executed" by Israel. Of these, 67 assassinations were carried out by the Israel Air Force and 59 of them were carried out by ground forces. In the course of these assassinations 85 additional Palestinians were killed, 75 of them in assassinations carried out by the Israel Air Force and 10 of them in assassinations carried out by ground forces.[85]

B'tselem's website does not mention whether any of these "additional Palestinians" caught in the close vicinity of the target victim – often in his car or office – were themselves involved in terrorist activity. In some cases additional victims have included the target's bodyguards and other members of his organization. Undeniably, some of the casualties have been innocent bystanders, even children.[86]

It is admittedly difficult to determine precisely how many innocent victims constitute a disproportionate cost in relation to the gains of the military operation, particularly when the efficacy of these operations is in itself a contestable issue. It is clear, however, that if it is to pass the test of proportionality, targeted killing, like any other military operation, must abide by at least the following two rules. First, as Paul Gilbert

---

[85] B'tselem – The Israeli Information Center for Human Rights in the "Occupied Territories", www.btselem.org.

[86] As noted in Chapter 2, in the worst of such cases to date, an Israeli attack in July 2002 achieved its goal of targeting Hamas leader Salah Shhada, but exceeded it, killing not only the arch-terrorist but also over a dozen civilians, including the man's wife and teenage daughter.

points out, "Military action is proportionate in-so-far as it employs only such force as is needed to secure military objectives."[87] Walzer, following Henry Sidgwick, describes this idea of proportionality as a requirement of the war convention: "we are to weigh the 'mischief done' against the contribution that mischief makes to the end of victory."[88] Admittedly, this aforementioned requirement is not a very restrictive one. Nonetheless, it prohibits at least any violence and destruction that is out of all proportion or relation to the requirements of combat.[89] Second, and not unrelated, is the additional requirement that military forces must not only refrain from targeting civilians, but also take care to avoid this outcome whenever possible. As with any attack on combatants, willful, or even negligent recklessness, with regard to collateral damage to civilians, is inexcusable.[90]

Once again, none of this sets targeted killing apart from conventional warfare. To the extent that this call for care and caution with regard to civilians draws a distinction between various military tactics, it does so in favor of pinpointed attacks on combatants. No doubt mistakes have been, and will continue to be, made. But choosing this form of military strategy, as opposed to any other, in itself exhibits a high regard for civilian well-being. Furthermore, in those cases in which terrorists are targeted by ground forces, the danger posed to civilians is reduced even further while soldiers assume a degree of risk I doubt even Walzer would require of them.[91] In the more common case in which the targeting is carried out from the air, due care for civilians can be, and often is, exhibited by the choice of weapon (the weight of a bomb, its precision, the flight altitude, etc.), as well as the timing of the attack and the precise location of the operation. Above all, targeting specific terrorists, as opposed to any other available military course of action, exhibits the distinct moral advantage of singling out and aiming for combatants, and it does so within a type of war in which such distinctions are increasingly blurred by the terrorists themselves. Certainly,

---

[87] Gilbert, *New Terror, New Wars*, p. 16. On the principle of proportionality in the Hague Convention, see also pp. 88–92.
[88] Walzer, *Just and Unjust Wars*, p. 129.   [89] Ibid., p. 130.
[90] Cohen, "Casting the First Stone," p. 14.
[91] It should be noted that nearly half of Israel's targeting operations have been carried out in this manner. See: www.btselem.org.

assassinating terrorists cannot be accused of being disproportionate in comparison with the terror strikes it is designed to combat.[92]

As for the impact of assassination on future mutual relations and the prospects for peace, one further source of opposition to targeted assassination may stem from the fear that the anger provoked by such operations might prevent future peaceful negotiation and political cooperation with the communities sympathetic to the terrorists and their leaders, who may themselves be terrorists. One must, however, bear in mind that conflicts involving terror are characterized by deep animosity, long-standing feelings of bitterness and injustice, and unsettled scores. Within this context, particular resentments brought about specifically by assassination are likely to be negligible, aside from being indistinguishable and immeasurable within the sea of existing hostilities. It is, for instance, improbable that conflicts with groups such as al-Qaida, and the deeply felt hatred they foster towards the West and its ways, are affected by any specific strategy adopted by the US in response to September 11. Even in the Israeli case, it is doubtful that targeting terrorists in particular contributes significantly to the existing list of Palestinian grievances against Israel. On a more optimistic note, it is unlikely that acts of assassination (or perfidy, or treachery or anything else) will destroy the necessary basis for establishing future peace. As Gross points out, "Nations commit unspeakable horrors and still cease fighting and restore relations when it is in their interest to do so."[93]

Morality and legality

I have argued that assassinating avowed terrorists in the course of an armed conflict as a preventive, rather than a punitive, measure is a legitimate act of self-defense, no less, and perhaps more, than is killing soldiers in combat. Certainly, it is more defensible than related acts of political assassination, which we tend to condone when we share the assassin's judgment of his victim. In the case of terrorists, there is little possibility of disagreement among liberals concerning the moral evaluation of the targets in light of the horrific nature of their deeds. While the

---

[92] Proportionality is conceded by Gross, "Fighting by Other Means," p. 357. For the Israeli High Court discussion of the proportionality requirement and its application to the targeted assassination of Palestinian terrorists, see: HCJ 769/02 [2005], Para. 41–6.

[93] Gross, "Fighting by Other Means," p. 356.

debate over the expediency of targeted killing remains inconclusive and contested, there are at least good reasons to believe that targeting terrorists is conducive to defense, which is all that can be reasonably required of any military strike. Moreover, since military operations – specifically those aimed at terrorists – are often something of a gamble, assassination bears the distinct moral advantage of aiming narrowly at combatants and minimizing civilian casualties.

Should the assassination of terrorists, then, be internationally endorsed in legislation? International moral and legal clarity would indeed send a brave and welcome message to terrorists and their accomplices worldwide that the civilized world is unanimously determined to root them out, as it did with piracy in the nineteenth century. There may, on the other hand, be grounds for shying away from publicly initiating new rules that would adopt targeted killing as a recommended form of combat. Assassination remains an act of deviation from limited warfare. As such, we might do well to refrain from adopting any general rule which could be interpreted as a new "free for all" endorsement of assassination within international law. Acts of war, however legitimate, need not be celebrated and encouraged by the introduction of new permissive rules. In the end, there may be a lot to be said in favor of ambiguity. The existing vagueness that characterizes the legal attitude towards assassinating terrorists – both internationally and internally – may in fact be the most appropriate one.

Vagueness, however, is not tantamount to total darkness, and ambiguity need not mean complete obscurity. While the international community need not explicitly endorse the targeting of terrorists, it could do more to adapt international law to the reality of modern warfare. International law could do a great deal more to support nations confronting terrorism without explicitly endorsing targeted killing. It could even lend its tacit consent to the targeting of genuine terrorist chieftains, while at one and at the same time narrowing the legitimate scope of targeting policies so as to avoid potential abuse. Surrounding legislation on terrorism, which is sorely lacking, could assist those combating it, and at the same time demarcate the legitimate boundaries for doing so. Legally defining terrorism would be a very good place to start. As far as targeted killing is concerned, an orderly definition would imply the category of persons who might legitimately be subject to this type of action, as opposed to those who would categorically be immune from it. In the absence of a universally agreed upon definition, one man's freedom fighter is, indeed, another's terrorist, as the old aphorism goes. As long as this is the case, endorsing the killing of terrorists, even tacitly, runs the risk of eroding the more general norm against political assassination. A definitive description of terrorism, on the other hand, would enable us to condone policies designed to combat it, without lending our hand to related practices, such as the murder of political enemies, which we ardently condemn.

An internationally agreed-upon definition of terrorism is a first necessary step in the right direction. I suggested at the outset that this definition ought to be a narrow one. In the present connection, another good reason for adopting a stringent definition is to deter the cynical use of the term terrorism for purely political purposes, namely dubbing any enemy a "terrorist" in order to de-legitimize their cause and legitimize their assassination. A strict definition of terrorism, like the one suggested in Chapter 1, would serve to distinguish between various instances of targeted killing and to condemn those that would be truly outrageous, such as the targeting of political opponents. It would enable at least silent support for policies which sincerely target terrorists – properly so called – in self-defense, while avoiding the dangers of a potential slippery slope.

I suggested at the outset that an appropriately restrictive definition of terrorism – one that would considerably narrow the scope of legitimate candidates for assassination – would include at least the following four accumulative elements. Following Michael Walzer's classic definition, terrorism properly understood was described as:

(a) The deliberate targeting of defenseless non-combatants; (b) the random choice of those victims (as opposed to the targeting of a specific, named individuals); (c) the intent of the action is to spread fear of mortal peril amidst a civilian population; (d) political purpose.[94]

This list may not be conclusive. State leaders would, no doubt, aspire to add the requirement (e), whereby the perpetrator is a non-state actor. I doubt they should be allowed the prerogative of doing so. Others would have us stipulate that the agent involved be a member of a recognized organization with a hierarchical chain of command. Be that as it may, any restrictive definition along these lines would at least imply the class of persons subject to targeting policies, while avoiding the potential ills of abuse.

[94] Walzer, *Just and Unjust Wars*, p. 197.

While an internationally agreed-upon, stringent definition of terrorism is highly desirable, it is not the only type of legislation that could shed light on the issue at hand without expressly authorizing it. As the previous chapter suggests, related legislation ought to recognize explicitly the distinction between combatants who play by the rules of war and those who disregard them. Essentially, this involves specifying the criteria for lawful behavior in combat and the benefits that attach to it, along with those benefits withheld from combatants who do not abide by the rules. On the most practical level, it comes down to drawing the appropriate conclusions regarding the rights of irregulars, and lack thereof, in battle and in its aftermath. Specifically, the lawless status of irregular combatants ought to be legally distinguished from their lawful counterparts by explicitly denying irregular combatants the conventional rights of soldiers. This might implicitly legitimize non-conventional action towards terrorists without explicitly endorsing targeted killing in law.

But if the international community has cause to refrain from positively endorsing assassination in written law, it must also refrain from condemning operations that specifically target the members of recognized terrorist organizations. This chapter argued at length against each and every moral argument raised against bona fide terrorist targeting policies. From a moral perspective, the appropriate international response to targeting *terrorists*, in the strict sense of the word, must, at the very least, be that of silent acquiescence.

6 | Torturing terrorists

Suppose British security services apprehend a terrorist carrying a load of explosives at one of the entrances to the London Underground. Would they be justified in torturing him in order to prevent other terrorists from inflicting imminent large-scale suffering and loss of human life on the public transport system? Should liberal democracies refrain from using torture in all circumstances, either regardless of the consequences or because the overall ill effects of its use always outweigh its advantages? Nearly three decades ago Henry Sue invoked a standard philosophical example just like this one in his essay on torture.[1] More recently, Alan Dershowitz asks: what if on September 11 law enforcement officials had "arrested terrorists boarding one of the planes and learned that other planes, then airborne, were heading towards unknown occupied buildings?"[2]

As Jean Bethke Elshtain observes, this is the way the debate on torture was usually carried out, even before September 11, 2001, and it is indeed difficult to find an essay on torture that does not contain its own variation on the theme of these examples.[3] Elshtain continues,

What usually followed the presentation of this, or some other vivid example was a discussion of options within the framework of the two dominant and competing moral philosophies of modernity: deontology and utilitarianism. The deontologist says "never" – one is never permitted to use another human being as a means rather than an end in himself. The utilitarian says that the greatest good for the greatest number will be served by torturing the creep ... so where do you stand? With Kant or with Bentham?[4]

---

[1] Henry Shue, "Torture," *Philosophy and Public Affairs* 7 (2) (1978), p. 141.

[2] Dershowitz, *Shouting Fire*, p. 477.

[3] In another example, Michael Walzer, "Political Action: The Problem of Dirty Hands," *Philosophy and Public Affairs* 2 (2) (1973), pp. 160–80, p. 167, reprinted in Sanford Levinson (ed.) *Torture – A Collection* (Oxford University Press, 2004), pp. 64–5.

[4] Jean Bethke Elshtain, "Reflection on the Problem of 'Dirty Hands'," in Levinson, *Torture*, p. 78.

Elshtain herself stands with neither, arguing that while deontology makes torture impossible, utilitarianism makes it too easy and too tempting.[5] While Kantians usually hold that torture is absolutely prohibited whatever the circumstances, utilitarians argue that the torture of one person may be justified if it prevents even more severe suffering to others, though they might not agree on the overall balance of consequences in any given case, all things considered.[6] As Jeremy Waldron comments, "Philosophy classes studying Consequentialism thrive on hypotheticals involving scenarios of grotesque disproportion between the pain that a torture might inflict on an informant and the pain that might be averted by the timely use of the information extracted from him: a little bit of pain from the electrodes for him versus five hundred thousand people saved from nuclear incineration."[7] For those of us who are neither strict Kantians nor blanket utilitarians, the choice between them is even harder, as both sides appear to have a very strong case, while moral intuitions pull in conflicting directions. I think Sanford Kadish was right when he commented, in response to Israel's Landau Commission report concerning the means employed by its general security services, that it is not difficult to defend one or the other horn of the dilemma: what is difficult is to choose between them.[8]

The right to remain silent

As the opening examples demonstrate, the issue at hand is a most difficult one; it is also, however, very specific. Could it ever be justified to torture a terrorist (or perhaps a terrorist suspect) for the sole purpose of extracting information concerning future attacks and preventing large-scale suffering? While this question cuts to the very core of liberal–humanist morality, it is not primarily concerned with the right to withhold self-incriminating evidence that can then be used against the suspect in a court of law. The privilege against self-incrimination, guaranteed by the US Fifth Amendment and by English common

[5] Elshtain, "Reflection," pp. 78–9.
[6] For a classic utilitarian piece on torture, see Jeremy Bentham, "Of Torture," in W.L. and P.J. Twining, "Bentham on Torture," *Northern Ireland Legal Quarterly* 24 (3) (Autumn 1973), pp. 305–56.
[7] Waldron, "Security and Liberty," pp. 191–210, esp. p. 206. See also Waldron, "Torture," pp. 1713–14.
[8] Sanford A. Kadish, "Torture, the State and the Individual," *Israel Law Review*, 23 (1989), pp. 345–56, esp. p. 346.

law,[9] need not apply to information regarding the criminal actions of *others* or their *future* plans. To the extent that divulging such information will often be self-incriminating for the subject of interrogation (which, in all likelihood, it will be), the right against self-incrimination could easily be preserved by a rule that self-incriminating evidence extracted under duress is inadmissible in a court of law.

Punitive torture, I assume here rather than argue, has long been regarded by liberalism, perhaps since its very inception, as a cruel and unusual punishment. Aside from that, security forces are not, nor should they be, authorized to judge and punish.[10] This discussion of torture deals exclusively with the contemporary debate over torturing terrorists for the purpose of divulging information. It excludes the issue of punishing, or torturing, the innocent (a child, for example) on utilitarian grounds. It most certainly excludes the possibility of purely gratuitous torture of the type recently carried out in Abu Ghraib prison, as well as any use of torture as a form of punishment, or for purely terroristic motives, that is, in order to intimidate or deter a surrounding population.[11] The limited question before us concerns not punishment or intimidation but prevention. It precludes the use of force as a means of extracting confessions and as a penal measure, as well as for purposes of intimidating persons other than the interrogated victim of the torture. Let us agree that this is a liberal given. Intimidating, or "terroristic," torture, that is, torture aimed not at its direct victim but rather at others assumed to be influenced by the victims suffering (other dissidents, an insurgent population, or the father of a tortured child), must be rejected out of hand by anyone who is not entirely a utilitarian in his moral convictions. I have already argued against the moral validity of terror in general. As Shue puts it, "terroristic" torture is "the purest possible case of the violation of the Kantian principle that no person may be used *only* as a means. The victim is simply a site at which great pain occurs so that others may know about it and be frightened by the prospect."[12]

---

[9] Adrian A. S. Zuckerman, "Coercion and the Judicial Ascertainment of Truth," *Israel Law Review* 23 (1989), pp. 357–74, esp. pp. 363–4. Zuckerman notes that the immunity from self-incrimination has in recent years been considerably undermined throughout the common law world.

[10] Michael Moore, "Torture and the Balance of Evils," *Israel Law Review* 23 (2–3) (1989), p. 326.

[11] On "terroristic torture" and its inadmissibility, see Shue, "Torture," pp. 132–3.

[12] Ibid., p. 132.

In what follows I concentrate on interrogational torture, implemented solely for the purpose of extracting information about pending terrorist attacks, in which the potential victims of torture are themselves already implicated in creating the danger that the torture is intended to thwart. I will defend a categorical ban on hard-core torture regardless of circumstances. Drawing a parallel between the evil of outright torture and the evil of terrorism itself, I argue for the categorical impermissibility of both. On the other hand, this chapter suggests that when it comes to interrogating terrorists in a "ticking bomb" situation, security forces may, under highly restrictive conditions, be justified in resorting to some physical measures, particularly those that do no permanent damage and that are inflicted only to the minimal degree essential for extracting vital information. Furthermore, while this essay addresses the moral issue rather than the surrounding legal and political implications, it notes that institutional safeguards are essential in order to assure that interrogators never surpass these limits.[13]

The right to self-defense

One common way of distinguishing terrorism, as well as the legitimate means of combating it, from common criminal activity is by classifying it as a form of warfare. The previous chapters suggested that while terrorism is an irregular, perhaps unlawful, form of belligerency, it is nonetheless military, or paramilitary in character. The rules of war justify the use of measures that would be prohibited against civilian criminals. While we may oppose capital punishment and would not authorize the police to kill criminals on sight, we do tolerate killing of enemy combatants on the battlefield, even if they do not pose an immediate threat. Thus, it might be suggested that the "war on terror" justifies implementing certain measures, such as killing and perhaps torture, which would be wholly prohibited under normal criminal circumstances.

As in the debate over targeted killing, the present discussion is warranted only if we set out with the non-pacifist view whereby it is sometimes morally justifiable to fight and kill other people, at least in order to defend ourselves as well as others. If we may kill in self-defense, why

---

[13] Bentham pointed out long ago that arguments concerning potential abuse cannot serve as conclusive principled reasons against the use of torture: see Twining and Twining, "Bentham on Torture," p. 309. For Bentham on potential abuse of torture, see also pp. 326, 328.

should we refrain from torturing in order to prevent terrorist attacks? Shue argues that torturing another human being *is* actually more harmful to him than his total destruction in combat:[14] "Torture is usually humiliating and degrading ... while killing destroys life, it need not destroy dignity."[15] Michael Ignatieff makes the same point that "there is a moral difference between killing a fellow combatant, in conformity to the laws of war, and torturing a person. The first takes a life; the second abuses one."[16] More fundamentally, Shue continues, torture, unlike killing on the battlefield, necessarily violates a basic principle of just combat: the prohibition against attacking the defenseless.[17] The victim of torture is disarmed, and in that sense is unthreatening. As such he is also, in a very important respect, defenseless.

Shue raises and rejects the suggestion that supplying information, thus avoiding the torture, constitutes defense. Admittedly, ready informants will collaborate and thus avoid torture. However, for an ignorant victim no escape is possible, and there is no way of differentiating in advance between an uninformed victim and a dedicated enemy who is withholding valuable life-saving information.[18] As for the latter, Shue argues that even the knowledgeable terrorist is defenseless and helpless in the face of torture because, Shue assumes, the betrayal of one's ideals, values, and friends, whatever their moral worth, is such a dishonorable alternative that it cannot count as an escape route because it is effectively a denial of one's very self.[19] According to this account, disclosing the whereabouts of a bomb about to go off in the heart of a densely populated urban center is an unreasonable violation of integrity, which cannot constitute escape.[20]

---

[14] Shue, "Torture," p. 125.   [15] Ibid., pp. 125–6.

[16] Michael Ignatieff, *The Lesser Evil: Political Ethics in an Age of Terror* (Princeton University Press, 2004), p. 137.

[17] Shue, "Torture," p. 129.

[18] Ibid., pp. 135–6. This concern for the ignorant victim of torture was already raised by Bentham, who admitted that this worry poses a serious objection to the use of torture in general. Bentham cautioned that torture could be appropriately inflicted only after serious precautions have been taken to assure that the victim of torment is indeed capable of complying. Alternatively, Bentham suggests, there may be rare cases in which the public interest in preventing a harm is so great that it outweighs the dangers of torturing the innocent and legitimizes the torture of a suspect whom we are fairly sure, though not certain, is capable of preventing the large scale harm. See Twining and Twining, "Bentham on Torture," pp. 312–4.

[19] Shue, "Torture," p. 136.   [20] Ibid., p. 141.

However convincing one may find this argument, David Sussman argues that Shue overlooks a further aspect of regarding the tortured subject, specifically the tortured terrorist, as a helpless victim.[21] According to Sussman, an interrogated terrorist, albeit unarmed, may pose a realistic, at times even immediate, threat to his torturers and their kinsmen. In the case of terrorism, the information withheld from the interrogators can be construed as an ongoing threat, often more deadly than, and at times as immediate as, that of a fully armed opposing soldier.[22] Jeremy Bentham made this point when he argued in his defense of torture that when a prisoner declined to do what justice requires of him, what is in the interest of the community at large, he is in effect committing an ongoing offence against society: "Every moment that he persists in his refusal he commits a fresh offence, of which he is convicted upon much clearer evidence too than can be obtained in almost any other case."[23] Sussman argues that the terrorist need not be considered non-threatening or helpless. His continued silence constitutes part of his attack, which began with the placing of the bomb, but continues even when the terrorist is in the interrogation chamber.[24] This is so regardless of whether divulging such information ought or ought not to be viewed as a genuine avenue of escape from torture, which Sussman, contra Shue, argues that it should, remaining puzzled by Shue's great concern for the terrorist's sense of his own integrity.[25]

Like Sussman, I remain unconvinced that we should be so solicitous about the terrorist's sense of his own integrity when he himself has thwarted all rules of civilized combat. However, part of the logic of Sussman's response to Shue remains problematic. The idea that a terrorist bound to a chair is a threat to his interrogators (or their countrymen) just because of the information he holds, blurs the distinction between acts and omissions: because the terrorist omits to tell them where the bomb is, the bomb's explosion can be attributed to him. In Chapter 2, I argued against Ted Honderich and Jacques Derrida for disposing all too readily of the distinction between acts and omissions when attempting to justify terrorist violence. In the present connection, Sussman's response to Shue may be too quick on precisely the same account.[26]

---

[21] Sussman, "What's Wrong with Torture?" pp. 16–18.   [22] Ibid.
[23] Bentham, in Twining and Twining, "Bentham on Torture," p. 312.
[24] Sussman, "What's Wrong with Torture?" pp. 16–17.   [25] Ibid., p. 18.
[26] I am grateful to Jeremy Waldron for pointing this out to me.

In "Torture and the Balance of Evils," Michael Moore attempts to gain insight into the moral basis of self-defense by drawing our attention to the classic case in which an aggressor trying to kill someone ends up being killed himself. Moore argues that self-defense constitutes a legitimate exception to moral prohibitions such as "never kill" (or "never torture") when an "aggressor creates a situation in which someone must be killed, either he or his intended victim. He has wrongfully created a threat of harm that his intended victim can now only redirect, but not eliminate. Since he is the one creating such a threat, he in all fairness is the one to be selected when someone has to bear the harm threatened."[27] The terrorists created a situation in which someone – either themselves or their defense-less victims – must suffer physical pain, maiming, and, perhaps, death. Self-defense is thus, if not literally applicable to state officials practicing torturous investigative methods on terrorists, at least analogous, and it suggests a possible basis for an exception to the prohibition on torture. As Moore puts this:

Terrorists who are captured do not now present a threat of using deadly force against their captors or others. Thus, the literal law of self-defense is not available to justify their torture. But the principle uncovered as the moral basis for the defense may be applicable. For if the terrorist knows the location of hidden bombs, or of buried hostages, or of caches of arms, or if he knows of future terrorist acts to be executed by others that he has aided, he has culpably caused the situation in which someone must get hurt. If hurting him is the only means to prevent the death or injury of others put at risk by his actions, such torture should be permissible, and on the same basis that self-defense is permissible.[28]

Moore admits that such an exception would apply only to a case in which we *know* that the subject of interrogation is indeed a knowledge-able terrorist, and this will often be difficult to ascertain: "Such an exception to the norm against torturing has of course no application to the torturing of the innocent."[29] On the other hand, Moore does take this self-defense-based exception to apply to "someone who had no hand in the terrorist activity that gave rise to the threat but who none-theless possesses information that, if disclosed, would prevent the threa-tened harm from occurring."[30] The rationale similarly addresses Shue's concern about attacks upon the defenseless. The informed bystander "is

[27] Moore, "Torture," pp. 321–2.   [28] Ibid., p. 323.   [29] Ibid.
[30] Ibid., p. 324.

unlike other civilians in that she could prevent the harm by no greater an act than speaking up."[31] On this account, even an omission from the act of speaking up suffices to justify torture: "The bad Samaritan who could prevent *anyone* dying and who refuses to do so for no good reason becomes part of the threat to be defended against, and should be treated accordingly."[32] Apparently for Moore, as for Sussman, dedication to the terrorist cause, as well as integrity and camaraderie, do not constitute a sufficient reason for threatening the lives of innocent civilians. As he puts this later on: "those who could remove the threat at little cost to themselves are also less wronged if they are tortured to induce them to do what morally they ought to do anyway."[33]

What's wrong with (interrogational) torture?

In "What's Wrong with Torture?" Sussman rejects Shue's characterization of the wrongness of torture as essentially an assault against the defenseless. Apart from denying Shue's claim that interrogated terrorists are helpless, Sussman argues that neither utilitarian nor Kantian objections to torture fully capture the core concept of torture as a distinctive kind of moral wrong, which bears a higher burden of justification than other forms of violence, warfare, and even killing.[34] While the utilitarian clearly captures an important aspect of the ills of torture – the harm it causes, both directly (the immediate pain it inflicts) and indirectly (its long-term psychological and political effects), his account cannot explain sufficiently how torture is categorically worse than other forms of warfare that conceivably deliver the same level of suffering (pain, mutilation, and death) as some torture can.[35] The Kantian, for his part, "argues that what is essentially wrong with torture is the profound disrespect it shows the humanity or autonomy of its victim. Here torture is wrong as the most extreme instance of using someone as a mere means."[36] While this account highlights an important immoral aspect of torture, regardless of the consequences, it does not sufficiently account for the fact that torture intrinsically involves pain. Theoretically, the Kantian should be just as opposed to any other type of unwanted imposition, which would equally disrupt the agent's autonomous agency (such as administering a harmless truth serum; perhaps the infliction of extreme unsolicited

---

[31] Ibid., p. 324.   [32] Ibid., p. 325.   [33] Ibid., p. 333.
[34] Sussman, "What's Wrong with Torture?" pp. 1–33.   [35] Ibid., p. 13.
[36] Ibid., pp. 13–14.

ecstasy that makes its victim liable to suggestion; inducing an unwanted drunken state, or even tickling the victim into confessing). The furthest a Kantian can go towards accommodating the special significance of pain is to argue that pain characteristically undermines the very capacities constitutive of autonomous agency itself.[37] Nevertheless, the Kantian cannot really account for something we intuitively consider to be a primary feature of the wrongness of torture, namely, the badness of inflicting pain in and of itself, regardless of its disruption of the victim's agency. As Sussman puts it, "The Kantian seems unable to do justice to what we would normally take to be a clearly non-accidental truth: the fact that torture *hurts*."[38]

Additionally, if what is wrong with torture is merely the disruption of autonomous agency then, according to Sussman, the Kantian cannot hope to explain how torture could ever be worse than killing, since the latter is the ultimate disruption of autonomy, as it is a total annihilation of the agent.[39] This may or may not be the case, as the Kantian might argue that the destruction of dignity involved in most torture is actually worse, on Kantian grounds, than is killing. Be that as it may, we can agree with Sussman that a notoriously unemotional moral theory may fail to take full account of our intuitive moral revulsion from torture as inherently painful.

Sussman's own view remains broadly Kantian, extending the thought that torture offends the dignity of its victim as a rationally self-governing agent: "Torture forces its victim into the position of colluding against himself through his own effects and emotions, so that he experiences himself as simultaneously powerless and yet actively complicit in his own violation."[40] Torture does not merely use its victim as a mere means, or simply disrupt his autonomy, though it is an important feature of its wrongness that it does so. According to Sussman, what is special about torture is that its victim is used as a means specifically through his own distressing effects and painful bodily functions.[41] Pain is an essential feature of this moral wrong, as it is an aspect of our own agency. Torture is a perversion of the value of self-respect, rather than merely a violation of it, in that through the use of pain specifically it turns the victim's own dignity against his person in a way that makes him an accomplice in his own destruction. Like rape, torture often involves "pitting the victim against himself, making him an active participant in

---

[37] Ibid., p. 14.   [38] Ibid., p. 15.   [39] Ibid., pp. 15–16.
[40] Ibid., p. 4.   [41] Ibid., p. 19.

his own abuse."[42] It always "puts the victim in the unavoidable position of betraying or colluding against himself, an experience the victim undergoes whether or not he actually informs or confesses."[43] Sussman goes on to state that "What the torturer does is to take his victim's pain, and through it his victim's body, and make it begin to express the torturer's will."[44] This must be particularly offensive to a moral theory that honors dignity and autonomous will.[45]

Sussman's account of the moral character of investigative torture is illuminating. His articulation of the distinct moral abhorrence involved in interrogational torture sets it apart derogatively from other forms of violence and even killing, which we often sanction in just wars. The pain-induced humiliation involved in torture – exploiting the victim's participation in his own violation – distinguishes it for the worse from both non-painful forms of disrupting autonomous agency and from other forms of painful and destructive violent weapons, such as bullets and bombs, which do not require their victims to collaborate in their own downfall.[46] This explains not only what is especially wrong about torture, but also why it is often assumed that torture bears a higher burden of justification than other forms of violence, warfare, and, even, killing. However, by Sussman's own admission, it does not categorically rule out the possibility that in some rare instances torture might be morally justifiable.

Threshold deontology

In his aforementioned essay, Michael Moore argues that even a non-consequentialist can accept that horrendous consequences would justify a breach of what he takes to be a moral prohibition on torture. Furthermore, he holds that when the potential consequences are disastrous enough, they would justify even the torture of innocents. This is what Moore calls "threshold deontology" which, as he explains at length, is a non-consequentialist agent-relative view of morality whose rules – justified on non-consequential grounds – can nonetheless be overridden in rare and extreme cases of pending catastrophe.[47] This agent-relative view is non-consequentialist in nature because it (initially) regards certain actions as right or wrong irrespective of their

---

[42] Ibid., p. 22.   [43] Ibid., pp. 24, 30.   [44] Ibid., pp. 20–1.
[45] Ibid., p. 19.   [46] Ibid., p. 30.   [47] Moore, "Torture," pp. 327–32.

consequences. However, it is a softened, or non-absolute, form of deontology because it rejects the Kantian notion whereby moral norms are phrased without any reference to consequences: "It just isn't true that one should allow a nuclear war rather than killing or torturing an innocent person," Moore argues.[48]

Whether one accepts this view of morality or its claim to separate itself sufficiently from all forms of utilitarianism, Moore does seem to have at least an intuitive point. Indeed, it is difficult to subscribe as absolutely as Kant did to the "though the heavens may fall" aspect of strict deontology, though there may be better ways of resolving conflicts among moral norms than the concept of thresholds. Furthermore, Moore himself admits, threshold deontology leaves us with the open question of what this threshold should be. (Do 300 or 3,000 or 3,050 potential casualties constitute a sufficient threshold for breaching the moral ban on torture?)[49] Admittedly, such indeterminacies do not form a conclusive objection to threshold deontology as a moral theory but, as Moore himself acknowledges, they do disturbingly conjure up the medieval worry about how many pebbles constitute a heap.[50] While we would not deny the existence of heaps just because it is difficult to determine whether they are made up of three or four or five pebbles, we might worry more about adopting a moral theory intrinsically structured around uncertainties of this kind, which become particularly acute just as we most urgently require its guidance, as when confronting such grave issues as torturing innocents and saving countless lives.

Moore intends his theory of threshold deontology to apply primarily to the possibility of torturing the innocent in order to divulge information that would prevent large-scale tragedy. In such cases, he says, there is a (very high) threshold beyond which our prohibition on torturing the innocent cannot be legitimately upheld.[51] Only the most horrendous consequences could justify the torture of innocents and the "likelihood of such horrendous consequences ever actually following from not torturing an innocent are so remote that no interrogator is likely to have faced such a situation."[52] The highly exceptional nature of such a situation, calling for the torturing of innocents as a necessary condition as well as a last resort to avoid totally horrendous consequences, renders it somewhat uninteresting for practical ethics. (I really do not

[48] Ibid., p. 328.   [49] Ibid., p. 332.   [50] Ibid.
[51] Ibid., p. 328.   [52] Ibid., p. 333.

know what we should do if the only way to prevent another imminent September 11 is to torture a baby from the bin Laden family, nor am I particularly troubled by this lack of moral knowledge.) The present discussion focuses only on the real-world dilemma of torturing terrorist activists. It is primarily this type of torture which we are currently tempted to think might sometimes be morally justified in combating terrorism.

Despite his comprehensive characterization of torture as an attack against the defenseless, even Shue entertained the possibility that such an assault on terrorists could, conceivably, be justified in extreme cases. This qualification is hedged around with a list of stringent necessary conditions that would have to obtain if torture were ever to be justified by its desirable effects. These include, "its serving a supremely important purpose, its being the least harmful means to that goal, its having a clearly defined and reachable endpoint."[53] While Shue worries about torture's metastatic tendency and warns of its allure for interrogators as the "ultimate shortcut," he concludes nonetheless that "it cannot be denied that there are imaginable cases in which the harm that could be prevented by a rare instance of pure interrogational torture would be so enormous so as to outweigh the cruelty of the torture itself and possibly, the enormous potential harm that would result if what was intended to be a rare instance was actually the breaching of a dam which would lead to a torrent of torture."[54]

Ultimately, Shue remains relatively unbothered by scenarios such as those sketched at the outset, as he regards them as highly artificial and therefore non-instructive for practical ethics. Unfortunately, he was probably wrong. In the post-September 11 age of terror it is not academic to contemplate the capture of an evidently involved potential informant whose torture could save the inhabitants of a city, or a significant part thereof. In such a case, Shue continues, "I can see no way to deny the permissibility of torture in a case *just like this* one. To allow the destruction of much of a great city and many of its people would be almost as wicked as purposely to destroy it."[55]

---

[53] Shue, "Torture," p. 141. Moore lists similar qualifications for torturing the *innocent*; Moore, "Torture," pp. 333–4.
[54] Shue, "Torture," p. 141.   [55] Ibid.

Moore's solution to such dilemmas does not rely on the problematic concept of a threshold, nor does it necessitate a direct weighing of consequences, though it does allow for their consideration in a way that a strict Kantian would not. With regard to terrorists, Moore argues essentially that torturing the culpable is simply not that wrong. Clearly, one cannot view the past, or intended, deeds of terrorists as in themselves justifying torture. As stated at the outset, torture is not a legitimate form of punishment, nor are interrogators rightful punishers. This rules out the possibility of adopting a formal exception to the norm "never torture" which would allow for the torture of culpable terrorists whether or not they possessed life-saving information.[56] Torture cannot be justified as a form of prepaid punishment pending trial.[57] On the other hand, Moore argues that "exceptions to moral norms needn't operate in an all-or-nothing fashion, perhaps it is *less* wrong to torture the culpable than the innocent. Put crudely, their lives and rights are worth less precisely because they are morally odious individuals deserving of punishment, even if we are not their rightful punishers and even if death or torture is not their rightful punishment."[58]

Moore formulates his justification for this view in semi-consequentialist terms: "while the killing or torture of another is wrong, where it is the killing or torture of someone deserving serious punishment, it is significantly less wrong, so much so that good consequences may justify the doing of it."[59] For Moore, the terrorist's culpability explains why we may weigh consequences when contemplating his torture, while we may not do so, for the most part, when contemplating the torture of innocents (at least as long as we have not reached a very high threshold of disaster). As Moore summarizes: "the moral ban against torture applies less firmly to those who culpably cause the need for torture by planting the bomb that needs removal."[60]

Notice that this justification for torturing terrorists is not primarily consequentialist. It is not, as in the case of torturing the innocent, initially the negative consequences that are doing the justificatory work here. This justification for torturing terrorists is based initially on a premise about the agent's guilt and culpability. It is an argument about the terrorist's responsibility and what he consequently deserves. Consequences function in this argument, but only at a second stage.

---

[56] Moore, "Torture," p. 326.   [57] Ibid.   [58] Ibid.
[59] Ibid., p. 300.   [60] Ibid., p. 333.

There is a non-consequential consideration – the agent's culpability – that serves to lower the threshold, which is then outweighed by consequence-related considerations. The terrorist's actions or guilt explain why we are permitted to weigh the consequences of torturously interrogating him. Culpability and consequence-related considerations work together here. If the potential victim of torture was innocent, we would be wrong to weigh his suffering against the potential benefits of divulging information (at least until we reach some cataclysmic threshold). It is *because* he is a terrorist (rather than because of the good consequences to be gained by his torture) that we may consider the relative utilities to begin with. Tibor Machan expresses a similar intuition when he remarks that torture may be justified only when "some measure of moral guilt is present or highly probable on the part of the party about to experience the violence."[61] Clearly, the justification for torture suggested here does not rely exclusively on the balance of evils. It does not rest initially on weighing the evil of torture against the prospect of thousands of casualties. If it did, such a utilitarian justification could serve as easily to justify the torture of innocents. Instead, Moore, as well as Machan, suggests that the initial consideration, prior to any possible balance of consequences, concerns the liability of the potential victim of torture.

Earlier, I discussed Shue's contention that torture always constitutes an assault against the defenseless, which is anathema to the laws of war. Even Shue, however, is willing to distinguish between the innocent and the terrorist in an extreme case of dire peril, and entertains the use of torture against a terrorist fanatic whose silence would result in a catastrophe that the terrorist himself set up.[62] Shue's argument for allowing the torture of terrorists in such rare instances is presented in purely utilitarian terms, concerning only the weighing of relative harms.[63] However, for some unarticulated reason it allows only for the torture of a "fanatic" – that is, a culpable dedicated terrorist – rather than for torturing anyone in order to prevent catastrophic harm to others, as a utilitarian would be committed to do.

---

[61] Tibor R. Machan, "Exploring Extreme Violence (Torture)," *Journal of Social Philosophy*, 21 (1990), p. 94.
[62] Shue, "Torture," pp. 141–2.   [63] Ibid., p. 141.

Clearly, despite the utilitarian rhetoric, consequences do not bear the primary burden of justification in such arguments. The hidden assumption appears to be that terrorists, as opposed to criminals, are guilty of a unique type of moral transgression that ultimately enables even non-utilitarians to balance their suffering against the potential harm to others. The terrorist, it is implicitly assumed both by Moore and Shue, has through his deplorable actions sacrificed his immunity from torture, rendering him vulnerable to considerations that are ruled out in the case of other agents, even criminals. Apparently, the terrorist has sunk so morally low that even the non-consequentialist can justify the balancing of his well-being against the welfare of others.

This point about guilt explains not only why liberal democracies and their philosophers entertain the torture of terrorists, though they have long prohibited the torturing of criminals. It also explains why, though combating terrorism may be regarded as a form of war (and as such is distinguishable from civilian crime), we contemplate torturing terrorists but not enemy soldiers. If consequences were the primary moral factor here, as the utilitarian would have us believe, we could easily find wartime examples analogous to the ticking bomb situation, which would equally justify the torture of enemy soldiers on utilitarian grounds. Nevertheless, I believe most people would recoil from torturing an enemy pilot or a high-ranking officer in order to obtain valuable information that could prevent large-scale casualties on our side and help us win the war (e.g. information regarding enemy tactics, strategy, or pending attacks).[64] This is precisely because soldiers, as opposed to terrorists are, in an important sense, *innocents*, as long as they abide by the rules of war.

One of the basic assumptions of the distinction between *jus ad bellum* and *jus in bello* is that soldiers and officers do not carry any responsibility for the war itself. As long as they fight fairly, according to the rules of *jus in bello*, they are not morally blameworthy and are not to be charged with any criminal offence. Leaders and politicians are responsible for going to war and hence for its justification. While this basic assumption of the traditional theory of war has admittedly been challenged in recent

---

[64] I borrow this example from Daniel Statman, "The Absoluteness of the Prohibition against Torture," *Mishpat Umimshal* 4 (1997), pp. 161–98, p. 186.

years, it is nonetheless widely accepted.[65] Be that as it may, there is little doubt that terrorists are often more closely involved in waging the struggle they are involved in than are soldiers. Far more importantly, they are by definition guilty of violating the laws of war, as well as some basic rules of morality. It is their warlike character that distinguishes terrorists, and the means by which they may be combated, from civilian criminals, however vicious. It is the terrorist's guilt, not the severe consequences of his silence, which distinguishes him from the captured soldier or officer, whose torture would not be tolerated by a non-utilitarian.

The premise that underlies Shue's, Machan's, and Moore's arguments, as well as many common intuitions, is that it is less wrong to torture a terrorist than anyone else.[66] It is not only that a terrorist can prevent great harm from ensuing (perhaps an innocent bystander or a captured pilot could prevent it as well). It is not only that he has set a threat in motion, so that it is now legitimate to redirect the danger away from his innocent victims and towards himself. A common criminal might be able to prevent a large-scale crime he has set in motion by confessing under torture, yet liberal intuitions, as expressed in philosophers' frequent examples, single out the terrorist as the only potentially legitimate victim of torture. This is not a ploy to safeguard our system of civil liberties by artificially preserving torture for foreign nationals rather than local criminals,[67] and it does not rest on the distinction between the

---

[65] Walzer, *Just and Unjust Wars*, p. 138; Gilbert, *New Terror, New Wars*, p. 14; Statman, "The Absoluteness," p. 186. This premise concerning the innocence of soldiers has admittedly been criticized, most recently by McMahan, "The Ethics of Killing," pp. 693–733, who challenges the distinction drawn by the traditional theory of war between principles governing the resort of war (*jus ad bellum*) and those governing the conduct of war (*jus in bello*), and the related combatant–noncombatants dichotomy upheld by the rules of war. McMahan argues that at the deepest moral level considerations governing the justness of the war and those governing its conduct necessarily converge and are not independent of one another. Morally speaking, he suggests (contra Walzer), one cannot fight "justly" in an unjust war. Ideally, McMahan aspires to place greater responsibility on the individual soldier for his participation in any given war.

[66] Moore, "Torture," pp. 300, 333.

[67] See Waldron, "Security and Liberty," pp. 194, 200, 204. Waldron worries that talk of restricting civil liberties specifically in order to combat terrorism has a disturbing distributional character. Rather than reducing everyone's liberty in order to enhance general security, talk of rebalancing liberty and security actually has the effect of diminishing the procedural rights of minorities (e.g. Muslims) in order to enhance a (perhaps false) sense of security for the rest of us. We do not worry enough about giving up certain procedural rights (in the extreme, the ban

laws of war and those of the criminal justice system, both of which prohibit torture. The terrorist is singled out because of the belief that his crimes are so horrendous, his project so fiendish, as to differentiate him for the worse from the common criminal, as well as the soldier, not to mention the innocent bystander. The terrorist not only flouts the laws of war. Once again, his entire method of operation specifically marks civilians, including those who are helpless and innocent even by the terrorist's own standards (children, infants, the elderly, the infirm) for death or maiming as a means of obtaining his political goals.[68] Not only do "the rules of *jus ad bellum* and *jus in bello* have no meaning to them. The whole point of terror is the purposeful, random killing of innocents, defined as those in no position to defend themselves."[69]

There is a striking parallel to be found here between torture and terrorism. The harm inflicted by terrorism and extreme torture is similar – excruciating pain, maiming, bodily amputations, and, ultimately, death. It is precisely this similarity which enables utilitarians to weigh the one against the other with such seeming accuracy. Furthermore, principled objections to torture parallel much of the contemporary political condemnation of terrorism. In both cases we worry about bodily assaults against the defenseless, both are regarded as prohibited uses of human beings as mere means towards the ends of others. This is why liberal states often claim to, and I believe should, uphold an absolute ban against terrorism, as well as outright torture, whatever its goal, however noble, and no matter that the heavens may fall. This conclusion will not turn out to be as harsh as it seems. It is not "deontology run amok"[70] and I will attempt to show that it squares better with our moral intuitions than either simple deontology or utilitarianism. It neither allows for the crude interpersonal calculation of pleasure versus pain, nor ignores the reality of our often dangerous and violent world.

To conclude this section: It is plausible to assume (as we do in the case of punishment) that what may legitimately be done to us *in a*

on torture, for example) because the potential ill effects will befall only "terrorists" whose profile, we assume, is very different from our own. I argue here that there are indeed good reasons to grant terrorists fewer procedural rights than common criminals, i.e. to reserve the use of harsh interrogational methods for terrorists only. This, however, is not because they are ethnically different, but rather because they are morally different.

[68] See Walzer, *Just and Unjust Wars*, p. 197.
[69] Elshtain, "Reflection," p. 80; Walzer, *Just and Unjust Wars*, pp. 197, 203.
[70] See Elshtain's critique of strict deontology, in "Reflection," p. 79.

non-consequentialist account of morality is determined, *inter alia*, by what we ourselves have done. This point emerges plainly from Moore's defense of investigative torture. Francis Kamm goes so far as to suggest that "it is permissible to use someone who has acted sufficiently unjustly as a mere means to save his victims or potential victims."[71] How far this non-consequentialist consideration can be pursued towards justifying the interrogational torture of culpable terrorists, and what the limits of such a license should be, remains to be seen.

Can torture ever be justified?

All the philosophical hypotheses, from Shue in 1978 and up to the present, imply that under certain strictly defined circumstances we might be justified in torturing a terrorist in order to divulge life-saving information that we cannot obtain in any other way: "The circumstances are desperate. The villain is thoroughly villainous. The probability that he knows where the bomb is planted is as close to a certainty as human beings can be in such situations."[72] The emergency is supreme and torture is the least harmful means to prevent catastrophe.[73] Even the deontologists are pressed for an answer. Can we now ignore our prisoner's humanity and submit him to any torturous methods of investigation in order to save innocent lives? I, for one, remain reluctant.

I have suggested, following Moore, Machan, Shue, and Kamm, that certain crimes, specifically terrorism, are so intrinsically deplorable – and on grounds similar to those on which we deplore torture – that those involved in them may deserve harsher treatment when this is necessary in order to save innocent lives that the terrorists themselves have placed in danger. Nonetheless, I argue that while the moral culpability of a terrorist, incurred by his selection of particularly inhumane methods of combat, may under circumstances of dire peril justify subjecting him to harsh methods of investigation that we would condemn in criminal cases, there remain certain measures we cannot resort to, no matter what the consequences.

Those of us who are not entirely impervious to religious arguments might want to think about this point, as Jeremy Waldron does, in terms of the sacredness of the human person,[74] and there is certainly a secular

---

[71] Kamm, "Failure of Just War Theory," pp. 650, 659.
[72] Elshtain, "Reflection," p. 78.   [73] Shue, "Torture," p. 141.
[74] Jeremy Waldron, "What Can Christian Thinking Add to the Debate about Torture?" *Theology Today* 63 (2006), pp. 330–43, esp. pp. 337–8.

notion of this within liberal humanism as well. As Waldron puts this: "The case against torture is rooted in respect for human dignity," understood from a religious perspective as "the holy presence of the image of God (*imago Dei*) in every human person".[75] Waldron continues,

There is no doubt that we may treat the guilty in ways that it would be wrong to treat the innocent. But it does not follow that we may treat the guilty any way we like or that it is permitted to exploit and instrumentalize their pain and terror for our purposes ... The most fundamental concerns invoked by the image of God in each human being and the commandment to respect and pay tribute to that image are utterly indiscriminate.[76]

Certainly there are secular equivalents to this argument regarding the sacredness of persons, human dignity, and the affront to this which torture poses, though Waldron leaves open the question as to how far one can get with secular equivalents to his argument.[77] Some secular arguments regarding respect for persons and human dignity, those that pertain to torture specifically, were cited in the previous sections as part of the attempt to pinpoint the particular wrong involved in torture, as opposed to other forms of human violence often sanctioned in war.[78] The burden of my argument here is that these features of torture ought to be regarded as conclusive reasons for its absolute prohibition. In terms of Waldron's Christian argument, we might say that while the essence of God is pure good, nonetheless, evildoers cannot degrade themselves below the implications of the image of God.[79] In secular terms, their criminality cannot erase their humanity altogether; nor can we.

Nowhere has the issue of torturing terrorists been more real and more pressing than it has been in Israel in the past few decades. For Israelis, the ticking bomb hypotheticals are far from fantasies; rather they are real-life dilemmas that confront Israeli security forces, at times on a daily basis, when they receive concrete intelligence information that a suicide bomber has left the territories, but do not know where his target is. Even in Israel, however, torture has been entirely ruled out on these same grounds of respect for human dignity. I have already referred, in connection with

---

[75] Waldron, "What Can Christian Thinking Add," p. 338.   [76] Ibid., p. 340.

[77] Ibid., p. 338. For Waldron on dignity, see Jeremy Waldron, "Dignity and Rank," *Archives européennes de sociologie* 48 (2) (2007), pp. 201–37.

[78] Shue, for example, "Torture," pp. 125–6; Ignatieff, *The Lesser Evil*, p. 137; Sussman, "What's Wrong with Torture?" throughout. All address the particularly degrading aspects of torture and its direct affront to dignity.

[79] This is more than implied by Waldron, "What Can Christian Thinking Add," p. 340.

unlawful combatants, to Israeli Supreme Court Justice Aharon Barak's statement that "unlawful combatants are not beyond the law ... God created them as well in his image; their dignity as well is to be honored; they as well enjoy and are entitled to protection, even if most minimal, by customary international law."[80]

As counter-intuitive as this may seem to the utilitarians among us, I am arguing that there are some things we may not do to others, regardless of their actions, and whatever the circumstances. An important point to consider here, as Waldron reminds us, is that absolute opposition to torture is not just a moral or religious view, or the view of an ethically sensitive Kantian conscience, but is in fact what the law requires:[81]

I am told that this is an idealistic position, a sort of naïve Kantianism utterly inappropriate for use as a standard for public action in the real world. Yet the absolutist position is not just conjured up out of my own personal fastidiousness. It is what the law requires, and it is found in all human rights conventions. These, we should remember, are **public** documents; they are not treatises of personal ethics but conventions establishing minimum legal standards for the exercise of state power. As such, they prohibit torture categorically and absolutely, explicitly withholding from the prohibition on torture the provision for derogation in time of emergency that they allow for other human rights norms. They do this on the basis of the most elementary regard for human dignity and respect for the sacredness of the human individual, even in extremis, when the individual is at his most isolated, dangerous and despised.[82]

Consequently, we err to begin with by asking why these Kantian moral views should apply in the hard situations of political decision making. We would do better to question why those making hard political decisions should be exempt from the obligation to obey the law.[83] I return to the question of whether it is ever excusable to disobey the absolute legal prohibition on torture in the following chapter. For now, it is important to note that an absolute and categorical prohibition on torture already

---

[80] HCJ 769/02 [2005], Para. 25.
[81] International Covenant on Civil and Political Rights, Articles 7 and 4(2); and the United Nations Convention against Torture and Other Inhuman or Degrading Treatment or Punishment, Part I, Article 2. See also Waldron, "Torture," p. 1688.
[82] Waldron, "What Can Christian Thinking Add," p. 336.
[83] I am grateful to Jeremy Waldron for pointing this out to me.

exists, as a matter of positive law, within internationally agreed-upon human rights conventions.[84]

Part of the trouble with resolving this issue, as Elshtain points out, lies in the word "torture" itself:[85] "Is a shouted insult a form of torture? A slap in the face? Sleep deprivation? A beating to within an inch of one's life? Electric prods on the male genitals, inside a woman's vagina, or in a person's anus? Pulling out fingernails? Cutting off an ear or a breast?"[86] The Geneva Convention makes no distinction between these tactics.[87] Adrian Zuckerman defends this inclusive view and criticizes the conclusions of Israel's Landau Commission report on the methods employed by its general security services in interrogating suspects of hostile terrorist activity: "The commission thought that 'a moderate measure of physical pressure' during interrogation is different in kind from torture ... and does not offend the human values reflected in our legal system in the same way."[88] Zuckerman argues that since the entire point of an interrogator's inflicting any physical pressure is to overcome the suspect's resistance to providing information, then obviously a determined suspect, of the type we have in mind, will succumb only when the pressure becomes, from his point of view, unbearable. There is no qualitative difference between "moderate" and torturous physical force, Zuckerman argues, nor is there any objective scale for quantifying torture because pain is a subjective concept.[89]

Admittedly, it is difficult to differentiate between a persistent, perhaps harsh, investigation and outright torture. One man's discomfort is another's excruciating pain; one man's mild intimidation is the realization of another's deepest fear. Nevertheless, Elshtain argues that human rights activists who take this line do a disservice both to the prevention of real torture and to the protection of honest citizens in a dangerous and violent world. Furthermore, "by failing to distinguish between sleep deprivation and amputation and burning or some other horror, they elevate the former and diminish the latter."[90] This non-distinguishing view is also inconsistent with the way we usually practice law and morality.[91] The law, as well as moral philosophy, frequently makes fine qualitative distinctions between activities that may appear different

---

[84] See note 81, above.   [85] Elshtain, "Reflection," p. 79.   [86] Ibid.
[87] Ibid., p. 85, critiques this approach.
[88] Zuckerman, "Coercion," p. 371.   [89] Ibid.
[90] Elshtain, "Reflection," p. 86.   [91] Ibid., p. 79.

only quantitatively.[92] We differentiate between insults and hate speech, between slapping and child beating, between flirtation and sexual harassment. And we take these distinctions to be both qualitatively meaningful and practically invaluable, despite the indeterminacy and the subjective manner in which these various forms of treatment may be perceived by their recipient.

To return to torture, at least two parameters for distinguishing justifiable forms of physical pressure from hard-core torture arise from Shue's classic essay. First, that no irreparable damage is caused. Second, that the defenseless victim is nonetheless not entirely helpless, in that the pain may be inflicted only "up to the point at which the necessary information is divulged" and no further. The victim has an escape route, whatever the cost to his questionable sense of integrity.[93] Although Shue never says so, these features may serve to distinguish qualitatively harsh investigative methods, which may at times be justifiable, from the core concept of torture, as well as from terror itself.

Consider, as Mark Bowden does, "sleep deprivation, exposure to heat or cold, the use of drugs to cause confusion, rough treatment (slapping, shoving or shaking), forcing a prisoner to stand for days at a time or sit in uncomfortable positions, and playing on his fears for himself and his family. Although excruciating for the victim, these tactics generally leave no permanent marks and no lasting physical harm."[94] Horrific as these tactics are (Bowden dubs them "torture lite"), compare them, as Elshtain does, with rape, breast burning, extracting fingernails, hanging for hours from the arms, crucifying, and actually torturing a spouse or children rather than merely threatening to do so. Most vividly and effectively (for

---

[92] Bentham distinguished between hard-core torture and what he called "compulsive durance" (e.g. incarceration in order to compel a suspect to divulge useful information), which he thought in some cases could be more effective than torture. As one would expect, however, he also sanctioned the use of torture in some rare cases, particularly when the danger to be thwarted is great and immediate and when we are as sure as possible that the potential victim of torture possesses the information necessary in order to protect the community from the imminent threat. The threat must be to individuals rather than to a particular government. Torture can be justified only when there is no alternative and it must be, as far as possible, effective. See Twining and Twining, "Bentham on Torture," pp. 308–37; 346–7.

[93] Shue, "Torture," p. 142.

[94] Mark Bowden, "The Dark Art of Interrogation", *Atlantic Monthly*, October 2003, pp. 53–4. Cited by Elshtain, "Reflection," p. 85.

those of us who saw the film), she conjures up the image of a sadistic Lawrence Olivier grinding down and pulling teeth, as he does to Dustin Hoffman in *Marathon Man*.[95] Elshtain asks, "In an exceptional and truly extreme circumstance, would it be defendable to do any of these things? Everything in me says no and tells me that when we think of torture it is these sorts of extreme forms of physical torment we are thinking of."[96] Elshtain calls this category "torture 1 – the extreme forms of physical torment", distinguishable from torture 2 "for which we surely need a different name, like coercive interrogation."[97] While the former is always prohibited, she argues that in dire circumstances in which a potential informant most probably holds information that would save innocent human lives, the latter, "torture 2", may regrettably be used.[98]

I join Elshtain in her categorical rejection of "torture 1." There are certain things we cannot do to others, ways in which we cannot use them, whoever they are and whatever their crime, simply because they are human beings. I am, however, somewhat hesitant about differentiating between tortures 1 and 2, or hard-core and lite, on the basis of refraining from long-term damage or as distinguishable in terms of physical versus "merely" psychological abuse. At least some research conducted on survivors of torture indicates that this distinction may be only apparent. According to a recent psychiatric study, the long-term mental effects of ill-treatment during captivity, such as use of the stress position, exposure to adverse environmental conditions, and severe psychological manipulation, do not differ significantly in terms of the severity of trauma and depression from the long-lasting effects of hard-core physical torture.[99] Consequently, it is argued that these techniques (or perhaps some of them, or their use beyond some minimal threshold) amount to torture, thereby lending support to their absolute prohibition in international law.

However, no form of interrogation is likely to be pleasant, particularly when the information sought is urgent and the victim reluctant. This is not a defense of contemporary practices, some of which are admittedly abhorrent. Certain forms of pressure regarded at times by liberal democracies, such as the US, UK, and Israel, as moderate physical

---

[95] Elshtain, "Reflection," p. 85.   [96] Ibid.
[97] Ibid., p. 87.   [98] Ibid.
[99] http://archpsyc.ama-assn.org/cgi/content/full/64/3/277?eaf (accessed May 10, 2007).

pressure may in the end constitute forms of unacceptable torture. Depriving a suspect of sleep for extended periods, exposure to unpleasant temperatures, hooding, holding a suspect in extremely uncomfortable positions for lengthy periods of time, may indeed be unbearable forms of physical force. Additionally, methods that require prolonged endurance, can rarely, if ever, be justified by any argument about immediate necessity. They are more likely to be used in order to gather general intelligence information. This is an important point, which is often missed and rarely stressed. Returning to the examples with which I opened this essay suggests that the only justification for the use of any physical force is the prevention of an immediately pending disaster. In such cases, methods that challenge the suspect's level of endurance over time are of no use. Depriving a prisoner of comfort for long stretches of time is largely irrelevant to any "ticking bomb" situation.

On the other hand, the same examples suggest that under such highly restricted circumstances of imminent danger, it is not unreasonable to extend interrogators greater leeway in the use of harsh investigative methods than would be permitted in any ordinary criminal circumstance. While I (gladly) lack the experience to determine precisely which of the lighter forms of interrogation are qualitatively different from torture, I also join Elshtain in concluding that some forms of moderate pressure may legitimately, though regrettably, be used against known terrorist activists, if they are indeed the only available means of saving innocents from torment and death.

Furthermore, harsh measures may be employed only when we are as certain as humanly possible that the interrogated subject is indeed involved in terrorism. My reason for this conclusion was explained in the previous section. Judicial involvement is then also essential in order to guarantee, as far as possible, that the interrogated subject is in fact a terrorist activist, that he is more than likely to possess the necessary information and, as such, normatively vulnerable to harsher treatment. I argued earlier that terrorists who specifically maim and kill innocents at random as means towards their ends, leaving their victims no escape route, transgress the most basic rules of humanist morality and offend the dignity and person of innocent human beings. I suggested that the conclusion of several accounts (Shue, Moore, Machan, and Kamm) is that terrorists are thereby less deserving of the legal immunities which would ordinarily prevent the balancing of their pain against the well-being of others – in this case their potential victims. Their own conduct enables us to weigh their suffering against the suffering of others, even if we are not utilitarians inclined to do so anyway.

The limits to this license ought not to be taken lightly. While this short chapter deals only with the moral impermissibility of torture rather than with the practical worries that surround it, it should be noted that even the most stringent license to resort to moderate forms of pressure, whether physical or psychological, in rare incidents of dire peril, must be limited to some extent by institutional guarantees, judicial and other-wise, which assure that security forces do not surpass these limits. These safeguards might include such requirements as acquiring a judicial war-rant prior to investigation, rather than after-the-fact authorization.[100] Judges who authorize the use of interrogational force might be required to supply written opinions, open to public scrutiny.[101] Sanford Levinson also suggests helpfully that when such a warrant is requested, "the person the state proposes to torture should be in the courtroom, so that the judge can take no refuge in abstraction."[102] Shue argues that even if torture can under rare circumstances be justified, it should be assured, among other things, that "the prime minister and chief justice are being kept informed; and a priest and a doctor are present."[103] Alan Dershowitz controver-sially suggests that interrogators ought to be required to obtain judicial "torture warrants" which would presumably enable them to inflict hard-core torture on their interrogated subjects.[104] I will return to this proposal in the following chapter, though I oppose the use of torture proper, whatever the safeguards. For now, suffice it to note that such safeguards are essential to the justification of any use of force in the interrogation chamber, not only hard-core torture, *inter alia* in order to guarantee that what sets out as moderate pressure does not end up as torture proper.

The utilitarian, however, and not only the utilitarian, poses one final challenge. How can one defend the counter-intuitive view that one

---

[100] Sanford Levinson, "Contemplating Torture," in Levinson, *Torture*, p. 37; Dershowitz, "Tortured Reasoning," in Levinson, *Torture*, pp. 257–77; Dershowitz, *Shouting Fire*, pp. 470–7. Here, as elsewhere, Dershowitz defends his position whereby since torture will, as a matter of empirical fact, inevitably be employed by liberal states combating terror, it ought to be under judicial supervision requiring the interrogators to obtain "torture warrants" prior to investigation. It should be noted that Dershowitz never actually defends the use of torture against terrorists.

[101] Levinson, "Contemplating Torture," p. 37.   [102] Ibid.

[103] Shue, "Torture," p. 142.

[104] See Alan Dershowitz, *Why Terrorism Works: Understanding the Threat, Responding to the Challenge* (Yale University Press, 2002), p. 248.

should refrain from torture proper (no. 1, and probably also certain methods hitherto regarded as no. 2 or "torture lite"), even in the most extreme circumstances? This conclusion is always resisted in the debate on torture, even by non-utilitarians, who do not wish to find themselves in Kant's awkward position of condemning lying even in order to protect an innocent man from murder. This overused example is inappropriate here. Other examples show that our intuitions, as well as our legal institutions, contain certain rules we believe in adhering to even if the consequences are truly disastrous.

Though the heavens may fall

Plainly, inflicting pain, of any kind, on another human being in order to obtain life-saving information nonetheless uses that person as a means towards others' ends. Worse still, as Sussman suggests, torture is perhaps best characterized as pitting the victim's own bodily functions and suffering against himself, so that he himself becomes the instrument of his own downfall.

Terrorism and torture are moral parallels in so far as they target individuals who are not directly involved in creating the plight that the aggressor is attempting to thwart, and as long as they inflict the type of severe detrimental pain and mutilation mentioned above. These are the root evils that ought to be categorically banned, whatever the consequences may be. I have argued that terrorism defies a most basic standard of liberal-humanist morality, at least since Kant and up to Rawls, which fundamentally forbids the use of human beings as means only, and commands their treatment as ends in themselves.[105] The same liberal democracies that contemplate the use of torture in their war against terror, usually regard terrorism itself as categorically wrong, regardless of cause, because it inflicts extreme and permanently mutilating suffering on victims who are not directly implicated in creating the plight the terrorist seeks to rectify, and who have no avenue of escape. As such, I have argued that we are justified in regarding terrorism as morally abhorrent, whatever its reasons. Regardless of our sympathies for the agent's cause (which may be justified and noble), representatives of Western democracies often say "never" terrorize, whatever the root

---

[105] See Kant, *Groundwork*, p. 96; Rawls, *A Theory of Justice*, p. 179.

cause, and similarly they should say "never" torture, whatever the danger.[106]

This, however, is as far as the analogy goes. As we saw, our intuitions about terrorism as an absolute wrong may change when the target of unconventional warfare is either military or political. In these instances, we should agree with Michael Walzer that the categorical imperative against terror, properly defined, does not apply to guerrilla warfare or political assassination, respectively, justifiable under certain circumstances and with reference to consequences.[107] We might also think that frightening, even coercing, a civilian population into action in ways that fall short of directly inflicting pain and death do not fall under this categorical ban on terror. (I doubt causing a power failure in New York City on the morning of September 11, 2001, with the presumed result of some injuries and deaths, would have brought about the sweeping condemnation of terrorism that demolishing two buildings did.)[108] This is not merely a difference of degree, but rather, we sense, a difference in kind.

The same goes for torture. For the reasons spelled out above, torture, properly defined, like terrorism, is an absolute violation of human dignity and the ultimately evil usage of its victim as a means towards his captors' ends. Aside from which it is also entirely ruled out by international law. However, just as unconventional, even illegal, warfare may be justifiable against a ruthless enemy – who would question the legitimacy of assassinating Hitler, or of the French Resistance? – the thrust of my argument has been that the terrorist has flouted the most basic distinctions and prohibitions of humanist morality, as well as international law. This may, under highly restrained circumstances, render the terrorist eligible for harsher methods of investigation (when this is absolutely essential to save innocent lives), which would be intolerable in the case of any other detainee. It is not implausible to hold that while torture is prohibited by liberal-humanist morality, individuals involved in terrorism need not be treated with kid gloves, at least if they are reasonably suspected of withholding vital life-saving information. On the other hand, the use of outright torture, I argue, is never justified even against those who have

---

[106] Waldron, "Torture," p. 1714: if the numbers of potential victims can justify the use of torture, then it can as easily be used to justify terrorism itself.

[107] See Walzer's *Just and Unjust Wars* for a triple distinction between guerrilla tactics, political assassination, and terrorism, which he categorically rejects, pp. 176–97.

[108] Kamm, "Failure of Just War Theory," p. 663.

engaged in precisely this type of categorical moral wrong themselves. There are certain things we simply cannot do, regardless of consequences and regardless of what others have done to us.

In a post-September 11 world, one need not be a utilitarian in order to question my categorical conclusion. Even Kantians start shifting uneasily when confronted by a variation on the familiar theme of the catastrophic examples presented at the outset. As Waldron observes:

> For a culture supposedly committed to human rights, we have amazing difficulty in even conceiving – without some sort of squirm – the idea of genuine moral absolutes. Academics in particular are so frightened of being branded "unrealistic" that we will fall over ourselves at the slightest provocation to opine that of course moral restraints must be abandoned when the stakes are high enough. Extreme circumstances can make moral absolutes look ridiculous, and those in our position cannot afford to be made to look ridiculous.[109]

Is an absolute prohibition on torture not the type of naïve "rule worship" that gave Kant's truth-teller a bad name? I do not think the prohibition on lying is the best analogy that can be invoked here. A far more challenging analogy is supplied by Kamm, who argues, in favor of torturing terrorists, that it is sometimes justified to use sufficiently unjust agents as mere means towards saving their victims or potential victims: "Suppose A deliberately takes B's crucial organs. A is captured and is no longer a threat. However, the only way to save B is to transplant all of A's organs into B. I think doing so is permissible."[110]

This challenge is indeed difficult to meet. While intuitions on what a state authority should do in any such particular situation may vary, I suspect most would join Kamm in favoring the dissection of the offender and, analogously, also the torture of a threatening terrorist. Kamm's hypothetical, however, is analogous only to a very restricted, somewhat far-fetched scenario, in which the captured terrorist is known in all certainty to be the very individual who has, by his own hands, endangered specific potential victims whom can now be saved only by his confession. Note that interrogated terrorists are rarely, if ever, tried and convicted prior to torture. In any slightly altered hypothetical, which would take into account the benefit of doubt, the possibility of less than direct involvement in the potential danger, as well as other uncertainties

---

[109] Waldron, "Torture," p. 1713.
[110] Kamm, "Failure of Just War Theory," p. 659.

concerning the prospects of attaining our life-saving goal, our intuitions might more easily pull in the direction of an absolute prohibition on using the state's judicial system in order to kill and coerce organ donation.

Consider the more familiar example of killing a person to obtain his organs in order to save the lives of several other people, or even removing them for that purpose against his will without killing him.[111] Most of us, I believe, hold to an absolute ban on such life-saving measures, even in the case of convicted criminals, and not for the reason a rule utilitarian might supply. Our reluctance to kill a healthy person, even one involved in illegal or immoral conduct, in order to obtain his life-saving organs, need not rely on the utility of a rule forbidding everyone to do so, or with any slippery-slope argument. In fact, we might find both the act utilitarian's necessary sanction of such acts, along with the rule utilitarian's explanation for demurring from them, a good cause for rejecting utilitarianism.[112] We may oppose such actions simply because they purport to use human beings as mere means towards attaining the happiness of others. Furthermore, they propose officially to employ the organs of state, hitherto regarded as liberal democracies, in order to do so. Moreover, compulsory organ donation would be an ultimate invasion of one's person and violation of integrity and dignity. This absolute conviction does not change even if the potential organ donor is a morally contemptible individual who has himself voluntarily violated the bodily integrity and dignity of other individuals.

There is no complete analogy between the tortured terrorist suspect and the unworthy potential organ donor. The point is that absolute prohibitions on the usage of individuals, even bad individuals, and the violation of individual dignity, autonomy, and integrity, are not as alien to our moral world and intuitions as some extreme examples would lead us to believe. As Waldron argues in favor of an absolute legal ban on torture, most "readers will draw the line *somewhere*, to prohibit *some* action even under the most extreme circumstances," even if we are at times tongue-tied, so to speak, at explaining precisely why we draw the line at this particular evil.[113] For some, the limit might be issuing judicial rape warrants (analogous to Alan Dershowitz's proposal of

---

[111] Moore, "Torture," p. 288.
[112] Bentham is a clear example of the former. See Twining and Twining, "Bentham on Torture" once again, for Bentham's view and also for some rule-utilitarian objections to institutionalizing torture.
[113] Waldron, "Torture," p. 1715.

attaining "torture warrants"); for others, the limit will be resorting to terrorism itself. But for most liberals, there are some measures that ought never to be resorted to, even against morally loathsome individuals, even though we know for certain that abstaining from them will result in the heavens falling for some innocent people.

Concluding remarks

I have tried to defend a categorical ban on torture regardless of circumstances. This defense may admittedly not cover the most horrendous potential consequences that can be conjured up in the wildest of philosophical examples. Nonetheless, I believe it holds for every real-world "ticking bomb" scenario we have experienced so far and are likely to experience in the foreseeable future.

On the other hand, I also suggested that in the regrettably more familiar cases of urgent interrogation, security forces may, under highly restrictive circumstances, be justified in resorting to some moderate physical or psychological methods of extracting essential life-saving information from terrorists, inflicted only up to the minimal degree essential for extracting the vital information. While I would not presume to offer interrogation techniques, I have in mind measures that under all ordinary circumstances would be regarded as police brutality but are, nonetheless, far from the horrors that the word "torture" usually conjures up. In the extreme, such measures might include slapping or shoving and shaking, imposing a certain degree of extended discomfort, or psychological pressures such as threats and insults; all, indeed, are harsher than the ordinary criminal justice procedure would allow for. Even this, however, would be permissible only where the interrogators can convince a judge that their prisoner not only possesses the information but is also involved in terrorist activity, that he is in fact knowledgeable, and that he is unlikely to divulge his information under ordinary criminal investigation tactics. Furthermore, the desired information must be vital to saving the lives of innocents, and the use of force must be the last resort and the minimal measure available for obtaining it. Hopefully, this will not be a very frequent occurrence. I suggested, hesitantly, that a very limited escalation in interrogation techniques might be justifiable against specific terrorists who have themselves voluntarily selected particularly inhumane (as well as illegal) methods of combat, morally akin to torturing the innocent, thereby placing the latter in immediate mortal peril. When urgently interrogating culpable terrorists, it may be justifiable to resort to somewhat harsher methods than one would employ towards a common criminal, though only when such treatment is regrettably essential in order to save the lives of innocents who have been placed at risk by the terrorist activity itself, and only after institutional guarantees against abuse have been secured. Notwithstanding this possible license, I argued against resorting to outright torture under any foreseeable circumstances and in favor of laws and moral rules that categorically prohibit such treatment.

What if we are holding the only terrorist whom we know for sure can prevent a nuclear incineration of the entire United States, and there is no other way of preventing this than by torturing him? Would I still uphold the ban on torture? Perhaps not, but under such circumstances we might also kidnap an innocent bystander and force him to donate an organ necessary to save the terrorist informer from dying before he supplies us with the life-saving information. Clearly, we would not attempt to deduce any statement of policy on organ donation from this hypothetical, nor should we derive any conclusions from it regarding torture. As Shue comments, "there is a saying in jurisprudence that hard cases make bad law, and there might well be one in philosophy that artificial cases make bad ethics."[114] The following chapter inquires further into the unforeseeable emergency scenarios, looked at from the perspective of a political leader or particular interrogator, rather than from the birds-eye view of ideal moral philosophy.

---

[114] Shue, "Torture," p. 141.

7 | Torture and the problem of dirty hands

It is widely agreed among liberals that torture is a moral wrong, even within a just war, as it is particularly degrading and humiliating even in comparison with actual killing. As we saw in Chapter 6, there is some disagreement among philosophers as to the characterization of the precise evil that is torture and regarding the limits of its prohibition. I argued that torture ought to be categorically prohibited by liberal democracies, even in the course of confronting ruthless and unscrupulous terrorists. The rise of international terrorism has brought forth the suggestion that liberal democracies may actually be justified in resorting to the use of torture against captured terrorists in order to obtain life-saving information. We saw that amongst academics such suggestions usually take a standard form of presenting a vivid example in which the torture of a known terrorist is pitted against the prospect of saving many innocent lives from violent death by terror.[1] The inevitable outcome, either implied or explicitly argued for, is a consequentialist, or semi-consequentialist, justification of specific acts of torture under certain, usually extreme, assumptions in which the outstanding suffering for many is taken to outweigh the suffering of the victim of torture.[2] Thus the issue is supposedly resolved with a clear conscience and the alternative is presented as morally untenable. I remained uneasy about regarding torture as morally justifiable under any conditions and argued in favor of an absolute ban on torture.

---

[1] Elshtain, "Reflection," p. 78.

[2] Shue, "Torture," p. 141; Dershowitz, *Shouting Fire*, p. 477. Some justifications are not primarily utilitarian but argue that consequences come in to play a secondary role, at least at some cataclysmic point. See, for example, Michael Moore's "soft deontology" in "Torture and the Balance of Evils," pp. 280–344; and Kai Nielson, "There Is No Dilemma of Dirty Hands," in Paul Rynard and David P. Shugarman (eds.), *Cruelty and Deception: The Controversy over Dirty Hands in Politics* (Peterborough, Ontario: Broadview Press, 2000), Chapter 8.

In the following I will continue to assume that all torture is wrong.[3] The issue to be unraveled here is of a different kind, and it presupposes, rather than argues for, a moral prohibition on at least some forms of torture. The position whereby some form of torture is absolutely wrong, always and under all circumstances, does not exhaust the range of moral query on this issue. The familiar examples present a different type of moral problem, rather than a solution, for theorists who view the prohibition on torture as a moral absolute. The latter may still be called upon to consider the perspective of the state leader, the politician, or the individual interrogator, forced to choose between the morally unjustifiable and illegal torture of an individual, perhaps even an innocent civilian, and the lives of many other innocent civilians for whom he has assumed responsibility. Michael Walzer presents this excruciating situation most clearly as "the dilemma of dirty hands," and it is this particular type of moral problem that will concern me throughout this chapter.[4] A similar task has recently been undertaken by Steven Lukes as part of his work on "Democratic Torture," where he asks whether torture is simply an instance of "the dilemma of dirty hands," defined as "a species of moral dilemma, where, in doing what appears to be the right, or best thing in the circumstances, we cannot avoid doing wrong."[5]

In the following I suggest that this notion of "dirty hands" best reflects our common intuitions on torture, as well as the moral complexity of the torture issue in an age of terror. Later, I will show that the variety of familiar philosophical examples referred to above, which pit torture against some potential terrorist catastrophe, are similar in form but not in purpose. While such examples are frequently invoked in order to justify the use of torture in terms of its desirable consequences, they are sometimes used in order to illustrate this more complex type of moral problem defined by Walzer. Within this approach, torture is morally unjustifiable but at the same time may, under certain circumstances,

---

[3] I address situations in which upholding what we take to be an absolute moral wrong – whether torture in general, torture of the innocent, torture of children, official rape – bears an unbearable price in terms of innocent human life.

[4] Walzer, "Political Action," p. 167, reprinted in Levinson, *Torture*, pp. 64–5. References are to this version.

[5] Steven Lukes, "Liberal Democratic Torture," *British Journal of Political Science* 36 (2005), p. 2.

remain in some sense the required course of political action. First, I will suggest, contra Walzer and Lukes, that the problem of dirty hands is not exclusively an absolutist predicament. It is in fact more universal and reflective of a wider range of moral positions than Walzer himself imagined. A utilitarian, I shall argue, particularly a rule utilitarian, can certainly suffer from dirty hands.

Dirty hands

Walzer's variation on the familiar theme asks us to:

Consider a politician who has seized upon a national crisis – a prolonged colonial war – to reach for power. He and his friends win office pledged to decolonization and peace ... Immediately the politician goes off to the colonial capital to open negotiations with the rebels. But the capital is in the grip of a terrorist campaign and the first decision the new leader faces is this: he is asked to authorize the torture of a captured rebel leader who knows or probably knows the location of a number of bombs hidden in apartment buildings around the city, set to go off within the next twenty-four hours. He orders the man tortured, convinced that he must do so for the sake of the people who might otherwise die in the explosions – even though he believes that torture is wrong, indeed abominable, not just sometimes, but always.[6]

Walzer's own answer is that the politician in such a situation may be right in doing what it is wrong for him to do. Rejecting the utilitarian approach, he insists that the politician in question has committed a definite moral wrong. By so doing he has, in Walzer's terms, tainted his hands with the blood of the interrogated victim. Paradoxically, Walzer tells us, the politician has acquired this moral blemish in the course of committing a wrong that it was actually right for him to commit.[7]

Kai Nielson criticizes Walzer on this very point. Claiming that "There is No Dilemma of Dirty Hands," Nielson argues, with much reference to the torture issue, that "dirty hands" is not a dilemma or a paradox but merely the problem of having to commit a necessary lesser evil in a political situation that requires choosing between two evils.[8] One need not be a utilitarian, Nielson points out, in order to concede that when faced with a choice between two evils, a political leader (indeed anyone) is justified, and not wrong at all, in choosing the option which, while

[6] Walzer, "Political Action," p. 167.
[7] Ibid., p. 63.
[8] Nielson, "There Is No Dilemma," pp. 139–55.

breaching a *prima facie* obligation, achieves the better (or less negative) all-round consequences.[9]

Many forms of soft, or weakened, deontology distinguish themselves from utilitarianism by adhering to rules which are not utility based, and yet concede that in unusual, usually extreme, circumstances these (*prima facie*) rules can, indeed should, be overridden by consequential considerations.[10] Also, rules and obligations can conflict and should in such cases be balanced against each other.[11] Any moral theory that enables the prioritizing of *prima* facie duties can allow for this.[12] The alternative, unacceptable to Nielson (as well as Walzer), is following moral absolutism to the point of catastrophe, rather than tolerating any breach of rules. Pointing out that Walzer himself rejects this course of action (he thinks the politician ought to order the torture), Nielson accuses Walzer of "paradox mongering," arguing that his "dirty hands dilemma" is fictitious and confusing.[13] Nielson does not deny the dirty work involved, only the existence of a paradox. The agent who chooses a lesser evil solution does not do right and wrong simultaneously, as Walzer suggests, but merely what is justified overall, and absolutely right, given the difficult circumstances.[14]

Howard Curzer recently attributes a similar stand to Walzer himself, pointing out that in opting for torture in his ticking bomb example, Walzer specifies this choice as the lesser evil, thus undercutting his own claim that the dilemma he presents is a moral no-win situation: "He takes torture to be the lesser evil, the greater requirement."[15]

The notion of dirty hands, however, properly understood, does not simply involve the prospect of doing a *prima facie* wrong in the process of, or for the sake of, achieving a greater good. If this were the case, dirty

---

[9] Ibid., pp. 140–1. For a specific discussion of torture within a "lesser evil theory," see Ignatieff, *The Lesser Evil*, pp. 135–44. It is interesting to note that Ignatieff, who dedicates an entire volume to his theory of "the lesser evil," resists justifying outright torture on these grounds.

[10] Nielson, "There Is No Dilemma," pp. 143–5. At various points I discuss Michael Moore's "threshold deontology" alongside his view on torture, which is also a form of "soft deontology."

[11] Ibid., p. 150.

[12] Coady, "Terrorism," discusses this approach toward exemptions from profound moral obligations, p. 83.

[13] Nielson, "There Is No Dilemma," p. 152.   [14] Ibid., pp. 151–2.

[15] Howard J. Curzer, "Admirable Immorality, Dirty Hands, Ticking Bombs, and Torturing Innocents," *The Southern Journal of Philosophy* XLIV (2006), pp. 31–56, p. 46.

hands would express little more than the classic question of whether the end justifies the means. At times Lukes appears to view the problem of dirty hands in such terms,[16] but Walzer clearly rejects the view that dirty hands involve the justification of immoral means by referring to their desirable ends, as well as the familiar attribution of such a stand to Machiavelli.[17] If Walzer were staking a lesser evil argument, there would be no interesting irresolvable dilemma to speak of, but merely the outweighing of a *prima facie* duty never to torture, by a weightier duty to protect the community, as Howard Curzer believes the case to be.[18]

The problem of dirty hands is genuinely paradoxical and far more elusive than justifying means in terms of their good goals. While Curzer argues that Walzer's decision to torture the rebel reveals a lesser evil position regarding torture, he also recognizes that Walzer denies the consistency of morality and its demands.[19] As Thomas Nagel suggests, the world – war and politics in particular – presents us with situations in which an agent cannot avoid doing wrong, whatever course of action he takes.[20] Nagel believes there is a genuine dilemma in such cases, which he describes in terms of the conflict between the principle of utility – instructing us to maximize good and minimize evil – and absolutist principles that place constraints on what we may do, whatever the consequences.[21] Both kinds of principle play a role in our normative thinking and form incommensurable parts of our moral intuitions. On the one hand, in certain situations, as when torture or murder is the only available means by which to save lives, absolutism requires us in effect to refrain from opting for the lesser evil. On the other, the pull of the consequentialist consideration is considerable, even for a non-utilitarian. In such cases, Nagel argues, the moral dilemma is acute and in fact insoluble, with both courses of action deemed to be wrong, and he regards torture in order to prevent disaster as a case in point.[22]

---

[16] "Perhaps we tend to associate dirty hands with politics because in political life the good to be attained tends to be framed in general terms and the wrongs committed highly specific: Spreading freedom around the world, social justice, the Defense of the Realm, the Cause of the Revolution, The Glory of the Republic." Lukes, "Liberal Democratic Torture," p. 3.

[17] Walzer, "Political Action," pp. 69–70.

[18] Curzer, "Admirable Immorality," p. 46.   [19] Ibid.

[20] Thomas Nagel, "War and Massacre," *Philosophy and Public Affairs* 1 (2) (Winter 1972), p. 143.

[21] Ibid., p. 124–5.

[22] Ibid., pp. 125–6, 129, 136–7; see esp. p. 143. For his reference to torture, see pp. 124, 137.

For Nagel, the dilemma is clearly an internal moral one and apparently has no solution. Morality itself pulls in two opposing directions.
Walzer's example illustrates a similar point, but not necessarily an
equivalent one. According to Walzer, a politician will necessarily be
called upon in the course of his office to commit what are unmistakably
immoral acts. In Nagel's terms, he will sometimes necessarily do wrong,
whatever he does.[23] But Walzer, unlike Nagel, instructs him clearly as to
which wrong he is to choose. His take on the familiar torture example,
however, is not intended as a justification of torture under any circumstances. He regards torture as a moral wrong and assumes that its
prohibition is widely held as a moral absolute. Unlike Nagel's situation,
it is unclear whether Walzer believes the problem to be internally moral
or whether it reflects a conflict between morality and other directives.
Perhaps, for Walzer, like Machiavelli, "his political judgments are
indeed consequentialist in character, but not his moral judgments."[24]

Walzer's frequent reference to Machiavelli is telling. For however
else he is interpreted, Machiavelli clearly denied the overriding nature
of moral obligations in political life. It is somewhat unclear whether
Walzer follows wholeheartedly in his footsteps, suggesting that torture
is immoral but that it is nonetheless politically required under certain
circumstances. He appears to hold simultaneously to the non-overriding
view of morality alongside the Nagel-type argument that morality itself
is internally inconsistent. These two views are theoretical alternatives,
though they need not be mutually exclusive. Morality might be both
inconsistent in its demands as well non-overriding in its scope.

Curzer argues against Walzer in support of the overridingness thesis.
Like Nagel, he describes the "dirty hands" dilemma in terms of a tension
within moral theory, though he denies that morality is inconsistent in its
requirements. He suggests instead that in the rarest of instances, moral
duty and moral virtue diverge, such that there may be vicious, morally
required acts (such as torture) and virtuous, morally wrong acts (refraining from torture at the expense of catastrophe). This tension is described
in terms of a conflict between *moral virtue* – understood as a disposition
enforced by habit, to act in a certain manner, and which is usually morally
required (i.e. never torture, which is normally right as well as virtuous) –
versus *moral duty*, understood as the product of careful reasoning in the
particular case (i.e. torture when necessary to avert disaster). Curzer holds

[23] Ibid., p. 143.   [24] Walzer on Machiavelli, "Political Action," p. 69.

unequivocally that torture is morally required when necessary to save the community. The remaining "dirt," associated with torture is then attributed merely to the viciousness commonly associated with torture by the virtuous. Torture is usually very wrong, thus the virtuous are habitually disposed to recoil from it. Resorting to torture when it is indeed required is thus out of character for the virtuous; hence the remaining feelings of shame, or dirt.[25] Walzer's dilemma of dirty hands exists only to the extent that it is indeed tragic for a good person to choose between virtue and duty. But there is no real moral deadlock because, according to Curzer's account, moral duty – which is the ultimate directive as to what ought to be done – unambiguously proscribes torture as the right course of action in a ticking bomb situation.[26]

Walzer does not pursue the issue of torture beyond the short passage cited above. Nonetheless, his theory of "dirty hands" grasps the moral complexities involved in the contemporary debate over investigative torture in liberal democracies, which is missed by simply regarding torture as emotionally repugnant, or "out of character" for the virtuous. The notion of acquiring a severe moral blemish in the process of taking a politically required course of action is stronger than the idea of merely doing a dirty, but morally necessary, job. It also highlights the excruciating moral and meta-moral issues involved in the choice of torture far better than any theory of lesser evils, justifying means by their good goals, or prioritizing duties. It raises questions concerning the priority of moral directives as well as the consistency of morality itself, even if it does not supply us with all the answers. Moreover, I will try to show that "dirty hands" reflects a wider scope of moral intuitions than even Walzer himself assumed, as it encompasses a familiar utilitarian approach as well as the absolutist one that he presents.

Rule utilitarianism and the problem of dirty hands

Nagel describes a moral dilemma that represents a conflict between two principles – utilitarianism and absolutism. Assuming that our moral intuitions may be mixed, he acknowledges that the dilemma he describes can be experienced not only by the devout absolutist but

---

[25] Curzer, "Admirable Immorality," esp. pp. 31–2, 47–9.   [26] Ibid., pp. 48–9.

also by the utilitarian.[27] However, he focuses primarily on the absolutist component of this dilemma.[28]

Walzer argues that the issue of politically dirty hands is exclusively an absolutist's dilemma, as utilitarianism cannot bring out the problem in its own terms. This is because, for the utilitarian, once the balance of utilities has been calculated, the moral prescription is definitive and there is nothing to feel bad, or dirty, about.[29] This is certainly the case for act utilitarians, as implied by the popular examples of torturing the few in order to prevent suffering for the many. If what morality requires is the simple comparison of the sum total of pleasure with the pain, there is nothing to feel guilty (or dirty) about when the calculation clearly indicates that the overall suffering can be reduced by torturing individual sentient beings in order to save many others from pain and death. Thus, they cannot suffer from dirty hands. As Lukes puts it: "The consequentialist simply asserts that what is morally required is that one always does 'simply what has to be done' in order to bring about the best outcome, all things considered. According to such a view, the ideas of an un-canceled wrong and regret at committing it have no place and no justification."[30]

Contra Walzer and Lukes, I suggest that rule utilitarians, and not only deontologists, can experience dirty hands, and thus that the "dirty hands" thesis is actually more widely applicable and illuminates a greater range of moral positions on issues such as torture than Walzer himself assumes. It is important to see how the problem of dirty hands plays out within rule utilitarianism because rule-utilitarian considerations, even when unarticulated, play an important role in the public debate on torture. Furthermore, as Nagel points out, few of us are pure, absolute deontologists, immune to utilitarian intuitions.[31]

After explaining why an act utilitarian who has acted in accordance with a successful set of calculations is free of dirty hands,[32] Walzer continues to argue that the same is true of rule utilitarians. It is true,

---

[27] Nagel, "War and Massacre," p. 143. [28] Ibid., p. 125.

[29] Walzer, "Political Action," p. 66.

[30] Lukes, "Liberal Democratic Torture," p. 5. See also Walzer, "Political Action," pp. 66–7. The act utilitarian may of course have psychological inhibitions about actions such as murder or torture, deriving from social conditioning or simple queasiness, but these cannot be justified in terms of his own moral theory, unless the feeling of guilt itself enhances utility.

[31] Nagel, "War and Massacre," p. 124. [32] Walzer, "Political Action," p. 66.

Walzer admits, that while act utilitarians hold that "every political choice ought to be made solely in terms of its particular and immediate circumstances,"[33] other forms of utilitarianism include moral rules. However, according to Walzer, utilitarian rules are no more than moral guidelines, summaries of previous calculations that ease our swift decision-making process in everyday cases. Such rules, according to Walzer, are merely convenient rules of thumb, which enable us to decide quickly and accurately in ordinary situations by simply referring to what was already found to be useful in the past, without having to make constant and repeated calculations. Perhaps such rules also have some general, educational, pedagogical purpose, but it is primarily expedient, rather than imperative, to adhere to such rules. Their convenience is their only purpose, "and so it cannot be the case that it is or even might be a crime to override them. Nor is it necessary to feel guilty when one does so."[34] If the rules are merely indications of greater utility based on previous calculations rather than moral prohibitions in any stricter sense, and if the calculated balance of utility is clearly different in the particular case, there can be no reason whatsoever to follow the (irrelevant) rule in an instance in which it clearly does not apply (that is, where greater happiness can be achieved by disregarding it). In fact it would be a mistake to do so and absurd to feel guilty about not doing so. But "this view" (that is, rule utilitarianism), Walzer worries, "captures the reality of moral life no better than the last one" (act utilitarianism). In other words, it makes no sense of the problem of dirty hands.[35]

Walzer assumes that the rules adhered to by rule utilitarians are merely summaries of previous calculations. But such rules of thumb are actually typical of act, rather than rule, utilitarianism, while the latter contains rules with greater normative force, which derives from the usefulness of the rules themselves.[36] On an indirect utilitarian account, a politician may find himself in a moral predicament very similar to the one experienced by the Kantian. In terms of Walzer's example, the rule utilitarian would be called upon to disregard a prohibition on torture in favor of the concrete utility to be gained by torturing the rebel in the individual case. But this would not merely be a breach of previous calculations, which indeed would not be problematic. The rule-utilitarian prohibition on

---

[33] Ibid., p. 66.   [34] Ibid., p. 67.   [35] Ibid.

[36] J.L. Mackie, *Ethics – Inventing Right and Wrong* (London: Penguin, 1990). See also Coady, "Terrorism," p. 82.

torture would be based on the far weightier moral consideration specifying that such individual acts of torture are wrong, regardless of their immediate utility, because the general performance of acts of this class (in our case, torture) would plainly have a negative effect on the general happiness.[37] This is indeed the standard form in which rule utilitarianism claims to escape the more violent conflicts that break out between act utilitarianism and our common moral intuitions. If the practice of torture is generally detrimental to the greater happiness, a rule utilitarian is committed, perhaps almost as strongly as the absolutist, to refraining from it, regardless of its immediate effects. Were this not the case, then rule utilitarianism would indeed simply collapse into act utilitarianism, as it has been, at times, accused of doing, and there would be little difference between act and rule utilitarianism regarding dirty hands or otherwise.

If the general tendency of torture is, as it is not unreasonable to assume, detrimental to the general happiness, then a rule utilitarian is committed to a rule with substantial merit, above and beyond the economy of swift decision-making.[38] If he decides, like Walzer's honest politician, to have the rebel tortured, he is not merely breaking some convenient rule of thumb. By his own moral standards, he has breached a prohibition far weightier in nature, and can certainly be said to have dirtied his hands considerably by doing so.

Rule utilitarianism, dirty hands, and torture

The difference between act and rule utilitarianism manifests itself in the prohibition on torture. There is no shortage of hypothetical cases, and (arguably) also some concrete ones, in which act utilitarians would unscrupulously prescribe the use of torture. Particularly in recent years, it has been suggested that the use of outright torture in the process of interrogating terrorist suspects and those associated with them can be highly expedient, and thus morally justifiable by act utilitarianism. Steven Lukes cites a case of torture from the mid-1990s in which Philippine authorities harshly tortured a terrorist into disclosing information that may have foiled plots to assassinate the Pope and to crash eleven commercial airliners, carrying approximately four thousand passengers, into the Pacific Ocean, as well as a plan to fly a private Cessna

---

[37] Mackie, *Ethics*, p. 137.   [38] Ibid., p. 136.

filled with explosives into CIA headquarters.[39] Similarly, the Israeli High Court, rejecting torture on moral-absolutist grounds, nonetheless acknowledged that there had been cases in Israeli history where physical methods of interrogation had actually saved lives.[40]

Notwithstanding this, as a matter of *policy* as opposed to any individual incident, torture has definite detrimental effects on any society's general happiness. It is unlikely that anyone could argue successfully, either historically or hypothetically, for the general utility of reintroducing torture as a rule into our criminal justice system, or even of enhancing its unfortunate use in combat situations. The practice of torture in particular, even in the specific cases of interrogating terrorist suspects, appears to be susceptible to a most dangerous slippery-slope effect. Aside from the first-order moral wrong of torture itself as a deliberate infliction of pain, the suffering it causes in the individual instance, its insult to dignity, and so on. Shue pointed out more than thirty years ago that: "There is considerable evidence of all torture's metastatic tendency" and warned of its allure for interrogators as the "ultimate shortcut."[41] Similarly, Waldron points to the "proven inability to keep torture under control, or the fatuousness of the suggestion made by Professor Dershowitz and others that we can confine its application to exactly the cases in which it might be thought justified."[42]

Many popular arguments against torture appear to run along similar lines. While it may at times be difficult, if not impossible, to resist the act-utilitarian logic behind some of the philosophical (and perhaps increasingly also real-world) examples in which torture is justified by weighing the suffering of one (at times guilty) individual against the lives of many potential victims, the overall balance of utility is questioned when considerations of general policy come into play. In short, the rule utilitarian may well have strong moral reasons for opposing torture above and beyond any rule of thumb indicating its inexpediency in previous cases. He may even be called upon to abide as strictly to his utility-based rules

---

[39] Lukes, "Liberal Democratic Torture," p. 12, citing Dershowitz, *Why Terrorism Works*, p. 137. Of course it could also be argued that the *Washington Post* may not have reported the facts objectively, and that one case over the past decade, cited repeatedly, hardly proves the scenario typical or the means employed efficient.

[40] Israel Supreme Court judgment on the interrogation methods applied by the GSS, September 1999; Statement of court president A. Barak, http://elyon1.court.gov.il/files_eng/94/000/051/a09/94051000.a09.HTM (accessed January 31, 2007). Also cited by Ignatieff, *The Lesser Evil*, p. 140.

[41] Shue, "Torture," p. 141.   [42] Waldron, "Torture," p. 1749.

as the absolutist adheres to his moral imperatives. It is in fact possible to make an accusation diametrically opposed to the one underlying Walzer's argument whereby the two forms of utilitarianism are ultimately similar. The opposite accusation, which asks whether rule utilitarianism ultimately collapses into some form of deontological moral theory, or something very similar to it, may be more warranted.[43]

For the purposes at hand it is clearly unnecessary to resolve this critique of rule utilitarianism. What is important is to see that a rule utilitarian can adhere to a moral prohibition on torture almost as strongly as an absolutist can, regardless of the expedience of torture in any concrete case. If, when placed in the position of Walzer's politician, he nonetheless proceeds to have the interrogated subject tortured in order to gain from the immediate utility of such an act, there is no reason to assume that his hands remain any cleaner than do those of his absolutist colleague. The problem of dirty hands presents itself with great force to the rule utilitarian, whose overall moral reasoning against torture may actually reflect a wider range of common moral beliefs than do the categorical imperatives against torture espoused by his Kantian counterpart.

Many of us hold a principled, deontological (or agent-relative-based) opposition to torture, and yet also find it difficult to meet the challenge posed by the variety of familiar catastrophic examples. Nagel's point about our mixed intuitions is well made.[44] Few in liberal democracies, I think, are "ruthless moralists," as Steven Lukes puts it.[45] Few are comfortable, as Kant claimed to have been, with the prospect of sacrificing the innocent rather than incurring a moral blemish. Fewer still, even among our civil libertarians, reject out of hand the torture option in the catastrophic case on strict deontological grounds. However, we also worry, like the rule utilitarian, about the effect of a single act of torture (however justifiable on consequentialist grounds in the particular case) on our society in general.[46] We worry about the effects a single act of torture would have on our constitutional spirit and commitments,[47] about our civil rights tradition and our legal

---

[43] For example, Coady, "Terrorism," p. 82, believes that the indirect utilitarian is ultimately for most, if not all, practical purposes, a bedfellow of the deontoligist.
[44] Nagel, "War and Massacre," pp. 124–8.
[45] Lukes, "Liberal Democratic Torture," p. 5.
[46] This is an effect the act utilitarian can also consider.
[47] Ignatieff, *The Lesser Evil*, pp. 18, 143.

system,[48] about interrogators acquiring the habit of using short cuts, about slippery slopes and metastatic tendencies.[49] In short, many of us, politicians included, have partially rule-utilitarian concerns.

If I am correct in arguing that the rule-utilitarian way of thinking, and not only the assumption of absolute prohibitions, brings out the moral problem of dirty hands, then the "dirty hands" thesis is even more attractive and applies to an even wider range of moral theories (which may be more popularly intuitive) than Walzer intended. The rule utilitarian placed in Walzer's example will have sullied his hands by breaking a rule (and thus endangering the anti-torture policy it represents), which is itself based on his highest moral directive – namely, the maximization of utility. By preferring the immediate advantages of torture, he thereby threatens the very useful general policy and practice of refraining from torture in general, which contributed to overall human happiness (his ultimate moral concern). This will definitely leave dirt on his hands.

Finally, it is worth pointing out that there is one extreme point at which the absolutist politician and the rule utilitarian will probably part company. In a catastrophic situation in which the utility of the torture in question clearly outweighs any advantages of adhering to the useful rules, the rule utilitarian will indeed be justified in breaking the "never torture" rule. In such a case, I am presuming, the harm, in terms of general utility or happiness, caused to the general practice of refraining from torture, will be outweighed by the particular large-scale utility to be gained by opting for torture in the individual situation. Henry Shue presents such a situation when he surmises that "it cannot be denied that there are imaginable cases in which the harm that could be prevented by a rare instance of pure interrogational torture would be so enormous so as to outweigh the cruelty of the torture itself and possibly, the enormous potential harm that would result if what was intended to be a rare instance was actually the breaching of a dam which would lead to a torrent of torture."[50]

In this case, rule utilitarianism will join with act utilitarianism in wholeheartedly prescribing the action. There could hardly be rational cause to do otherwise since utility (rather than the rules themselves) is ultimately the primary normative force of rule, as well as act, utilitarianism. For the former, as opposed to the latter, the rules have substantive merit above and beyond the economy of swift decision-making

---

[48] Waldron, "Security and Liberty," pp. 191–210.
[49] Shue, "Torture," p. 141.   [50] Ibid.

which Walzer attributes to them. But they are ultimately justified only with reference to the principle of utility, and therefore can be outweighed by extreme immediate advantages.

Notwithstanding the last point, it is unclear even in this situation that the rule-utilitarian politician could walk away from this decision with clean hands even if (from a utilitarian point of view) they had a clean conscience. The politician's hands may be less dirty than they would be if looked at from an absolutist moral perspective, but even from a rule-utilitarian point of view their hands may be slightly tainted, for clearly a moral price has been paid for this choice. Unlike the act utilitarian's choice, which is clean and clear-cut, leaving no traces of cost, the rule utilitarian has paid a moral price in terms of a personal moral theory – namely, the harm to the very useful rule.

Torture warrants and dirty hands

I am arguing that Walzer's thesis on dirty hands supplies the most illuminating perspective for contemplating contemporary investigative torture and that it does so from the widest range of moral theories. It offers a viewpoint which takes the academic hypotheticals beyond the narrow framework of repeatedly contrasting deontology and utilitarianism on this specific issue, and articulates more widely held moral intuitions than either strict Kantian principles or simple utilitarian considerations. So far I have argued that it operates within a wider range of moral theories than has so far been assumed.

I have already pointed out that the popular, vivid examples pitting torture against catastrophe, which are commonly enlisted in order to justify torture on consequentialist grounds, have also been solicited in order to present the different approach whereby torture is morally unjustifiable, but at the same time may, in certain circumstances, remain the inevitable course of political action. Walzer's own variant on the familiar theme explicitly makes this point.[51] In this section I will argue that Alan Dershowitz's controversial proposal that liberal democratic judicial systems ought to be officially authorized to issue "torture warrants" to low-level law enforcement officials represents the "dirty hands" approach to torture rather than any justification thereof. Understood as such, his widely publicized and extensively criticized approach emerges

---

[51] Walzer, "Political Action," p. 65.

as somewhat more plausible and palatable than has thus far been acknowledged, though, ultimately, it ought to be rejected.

In *Shouting Fire: Civil Liberties in a Turbulent Age*, Dershowitz asks: what if on September 11 law enforcement officials had "arrested terrorists boarding one of the planes and learned that other planes, then airborne, were heading towards unknown occupied buildings?"[52] And he has since proceeded to present his proposal that a system of judicial review ought to be set up, enabling and requiring those officials doing the torturing to obtain a "torture warrant" from the judiciary.[53] Dershowitz's proposal has been widely understood as, and criticized for, justifying torture on consequentialist grounds concerning the prevention of terrorism.[54]

In his recent "Tortured Reasoning," Dershowitz complains of having been accused and misrepresented in a variety of popular, as well as academic, publications of justifying, even prescribing, torture. One reviewer, he complains, went as far as to refer to him as "Torquemada Dershowitz."[55] Luckily for Dershowitz, he has himself as an advocate. He argues, quite convincingly, that he never intended, or presented, any justification or moral permission for torture of any kind.[56] In fact, in *Shouting Fire*, Dershowitz no more than entertains the possibility that law enforcement officials, if they had been faced with his highly specific "ticking bomb" scenario, might have had "an understandable incentive" to torture the terrorists in question.[57] Although he never says so, his "defense" – that is, his own explanation of his view – is in fact a variation on Michael Walzer's notion of dirty hands, presented in a contemporary light and with reference to the specific debate over the use of torture in the course of interrogating terror suspects in a ticking bomb situation.

In "Tortured Reasoning" Dershowitz states that he is a civil libertarian, opposed to torture as a normative matter, and that he would like to see its use minimized.[58] In the highly specific case of a captured terrorist

---

[52] Dershowitz, *Shouting Fire*, p. 477.   [53] Dershowitz, *Why Terrorism Works*, p. 248.

[54] Waldron, "Security and Liberty," p. 206; Waldron, "Torture," pp. 1713–18, esp. p. 1714, with reference to Dershowitz, *Why Terrorism Works*, pp. 143–6.
Elaine Scary, "Five Errors in the Reasoning of Alan Dershowitz," in Levinson, *Torture*, p. 284.

[55] Dershowitz, "Tortured Reasoning," p. 265.

[56] Ibid. I am grateful to Alan Dershowitz for some important clarifications regarding his proposal, and in particular for very useful critical comments on a previous version of this chapter.

[57] Dershowitz, *Shouting Fire*, p. 477.

[58] Dershowitz, "Tortured Reasoning," pp. 257, 258, 266, 274.

who refuses to divulge information deemed essential to prevent an avoidable act of mass terrorism, Dershowitz claims that he has at worst declined to take a definite position on the normative issue of whether he personally would approve of the use of non-lethal torture in such cases.[59] While examples such as his September 11 hypothetical have been taken by his critics to imply that torture is justified in such cases, Dershowitz is adamant that he has never explicitly condoned this practice and that he is actually opposed to it in principle.[60] As a matter of empirical fact, however, Dershowitz argues that liberal democracies confronting terrorism will inevitably resort to torture, at least in "ticking bomb" situations. Whatever the meta-moral truth of the matter, it is evidently clear that liberal-democracies do not subscribe to the over-ridingness thesis of morality whereby moral considerations always trump all others. In this non-ideal moral situation, Dershowitz suggests, it is better that they torture overtly and under judicial review than incur the greater ills of covert, unrestricted torture far from public scrutiny and supervision. The latter is also Shue's great concern when he cautions us to guarantee, even in ticking bomb situations, that "The torture will not be conducted in the basement of a small town jail in the provinces by local thugs popping pills."[61]

Regardless of whether one accepts Dershowitz's empirical assumption that democracies will inevitably resort to torture under certain circumstances, and his normative view that regulating torture is better than condoning its covert use (and there is clearly room for doubt regarding both propositions), no justification for torture is offered or required in order to sustain his proposal. For Dershowitz, torture is clearly a moral wrong, an instance in which someone's hands will get dirty. He suggests that a lesser evil is incurred when torture is performed within the framework of the rule of law, but the lesser evil argument is never presented as a justification of torture itself. When he put his proposal to Israel's Landau Commission back in the late 1980s, he reports, "The response, especially of Israeli judges, was horror at the prospect that they – the robed embodiment of the rule of law – might have to dirty their hands by approving so barbaric a practice in advance and in specific cases."[62]

---

[59] Ibid., p. 264.   [60] Ibid., throughout.
[61] Shue, "Torture," p. 142.
[62] Dershowitz, "Tortured Reasoning," p. 259.

What then of Dershowitz's alleged "justification" for torture in his September 11 hypothetical, and others like it? In fact, the law-enforcement officials in Dershowitz's September 11 hypothetical are no more justified in torturing the terrorist than Walzer's politician is in torturing the rebel leader. Dershowitz explains that his argument, at its core, is not in favor of torture of any sort.[63] He presents his view as best exhibited by a quotation he chooses to cite from former presidential candidate Alan Keyes, who "took the position that although torture might be *necessary* in a given situation, it could never be *right.*"[64] Dershowitz's background view on torture (as opposed to his specifically original legal proposal of torture warrants) is in essence a further, more contemporary spin on Walzer's classic view of dirty hands. Neither Walzer nor Dershowitz (nor Keyes) justifies torture, in any situation whatsoever. They are (as Dershowitz describes his own argument) engaged in a debate quite different from the old abstract one over whether torture can ever be justified.[65] Both Walzer and Dershowitz (albeit in their very different ways) are looking at the perspective of a state official confronted with the choice to torture, which is at least politically necessary, inevitable, or in some sense even required, either in utilitarian terms – in order to save the many – or in terms of their special responsibility for their public. Dershowitz seeks to minimize what he clearly takes to be an unquestionably evil practice and its ill effect by placing the moral responsibility for its inevitable use in the hands of the judiciary. Walzer asks about the soul and fate of a politician who is politically required to commit a moral wrong. Neither justifies the practices they debate; both believe those responsible for them are sullied by their deeds.

Viewed in light of the notion of dirty hands, Dershowitz's highly debated "torture warrant" suggestion deserves further reflection. As a dirty hands argument, it is coherently raised against the background moral view that torture is wrong. The argument assumes factually that this wrong will be perpetrated by liberal democracies experiencing terrorist threats and proceeds to question whether, from a practical legal viewpoint, it is better for the judiciary to officially and publicly

---

[63] Ibid., p. 275.   [64] Ibid., p. 272.

[65] Ibid., p. 266. Or perhaps Dershowitz, Keyes, and Walzer are debating torture not only within an imperfect world and in a non-optimal moral situation, but also in the framework of a non-ideal type of moral theory.

regulate the empirically inevitable moral wrong or for it to go on covertly and unrestrictedly. Relatedly, he asks whether the judiciary should be asked to dirty its own hands with the decision, or whether we should leave the filth to the interrogators themselves. I believe Dershowitz's proposal ought ultimately to be rejected. Israeli Judges were rightly horrified at the prospect of dirtying their hands and contaminating the Israeli judicial system and rule of law with such a barbarous, dangerous practice as torture.[66] Nevertheless, whatever the merits or demerits of the torture warrant proposal, it ought to be considered accurately as a "dirty hands" argument, which introduces a different perspective for considering contemporary moral and political debates.

Like Walzer, Dershowitz does not adopt a Benthamite line of defense for torture even in extreme cases. It is not incoherent to oppose a practice, even to regard it as utterly evil and unjustifiable, while at the same time holding that a public official could, in certain highly restrained circumstances, be excused, though never quite justified, in resorting to it. Both Walzer and Dershowitz clearly express this view.[67] In the following section I turn to this distinction between justifications and excuses.

Justifications and excuses

Thus far I have suggested that the notion of dirty hands is the appropriate perspective from which to address the modern debate over investigative torture, and that it may be well suited to account for the most widely held liberal intuitions on this issue. It assumes that torture is wrong (based on either deontological or rule-utilitarian reasoning) and that, if it occurs, for whatever reason and under whatever circumstances, its perpetrator cannot walk away from his deeds with a clean set of hands and a clear conscience. Catastrophic scenarios, whether real or hypothetical, express the classic problem of dirty hands, which in turn supplies the best way to address them. When considering these examples from the viewpoint of the decision-maker or his public, they ought never to be taken as a general moral justification for torture under any circumstances, but rather as an

---

[66] For all the good reasons to uphold an absolute legal ban on torture see Waldron, "Torture." For Waldron's critique of Dershowitz and torture warrants, see pp. 1713–17.

[67] Dershowitz, *Shouting Fire*, p. 475. Walzer, "Political Action," p. 67.

illustration of the paradoxical case in which a state official may be required, in the sense that his alternative is unacceptably disastrous, to commit a horrendous wrong.

In Shue's variant on the familiar theme of catastrophic hypothesis, torture is contemplated in order to defuse a nuclear threat to Paris. Recall that Shue found it difficult to "deny the permissibility of torture in a case *just like this* one. To allow the destruction of much of a great city and many of its people would be almost as wicked as purposely to destroy it."[68] In Shue's example, as in most, the potential victim of torture is a terrorist himself. However, on this logic, one may also find it difficult to deny, as Michael Moore explicitly does, the permissibility of torturing an innocent (imagine again a baby from the bin Laden family) for purposes of extracting life-saving information from the victim's reluctant relative in order to prevent absolute catastrophe for the many.[69] Can these examples justify the use of torture even against the innocent? Must we ultimately succumb to consequentialism, or admit that absolute imperatives yield philosophical conclusions that are wholly detached from the real world, as well as counter-intuitive in extreme cases? I believe the answer to both questions is negative.

Shue supplies us with the first piece of the correct answer with his comment about hard cases making bad law and artificial ones making bad ethics.[70] At the very least, I suggested in concluding the previous chapter, hypothetical cases are precarious bases for general policy decisions. Recall the analogy with killing a person in order to obtain his organs in order to save the lives of several other people.[71] What if we need to kidnap an innocent bystander and force him to donate an organ necessary to save a terrorist informer from dying before he supplies us with his life-saving information that could prevent a nuclear bomb on Paris?[72] First, there is Shue's well-made point about hard or artificial cases making bad ethics and law. Far-fetched examples do not serve well

---

[68] Shue, "Torture," p. 141.
[69] Moore, "Torture," p. 328: "It just isn't true that one should allow a nuclear war rather than killing or torturing an innocent person."
[70] Shue, "Torture," p. 141.   [71] Moore, "Torture," p. 288.
[72] Francis Kamm, "Failure of Just War Theory," uses a more specific analogy in order to defend the torture of guilty and knowledgeable terrorists: "Suppose A deliberately takes B's crucial organs. A is captured and is no longer a threat. However, the only way to save B is to transplant all of A's organs into B. I think doing so is permissible," pp. 650, 659.

towards forming general policy decisions. Second, it is questionable whether the hypothetical serves to *justify* the kidnapping and dissection, even under the specifics of the examples. This will depend, of course, on the background moral theory to which we adhere. It is quite plausible to view the decision-maker in such an instance as retroactively excusable, though less than morally justified, in carrying out the life-saving action.

Nagel puts this better than I can when he describes the conflict between absolute moral prohibitions and consequential considerations: "Even if certain types of dirty tactics become acceptable when the stakes are high enough, the most serious of the prohibited acts, like murder and torture, are not just supposed to require unusually strong justification. They are supposed *never* to be done, because no quantity of resulting benefit is thought capable of *justifying* such treatment of a person."[73] By its very definition, absolutism supplies moral requirements that no advantage can justify one in abandoning.[74] If there are such moral restrictions based, for instance, on our duties towards other persons (and Nagel suggests, as I have, that many of us are drawn, at least intuitively, to believing that there are such moral restraints), the prohibition on torture is a very likely candidate for such absolute prohibition. However, Nagel, like Walzer and indeed anyone aside from Kant's most devout followers, acknowledges that "there may be circumstances so extreme that they render an absolutist position untenable."[75] One may find then that one has no choice but to do something terrible. Nevertheless, even in such cases absolutism retains its force in that one cannot claim *justification* for the violation. It does not become *all right*.[76]

The lesson to be learned from the hypotheticals need not be the lesson of justification that they are usually enlisted to teach. The same hypotheticals may do better at expressing our intuitions and approximating the more complex moral truth of the matter if they are read as paradoxically *requiring* the commission of an unmistakable moral wrong, which leaves its perpetrator guilty of making the necessary decision. Perhaps some will agree with Bernard Williams that morality simply runs out at this point, that is, that it cannot supply us with guidelines for making quite such excruciating choices.[77] According to its precepts, both alternatives are

---

[73] Nagel, "War and Massacre," pp. 142–3.   [74] Ibid., p. 136.
[75] Ibid., p. 136.   [76] Ibid., pp. 136–7.
[77] J. Smart and B. Williams, *Utilitarianism: For and Against* (Cambridge University Press, 1973), p. 92.

simply wrong and here we find ourselves in what Nagel dubs "a moral blind alley."[78] Others reject this view, arguing that morality is of the utmost importance precisely in such hard cases and that, if it is to be taken seriously, it must have something to say about them.[79]

The hypotheticals looked at in the previous chapter might be read as taking the viewpoint of the decision-maker – the state leader, inter-rogator, or judge – rather than the bird's-eye view of pure moral theory. They can supply a perspective on the agent himself, rather than the act, and supply him with an excuse, rather than a justification for his action. Walzer himself raises this distinction between justifica-tions and excuses, though somewhat in passing, in the course of criticizing utilitarianism rather than with reference to torture specifi-cally. Citing Austin, Walzer reminds us that "an excuse is typically an admission of fault; a justification is typically a denial of fault and an assertion of innocence."[80] And Walzer adds, "When rules are overridden, we do not act as if they have been set aside, canceled, or annulled. They still stand and have this much effect at least: that we know we have done something wrong even if what we have done was also the best thing to do on the whole in the circumstances."[81] Dershowitz explicitly makes precisely this distinction, between justi-fying unlawful conduct and excusing it, in *Shouting Fire*.[82] Moore refers to the same distinction when explaining the legal defense of necessity: "a justification shows that *prima facie* wrongful and unlaw-ful conduct is not wrongful or unlawful at all ... By contrast, an excuse does not take away our *prima facie* judgment that an act is wrongful and unlawful; rather it shows that the actor was not culpable in his doing of an admittedly wrongful and unlawful act."[83]

Can a plea of necessity be invoked as an excuse, rather than a justification, for torture under dire circumstances? Both Moore and

[78] Nagel, "War and Massacre," p. 143.
[79] Ibid., pp. 123–44. See also Michael Moore, "Torture," who discusses these various views with regard to torture and rejects Williams's stand, pp. 337–8.
[80] Walzer, "Political Action," p. 67, quoting J. L. Austin, "A Plea for Excuses," in J. O. Urmson and G. J. Warnock (eds.) *Philosophical Papers* (Oxford University Press, 1961), pp. 123–52.
[81] Walzer, "Political Action," p. 68.   [82] Dershowitz, *Shouting Fire*, p. 475.
[83] Moore, "Torture," p. 284.

Dershowitz argue that it cannot.[84] Necessity is commonly regarded as a justification defense rather than an excuse, although admittedly the distinction between justifications and excuses is rough and controversial.[85] Moore argues that necessity is in fact primarily a moral justification rather than an excuse. It was certainly employed as such by Israel's Landau Commission report on torture, which Moore addresses. The report adopted the legal plea of necessity as a defense for Israel's security forces' repeated use of physical force in the process of interrogating Arab terrorist suspects. The Landau report clearly viewed the necessity of extracting vital life-saving information as a *justification* for the use of physical force in the investigating chamber. All things considered, they concluded, interrogators were justified, both legally and morally, in resorting to such measures in life-threatening situations.[86] This report was overturned, over a decade later, by Israel's High Court in favor of upholding an absolute ban on any form of torture.

I suggested earlier that some moderate degree of physical pressure, used specifically against knowledgeable reluctant terrorists, might be distinguishable from torture proper, and potentially justifiable under life-threatening circumstances. As for hard-core torture itself, if it is absolutely ruled out as a justifiable measure of interrogation, as I argued that it should be, can the extreme examples nonetheless point to an excuse, rather than a justification, for its use in absolutely extraordinary situations such as those invoked in the philosopher's hypotheses? And, if so, can this excuse be regarded as "necessity"?

Arguing against Israel's original ruling, Dershowitz, as well as Moore, opposes such a plea. For one thing, Dershowitz points out, necessity clauses are obviously a defense of the unusual, not of a systematic policy, such as the one carried out by Israel's security forces in the course of a prolonged struggle with terrorism. The usual cases are defined under specific laws. A plea of necessity enters only in some

---

[84] Ibid., pp. 283–6, where Moore raises a variety of arguments against employing the necessity argument as a defense of torture; Dershowitz, "Is It Necessary to Apply 'Physical Pressure' to Terrorists – And to Lie About It?" *Israel Law Review* 23 (2–3) (1989), pp. 193–200, esp. p. 197.

[85] See, for example, George Fletcher, *Rethinking Criminal Law* (Boston: Little, Brown, 1978), pp. 759, 762, 799–800, 810–11.

[86] Moore, "Torture," p. 282.

rare, unforeseeable cases:[87] "The necessity defense is, by its very nature, an *emergency* measure; it is not suited to situations which recur over long periods of time."[88] Leaving aside the specific Israeli case and law, Dershowitz raises a more general point about the nature of necessity arguments, which renders it, at least literally, inapplicable to the very agents whose viewpoint we are here considering, that is, state officials and officers of the law. As Dershowitz explains:

> The defense of necessity is essentially a "state of nature" plea. If a person finds himself in an impossible position requiring him to choose between violating the law and preventing a greater harm, such as the taking of innocent life – and he has no time to seek recourse from the proper authorities – society authorizes him to act as if there were no law. In other words, since society has broken its part of the social contract with him, namely to protect him, it follows that he is not obligated to keep his part of the social contract, namely to obey the law.[89]

Agents of the state, representatives of the law itself, cannot therefore employ such a defense. They cannot, strictly speaking, argue that they acted out of necessity in order to save innocent lives in an emergency situation in which there was no time for the law to intervene. This is not merely a point of law. It derives from the philosophical basis of this plea. The agents whose decisions we are scrutinizing cannot claim to have found themselves in a "state of nature," since they are themselves the representatives of the state. This is certainly true as regards a recurring policy of torture in order to extract life-saving information: "The point of the necessity defense is to provide a kind of 'interstitial legislation', to fill in 'lacunae' left by the legislative and judicial incompleteness. It is not a substitute legislative or judicial process for weighing policy options by state agencies faced with long term systematic problems."[90] Dershowitz's point about necessity functioning essentially as a state of nature plea is well made, even if the situation under which the interrogator finds himself is rare and unusual rather than a recurring situation.

To this one may retort that this "state of nature" objection is purely formal. One can easily envision a situation, like the many described above, in which the politician, state leader, interrogator, or judge is called

---

[87] Dershowitz, "Is It Necessary," p. 197. Moore, "Torture," p. 286, makes a similar point about necessity clauses referring to the unusual and unexpected.
[88] Dershowitz, "Is It Necessary," p. 197.
[89] Ibid., pp. 195–6.   [90] Ibid., p. 198.

upon to make a swift decision regarding torture in the face of an immediately pending large-scale terrorist catastrophe. In such a case, it has been put to me, the type of agent we are considering is placed in a situation that is, if not literally, at least morally analogous to the emergency situations in which necessity comes into play.[91]

From a legal point of view, however, there may be a further reason to reject necessity as a defense of torture in emergency situations, one which would strengthen Dershowitz's overall argument against a necessity defense. The International Convention on Civil and Political Rights, which includes an absolute ban on torture of any kind, specifically refers to times of emergency and explicitly precludes in advance the possibility of deviating from the prohibition on torture even in times of national crises.[92] Article 7 of the ICCPR states that "No one shall be subjected to torture or to cruel, inhuman or degrading treatment or punishment."[93] Article 4(1) provides that "In time of public emergency which threatens the life of the nation and the existence of which is officially proclaimed, the States Parties to the present Covenant may take measure derogating from their obligations under the present covenant to the extent strictly required by the exigencies of the situation."[94] But, Article 4 also includes a non-derogation clause regarding torture, whereby no derogation from Article 7 (among others) may be made under this provision.[95] It would seem, then, that this non-derogation for torture provision precludes the use of a particular defense of necessity, assuming that the defense raised in any particular case appealed to circumstances of the exact sort that the non-derogation clause refers to in general as a basis of exception.[96]

It may be questioned whether this non-derogation clause applies to the type of emergency under consideration here – the "ticking bomb" scenario. Strictly speaking, these are not usually situations of "public

---

[91] Israeli Supreme Court Justice Barak states in his judgment on the interrogation methods applied by the GSS, September 1999, that "necessity" can be invoked retroactively by agents of the state defending themselves against charges of torture. http://elyon1.court.gov.il/files_eng/94/000/051/a09/94051000.a09. HTM (accessed January 31, 2007).

[92] International Covenant on Civil and Political Rights.

[93] ICCPR, Article 7. [94] ICCPR, Article 4(1). [95] ICCPR, Article 4(2).

[96] I am very grateful to Jeremy Waldron for pointing all this out to me. See also his discussion of the prohibition on torture in the ICCPR in Waldron, "Torture," p. 1688.

emergency which threaten the life of the nation and the existence of which it is officially proclaimed."[97] However, I think it is plausible to assume that if the stipulation never to torture was intended to apply even in such dire emergency situations, which actually threaten the existence of the political community as such, it would certainly apply to the type of public emergency presently under consideration, in which only a certain portion of the nation is placed in danger. If so, the non-derogation provisions of the ICCPR comprehend the individual ticking bomb emergencies, as well as national emergencies. In any event, the United Nations Convention against Torture explicitly states that "No exceptional circumstances whatsoever, whether a state of war, internal political instability or any other public emergency may be invoked as a justification of torture."[98] And this should almost certainly be taken to apply to any necessity defense as well. Whatever the circumstances, resorting to torture is clearly a direct violation of international law.

The legal concept of duress may be more appropriate here, by analogy, than necessity. As we have seen, necessity is often thought of as a lesser-evil type of justification for otherwise criminal conduct, rendering the agent innocent. Having chosen the lesser of two evils we will have done the right thing. Duress, on the other hand, is commonly seen as an excuse for breaking the law or doing the wrong thing.[99] Hence, duress may be analogous (though admittedly not tantamount) to the use of investigative torture in extremely life-threatening situations. In the face of an imminent large-scale threat (say, the morning of September 11) ordinary, legal interrogation techniques may not suffice in order to extract the urgent life-saving information. Could a state leader, a politician (for example, the Minister of Defense), an individual interrogator or his supervisor, or a judge applied to for a torture warrant, be regarded as acting under duress, if not out of necessity, in the legal sense?

Whether or not the answer to this question is positive in the strictly legal sense, I suggest that in such difficult cases officials might be excused retrospectively for torturing under life-threatening circumstances, even against a background moral theory that prohibits torture and within

---

[97] ICCPR, Article 4(1).
[98] The United Nations Convention against Torture and Other Inhuman or Degrading Treatment or Punishment, Part I, Article 2.
[99] Meir Dan-Cohen, *Harmful Thoughts: Essays on Law, Self and Morality* (Princeton University Press, 2002), p. 47.

a system of positive laws that exclude the use of torture. Furthermore, I argue that legally excusing such officials retrospectively in very restrictive catastrophic situations is morally preferable (truer and more intuitive, as well as morally beneficial as a legal policy) to either justifying their actions in advance or to denying, as Kant did, that moral prohibitions can ever be breached, even under cataclysmic situations.[100]

Excuses and acoustics

When contemplating the desirable legal attitude towards torture, Moore suggests that we consider the option described by Meir Dan-Cohen as "acoustic separation."[101] Dan-Cohen distinguishes between two types of legal norms: conduct rules (aimed at the general public) and decision rules (aimed at the judiciary).[102] In some imaginary world there might be an acoustic divorce between the behavior rules aimed at the public and intended to gear them towards some desirable behavior (in our case, never torture), and decision rules, which are intended only for the ears of officials invested with the authority to justify, pardon or excuse the breach of a conduct rule under certain circumstances.[103] The defenses of necessity and duress that concern us here are decision rules in that they are not intended to shape the behavior of the general public (in our case, including the security services) who, in an ideal world, would not even be aware of their existence.[104] The policy advantage of such a separation would be to enable the legal system to advance a desirable mode of conduct (in our case discouraging torture) by requiring this behavior exclusively in a criminal prohibition. Conduct would then be guided exclusively by the relevant criminal proscription.[105] However, the conflicting values of fairness and compassion for individuals in unusual situations who break the law in cases where any one of us, even the judges themselves, would have done the same, is advanced by a decision rule aimed only at state officials.

---

[100] Although I differ on the language of "necessity" I think this conclusion is in keeping with Israeli Supreme Court Justice Barak's ruling on torture; see http://elyon1.court.gov.il/files_eng/94/000/051/a09/94051000.a09.HTM.

[101] Moore, "Torture," pp. 340–2, with reference to Meir Dan-Cohen, "Decision Rules and Conduct Rules: On Acoustic Separation in Criminal Law," *Harvard Law Review* 97 (1984), p. 625–677. Reprinted in Dan-Cohen, *Harmful Thoughts*, pp. 37–93 (references are to the latter).

[102] Ibid., pp. 37–40.   [103] Ibid., pp. 40–1.

[104] Ibid., pp. 42, 46–7.   [105] Ibid., p. 43.

In the case of torture, unlike purely personal instances of duress, not only fairness and compassion are at stake. We may actually want our security services to dirty their hands by breaching the prohibition on torture in situations analogous to necessity or extreme duress, for it is the general public, not the interrogator himself, who are endangered.[106] As Walzer comments, politicians act on our behalf and in our name (or at least they claim to).[107] What we do not want, either in the ordinary cases of duress or in our analogous case of torture, is for this tactic to be employed too lightly. We know that when attempting to avert an evil aimed at themselves, people naturally tend to err in favor of themselves (probably also of their compatriots), often exaggerating the danger or downplaying the evil involved in violating the relevant prohibition.[108] We know that in extreme situations they will preserve themselves even at the expense of committing murder or torture. We do not want them to hear that they may be pardoned for doing so, because such knowledge will encourage them to act too swiftly in their own interest or those of their countrymen at intolerable expense to others. We are willing to excuse them for preferring their own lives to those of others only when there was genuinely no alternative way for them to secure their survival. We ensure that they do not take the easy course in their favor, the ultimate short cut, by prohibiting it entirely and seeing to it that they do not hear any alternative. Judges know that defendants act genuinely out of duress precisely where they were prepared to breach a steadfast rule at the expense of placing themselves in grave personal risk of punishment.[109]

Of course, as Dan-Cohen as well as Moore readily acknowledge, judges are not separated from the rest of the public (interrogators included) in two acoustically separated chambers, and thus everybody hears everything.[110] Consequently, any such acoustic divorce can be maintained and benefited from only if, as Moore suggests, pardons or clemencies could be given without much public attention.[111] More

---

[106] Moore, "Torture," pp. 340–41. Note that Moore, unlike me, actually justifies some investigative torture.

[107] Walzer, "Political Action," pp. 62–3.

[108] Dan-Cohen, *Harmful Thoughts*, p. 47; Moore, "Torture," p. 341.

[109] Dan-Cohen, *Harmful Thoughts*, p. 47.

[110] Ibid., pp. 41–2, on the difference between the model of acoustic separation and the real world; Moore, "Torture," p. 341.

[111] Ibid.

likely, and more desirably to my mind, some acoustic separation between a hard and fast conduct rule prohibiting torture and a decision rule permitting clemency for torturers *in extremis* can be maintained if excuses are employed very rarely indeed.

Recall that Moore actually justifies the torture of terrorists and even of innocents in extreme situations in terms of his "threshold deonto-logy."[112] He then argues that acoustic separation will enable the legis-lator to achieve the desirable target, which in his view is: to torture only terrorists when necessary, and innocents when pending catastrophe reaches a certain threshold – but not otherwise.[113] I have suggested, to the contrary, that torture is never justified, but that when dealing with terrorists specifically, and under very rare and extreme life-threatening circumstances, particular agents of the state may be retroactively excused or pardoned for dirtying their hands with the wrong that is torture. Acoustic separation is then morally desirable in order to uphold an absolute legal ban on torture, and yet to leave a small loophole for those who dirty their hands in our name and for our sake in those rare instances in which the alternative course of action is truly cataclys-mic.[114] The agent in such cases will be guilty of doing what is unques-tionably a moral wrong, but nonetheless one which will have been committed on our behalf and which we may even want to be committed. We recognize this act as wrong, and aspire to minimize its occurrence. Hence the strict conduct rule prohibiting it. We do not believe it to be justified under any circumstances; we do not want it ever to be imple-mented within our society. But just in case the unbearable should in fact occur, we whisper another rule, a decision rule, to the judges, in the name of fairness, authorizing and asking them to legally excuse the agent who tortured on our behalf.

---

[112] Moore, "Torture," pp. 327–34.   [113] Ibid., p. 341.

[114] Note that, aside from his theory of acoustic separation, Dan-Cohen discusses the dilemma of dirty hands within the law, *inter alia* à propos the advantages (versus disadvantages) of the legal system's segregating normative messages by means other than acoustic separation, such as selective transmission (e.g. by vagueness). The problem of dirty hands, as he points out, exists not only in politics but also in law. I cannot possibly delve into this aspect of the dirty hands issue in this connection, nor am I convinced that there is reason to do so here. Nevertheless, it is worth pointing out that certain aspects of Dan-Cohen's discussion of dirty hands in law may have some bearing on the issue of legislation about torture. See Dan-Cohen on dirty hands, *Harmful Thoughts*, pp. 68, 75, 259.

Two final points must be emphasized regarding this plea for excuse as opposed to any justification of torture. First, justification is a matter of policy. As a matter of policy, we ought not to tolerate torture within liberal democracies under any general circumstances. Policy-making has both an instructive and a pedagogic function, and the strict liberal prohibition on torture ought to be upheld at this level within all civilized societies, whatever the threats they face, from terrorists or otherwise. Interrogators as well as all other state officials must be advised that torture is simply out of the question and that its use, at any level, will be treated harshly. This is where I part company with Dershowitz and his suggested policy of torture warrants. Only if a genuine situation analogous to immediate necessity or duress should arise, under which no alternative to torture is available other than enduring a cataclysmic loss of innocent life, will we want to excuse the individual official for making a truly excruciating decision to resort to torture in order to save our lives. On a purely moral level, as well as legally, he will never be entirely vindicated for his action; he will have dirtied his hands with the blood of his interrogated suspect. But we will excuse him for doing what we would do in his uncomfortable position. For he will have dirtied his hands (as Walzer explains) for us and in our name.

This leads me to the second crucial point about excuses versus justifications. Excuses operate retroactively. As opposed to justifications and policy considerations, they are essentially backward-looking. They supply an after-the-fact defense for breaking a valid moral rule rather than a license to violate it.[115] This point is both moral and practical. From a moral point of view, it is important to see that the circumstances do not make torture a rightful action, as the utilitarian or soft deontologist would have us believe.[116] From a practical point of view, an agent facing such a decision will have to consider not only the risk of punishment but also the need to explain and excuse his immoral and unlawful conduct if he is to avoid punishment. This places a heavy burden on the individual decision-maker, but so it should. Torture is wrong, and our primary commitment ought to be to its eradication rather than to excusing its abhorrent use. We do not require an interrogator, or any

---

[115] Moore, "Torture," p. 284. See also Justice A. Barak http://elyon1.court.gov.il/files_eng/94/000/051/a09/94051000.a09.HTM. "Necessity" cannot authorize the GSS in advance to use physical methods of interrogation.

[116] Nielson and Moore both believe that, however excruciating the decision, torture would be the right, justifiable action under the circumstances.

other official, to delve into moral theory, balance evils, or resolve moral dilemmas. He is not trained in ethical theory, nor is he authorized to make such decisions. The law should tell him that torture is absolutely wrong, and he must not ponder on this issue any further. He ought to be legally deterred from considering the various options and weighing moral considerations. The possibility of a retroactive excuse exists only in a rare and extreme situation in which any reasonable person would have virtually no choice but to opt for torture.

It might be argued persuasively that authorizing the judiciary to make such decisions, even in an immediate situation of crisis, is more appropriate, for judges are better versed in normative reasoning. I think this is a point well made by Dershowitz as well as others. Perhaps Dershowitz's suggestion could be modified so that we shy away from a policy of judicial torture warrants but nonetheless attempt to shift the decision-making, even in the unusual cases, towards the court rather than the individual interrogator. Thus we prohibit the interrogator from torturing, but invest in judges the authority to excuse a rare incident of torture *in extremis*.

Crime and punishment

To summarize: I assumed throughout that torture is wrong both on deontological and, for the most part, on rule-utilitarian grounds, and suggested that it can at most be retroactively excused, rather than justified, in the face of unmistakable extreme circumstances analogous to necessity or duress. I argued that even in such cases the decision-maker is not morally vindicated for his action, but merely legally exempt from the full repercussions of breaking the moral and legal rules. The most appropriate way of viewing this complicated situation, I suggested, following Michael Walzer, is as a case of political "dirty hands." What then, practically speaking, is to become of the agent – the interrogator, leader, politician or judge – who dirtied his hands with this life-saving decision? When should he be excused, and to what extent should he be immune from punishment?

Walzer argues that a politician's dirty hands are not washed clean by the successful consequences of his deeds, as Machiavelli is often understood to have believed.[117] Nor, according to Walzer, is it sufficient for

---

[117] Walzer, "Political Action," pp. 69–70. Note that Walzer is not convinced that this is the appropriate reading of Machiavelli, but he does admit that Machiavelli offers no account of the effect of bad deeds on the successful prince's soul or conscience.

him to feel guilty for his actions, as Nielson argues.[118] Walzer believes that some practical measure of punishment ought to be implemented by the state, or public, even if this means paradoxically that we are in effect punishing a state official for doing what, all things considered, he ought to have done, or at least what we wanted him to do. Furthermore (as if that irony were not enough), Walzer suggests that in doing so we in fact dirty our own hands, and in turn will have to find our own way of paying the price.

Walzer does not take any particular view of punishment, and it is clear that his imagery of an executioner is purely metaphorical.[119] He has in mind some course of political repercussion with the educational intent of deterring immoral deeds in politics. Perhaps we can reduce, though we cannot eliminate, dirty politics by denying the greatest power and glory to those with particularly dirty hands.[120] He also believes that a politician's own willingness to pay, to do penance, for his action, is the only indication he can offer us of his ultimate goodness, despite his dirty hands. In fact, Walzer tells us, we know a moral politician (or other state official) only by his dirty hands: "If he were a moral man and nothing else, his hands would not be dirty; if he were a politician and nothing else, he would pretend that they were clean."[121]

Let us set aside the question of the agent's real-world success and assume that our politician or interrogator acted in good faith, with utmost caution, and indeed opted for torture only when the only alternative was catastrophe. Whether he succeeded in preventing the disaster by extracting the information in time will be largely affected by reasons other than his own actions. Machiavelli is notorious for pointing out that political success is based on results and consequences rather than intentions or moral deeds.[122] Moral consequentialists may incorporate the actual results, not only the foreseeable ones, into their ethical calculations. I address the agent who acted as we undoubtedly would, and would want him to, in the very destructive "ticking bomb" scenario, regardless of whether he actually succeeded in preventing the catastrophe. I have already argued that in this very specific case such an

---

[118] Ibid., pp. 65, 71–2. See Nielson, "There Is No Dilemma," p. 148.
[119] Walzer, "Political Action," pp. 72–3.
[120] Ibid., p. 74.   [121] Ibid., p. 65.
[122] Ibid., p. 70, comments that Machiavelli's prince "must do bad things well. There is no reward for doing bad things badly."

agent may be excused as acting under duress, or something very closely analogous to it.

Unlike Walzer, I find the idea of punishment in such cases, whatever its educational value, totally counter-intuitive. In such a truly hard case, where there is no doubt that the agent acted in good faith and with the utmost caution, with risk to his own liberty and career, external punishment is not only unjustifiable (thus rendering our own hands ironically dirty, as Walzer believes) but also inexcusable. Unlike the official who can be excused for committing his crime, any subsequent punishment on our part strikes me as analogous to the indefensible case of punishing the innocent (even if our decision-maker can paradoxically be described as an innocent criminal, or as excusably guilty). Punishing him for what we ourselves would have wanted him to do is no longer an irony or a paradox; it is simply wrong.

Bibliography

Aristotle (1976), *The Nicomachean Ethics*, London: Penguin.

Austin, J.L. (1961), "A Plea for Excuses," in J.O. Urmson and G.J. Warnock (eds.), *Philosophical Papers*, Oxford University Press: pp. 123–52.

Barry, John, Michael Hirsh, and Michael Isikoff (2004), "The Roots of Torture – The road to Abu Ghraib began after 9/11, when Washington wrote new rules to fight a new kind of war: A *Newsweek* investigation," *Newsweek*, May 24. http://csjconference.thereitis.org/displayarticle269.html.

Becker, Lawrence C. and Charlotte B. Becker (eds.) (2001), *Encyclopedia of Ethics*, 2nd edn., New York: Routledge.

Berlin, Isaiah (1990), *The Crooked Timber of Humanity: Chapters in the History of Ideas*, London: Fontana.

Berman, Paul (2003), *Terror and Liberalism*, New York and London: Norton.

Borradori, Giovanna (2003), *Philosophy in a Time of Terror: Dialogues with Jürgen Habermas and Jacques Derrida*, University of Chicago Press.

Bowden, Mark (2003), "The Dark Art of Interrogation," *Atlantic Monthly*, October: pp. 51–76.

Chomsky, Noam (2001), *9–11*, New York: Seven Stories Press.

Coady, C.A.J. (2004), "Terrorism, Morality and Supreme Emergency," *Ethics* 114 (4): pp. 772–89.

Cohen, Gerald (2003), "Casting the First Stone: Who Can, and Who Can't, Condemn the Terrorists," in A. O'Hear (ed.), *Royal Institute of Philosophy Lectures, 2004–05*. www.royalinstitutephilosophy.org/index.php.

Curzer, H.J. (2006), "Admirable Immorality, Dirty Hands, Ticking Bombs, and Torturing Innocents," *The Southern Journal of Philosophy* XLIV: pp. 31–56.

Dan-Cohen, Meir (1984), "Decision Rules and Conduct Rules: On Acoustic Separation in Criminal Law," *Harvard Law Review* 97: p. 625.

   (2002), *Harmful Thoughts, Essays on Law, Self and Morality*, Princeton University Press.

David, Stephen R. (2003), "Israel's Policy of Targeted Killing," *Ethics and International Affairs* 17 (1): pp. 111–26.

Dershowitz, Alan. M. (1989), "Is It Necessary to Apply 'Physical Pressure' to Terrorists – And to Lie About It?" *Israel Law Review* 23 (2–3): pp. 193–200.

(2002a), *Shouting Fire: Civil Liberties in a Turbulent Age*, New York: Little, Brown.

(2002b), *Why Terrorism Works: Understanding the Threat, Responding to the Challenge*, Yale University Press.

(2004), "Killing Terrorist Chieftains is Legal," *The Jerusalem Post*, April 22: p. 18.

Dworkin, R. (2002), "The Threat to Patriotism," *New York Review of Books*, February 28.

Eichensehr, K.E. (2007), "On Target? The Israeli Supreme Court and the Expansion of Targeted Killings," *Yale Law Journal*, June 116 (8): pp. 1873, 1875–6.

Finn, J.E. (1991), *Constitutions in Crisis: Political Violence and the Rule of Law*, Oxford University Press.

Fletcher, George (1978), *Rethinking Criminal Law*, Boston: Little, Brown.

(2003), *Romantics at War: Glory and Guilt in the Age of Terrorism*, Princeton University Press.

(2006), "The Indefinable Concept of Terrorism," *Journal of International Criminal Justice* 4 (5): pp. 1–14.

Gilbert, Paul (2003), *New Terror, New Wars*, Edinburgh University Press.

Goodin, R.E. (2006), *What's Wrong with Terrorism?* Cambridge, UK and Malden, MA: Polity Press.

Gross, Michael (2003), "Fighting by Other Means in the Mid-East: A Critical Analysis of Israel's Assassination Policy," *Political Studies* 51: pp. 350–68.

(2004), "Assassination: Killing in the Shadow of Self-Defence," in J. Irwin (ed.), *War and Virtual War: The Challenges of Communities*, Amsterdam and New York: Rodopi.

Hamilton A. (1787), "The Necessity of a Government as Energetic as the One Proposed to the Preservation of the Union", no. xxiii, *New York Packet*, Tuesday, December 18, in *The Federalist Papers*.

Hobbes, T. (1991), *Leviathan*, ed. R. Tuck, Cambridge University Press.

Honderich, T. (2002), *After the Terror*, Edinburgh University Press.

(2003), *Terrorism for Humanity: Inquiries in Political Philosophy*, London: Pluto Press.

Hornby, A.S. (1991), *Oxford Student's Dictionary for Hebrew Speakers*, Tel-Aviv: Kernerman.

Ignatieff, Michael (2004), *The Lesser Evil: Political Ethics in an Age of Terror*, Princeton University Press,

Kadish, Sanford A. (1989), "Torture, the State and the Individual," *Israel Law Review* 23: pp. 345–56.

Kamm, Francis M. (2004), "Failure of Just War Theory: Terror, Harm and Justice," *Ethics* 114 (4) July.

Kant, Immanuel (1964), *Groundwork of the Metaphysic of Morals*, trans. H.J. Paton, New York: Harper and Row.

Laqueur, Walter Z. (1987), *The Age of Terrorism*, Boston: Little, Brown.

Levinson, Sanford (ed.) (2004), *Torture – A Collection*, Oxford University Press.

Locke J. (1960), *Two Treatises of Government*, ed. Peter Laslett, Cambridge University Press.

Lukes, Steven (2005), "Liberal Democratic Torture," *British Journal of Political Science* 36: pp. 1–16.

Machan, Tibor R. (1990), "Exploring Extreme Violence (Torture)," *Journal of Social Philosophy* 21: pp. 92–97.

Mackie, J.L. (1990), *Ethics – Inventing Right and Wrong*, London: Penguin.

Madison, J. (1788), "The Question of a Bill of Rights", letter to Thomas Jefferson, October 17. www.constitution.org/jm/17881017_bor.htm.

Mavrodes, George I. (1975), "Conventions and the Morality of War," *Philosophy and Public Affairs* 4: pp. 117–31.

McMahan, Jeff (2004), "The Ethics of Killing in War," *Ethics* 114 (July): pp. 693–733.

   (2005), "Just Cause for War," *Ethics and International Affairs* 19 (3): pp. 1–13.

Moore, Michael (1989), "Torture and the Balance of Evils," *Israel Law Review* 23 (2–3): pp. 280–344.

Nabulsi, Karma (1999), *Traditions of War*, Oxford University Press.

Nagel, Thomas (1972), "War and Massacre," *Philosophy and Public Affairs*, Winter 1 (2): pp. 123–44.

Netanyahu, B. (ed.) (1986), *Terrorism: How the West Can Win*, New York: Farrar, Straus, and Giroux.

   (2001), *Fighting Terrorism*, 2nd edn., New York: Farrar, Straus, and Giroux.

Nielson, Kai (2000), "There Is No Dilemma of Dirty Hands," in Paul Rynard and David P. Shugarman (eds.), *Cruelty and Deception: The Controversy over Dirty Hands in Politics*, Peterborough, Ontario: Broadview Press.

Norman, Richard (1995), *Ethics, Killing, and War*, Cambridge University Press.

Pape, Robert A. (2003), "The Strategic Logic of Suicide Terrorism," *American Political Science Review* 97 (3): pp. 343–61.

Primoratz, Igor (ed.) (2004), *Terrorism – The Philosophical Issues*, New York: Palgrave Macmillan.

Rawls, John (1989), *A Theory of Justice*, 9th edn., Oxford University Press.

Rousseau, Jean Jacques (1993), *The Social Contract and Discourses*, London and Vermont: Everyman.

Schmid, Alex P. (1984), *Political Terrorism: A Research Guide to Concepts, Theories, Data Bases and Literature*, Amsterdam: North-Holland Publishing.

Schmid, Alex P. and Albert J. Jongman (1988), *Political Terrorism: A Research Guide to Concepts, Theories, Data Bases and Literature*, 2nd edn., Amsterdam: North-Holland Publishing.

Shue, Henry (1978), "Torture," *Philosophy and Public Affairs* 7 (2): pp. 124–43.

—— (1980), *Basic Rights: Subsistence, Affluence and US Foreign Policy*, Princeton University Press.

Smart, J. and B. Williams (1973), *Utilitarianism: For and Against*, Cambridge University Press.

Smilansky, Saul (2004), "Terrorism, Justification, and Illusion," *Ethics* 114 (4) July: pp. 790–805.

Statman, Daniel (1997a), "The Absoluteness of the Prohibition against Torture," *Mishpat Umimshal* 4: pp. 161–98.

—— (1997b), "Jus in Bello and the Intifada," in Tomas Kapitan (ed.), *Philosophical Perspectives on the Israeli–Palestinian Conflict*, Armonk, NY: Sharpe: pp. 133–56.

—— (2003), "The Morality of Assassination: A Response to Gross," *Political Studies* 51 (4): pp. 775–9.

—— (2004), "Targeted Killing," *Theoretical Inquiries in Law* 5: pp. 179–98.

Sussman, David (2005), "What's Wrong with Torture?" *Philosophy and Public Affairs* 33 (1): pp. 1–33.

Twining, W.L. and P.J. Twining (1973), "Bentham on Torture," *Northern Ireland Legal Quarterly* 24 (3): pp. 305–56.

Waldron, Jeremy (1993), *Liberal Rights*, Cambridge University Press.

—— (2003), "Security and Liberty: The Image of Balance," *The Journal of Political Philosophy* 11: pp. 191–210.

—— (2004), "Terrorism and the Uses of Terror," *The Journal of Ethics* 8: pp. 5–35.

—— (2005), "Torture and Positive Law," *Columbia Law Review* 105 (6): pp. 1681–750.

—— (2006a), "Safety and Security," *Nebraska Law Review* 85: pp. 301–53.

—— (2006b), "What Can Christian Thinking Add to the Debate about Torture?" *Theology Today* 63: pp. 330–43.

—— (2007), "Dignity and Rank", *Archives européennes de sociologie* 48 (2): pp. 201–37.

Walzer, Michael (1973), "Political Action: The Problem of Dirty Hands," *Philosophy and Public Affairs* 2 (2): pp. 160–80.

(1977), *Just and Unjust Wars*, New York: Basic Books.
(1988), "Terrorism: A Critique of Excuses," in Steven Luper-Foy (ed.), *Problems of International Justice*, London: Westview.
Wellman, C. (1979), "On Terrorism Itself," *Journal of Value Inquiry* 13: p. 250–2.
Wilkins, B.T. (1992), *Terrorism and Collective Responsibility*, London: Routledge.
Zohar, Noam J. (1993), "Collective War and Individualistic Ethics: Against the Conscription of Self-Defence," *Political Theory* 21: pp. 606–22.
Zuckerman, Adrian A.S. (1989), "Coercion and the Judicial Ascertainment of Truth," *Israel Law Review* 23: pp. 357–74.

Further sources

Barzilai, Gad, "Islands of Silence: Democracies Kill?" paper presented at the annual meeting of the Law and Society Association, Budapest, 2000.
B'tselem – The Israeli Information Center for Human Rights in the "Occupied Territories," www.btselem.org.
Fletcher, George, "The Problem of Defining Terrorism," paper presented at Tel-Aviv University at the conference on "Terrorism – Philosophical Perspectives" (organized by the Department of Political Science and the Minerva Center for Human Rights, Tel-Aviv University Law Faculty), March 2004.
Geneva Convention relative to the Treatment of Prisoners of War, adopted on 12 August, 1949, www.unhchr.ch/html/menu3/b/91.htm.
Hague Convention, October 18, 1907, http://net.lib.byu.edu/~rdh7/wwi/hague.html.
Harel, A., "Is Terrorism a Moral Category", paper presented at Tel-Aviv University at the conference on "Terrorism – Philosophical Perspectives" (organized by the Department of Political Science and the Minerva Center for Human Rights, Tel-Aviv University Law Faculty), March 2004.
HCJ 769/02 (December 11 2005), http://elyon1.court.gov.il/Files_ENG/02/690/007/a34/02007690.a34.pdf.
International Covenant on Civil and Political Rights (ICCPR), adopted December 16 (1966), www.unhchr.ch/html/menu3/b/a_ccpr.htm.
Jackson J. (1949), in *Terminiello* v. *City of Chicago*, 337 US 1.
(1963), in *Kennedy* v. *Mendoza-Martinez*, 372 US 144.
Protocol I – Addition to the Geneva Conventions (1977), Part IV: Civilian Population, www.unhchr.ch/html/menu3/b/93.html.
Public Committee against Torture in Israel, The Supreme Court sitting as the High Court of Justice (draft document) (May 5, 1998, January 13 1999, May 26, 1999) before President A. Barak, Deputy President

S. Levin, Justices T. Or, E. Mazza, M. Cheshin, Y. Kedmi, I. Zamir, T. Strasberg-Cohen, D. Dorner, http://elyon1.court.gov.il/files_eng/94/000/051/a09/94051000.a09.HTM.

United Nations Convention against Torture and Other Inhuman or Degrading Treatment or Punishment, Part I, Art. 2 (1975), www.hrweb.org/legal/cat.html.

Index